Knowing and Not Knowing

The social world is saturated with powerful formations of knowledge that colonise individual and institutional identities. Some knowledge emerges as legitimised and authoritative; other knowledge is resisted or repressed. Psychosocial approaches highlight the unstable basis of knowledge, learning and research; of knowing and not knowing. How do we come to formulate knowledge in the ways that we do? Are there other possible ways of knowing that are too difficult or unsettling for us to begin to explore? Do we need the authority of legitimised institutions and regularised methods to build secure knowledge? What might it mean to build *in*secure edifices of knowledge? How might we trouble notions of knowledge in processes of teaching, learning and research?

This collection addresses these questions, drawing on a range of psychoanalytic and social theory, from Bion, Freud and Lacan, to Derrida, Kristeva and Žižek. Showcasing work from North America, Europe and Japan, contributors explore: writing as a practice that can stabilise *or* unsettle subjectivities; the unconscious relations between school practices, subjectivities, educational spaces and ideologies; implications of the productive energies and the deadening inwardness associated with mourning and melancholia for formal and informal learning; and the authority we invest in apparently rigid or ephemeral institutional spaces. Strongly empirical as well as theoretical in approach, this collection will be of interest to students and academics seeking ways to resist normative orders of legitimacy and coherence in education and research.

This book was originally published as a special issue of *Pedagogy, Culture & Society*.

Claudia Lapping is a Senior Lecturer in the Department of Culture, Communication and Media at the Institute of Education, University College London, UK. Her main research interests are the sociology of knowledge, reflexivity and the use of psychoanalysis within empirical social research. She is author of *Psychoanalysis in Social Research: Shifting theories and reframing concepts* (Routledge, 2011); and of recent journal articles in *Psychoanalysis, Culture and Society* and *Qualitative Inquiry*.

Tamara Bibby is a Senior Lecturer in the Department of Early Years and Primary Education at the Institute of Education, University College London, UK. She has a background in primary education and is particularly interested in psychosocial dimensions of student and teacher experiences of learning. She is currently completing an ESRC funded seminar project: 'Bridging the Structure/Agency Divide: Interdisciplinary Approaches to Disadvantage and Education'. She is author of *Education – An 'Impossible Profession'?: Psychoanalytic explorations of learning and classrooms* (Routledge, 2010); and of a recent journal article in *Psychoanalysis, Culture and Society*.

Knowing and Not Knowing
Thinking psychosocially about learning and resistance to learning

Edited by
Claudia Lapping and Tamara Bibby

LONDON AND NEW YORK

First published 2016
by Routledge
2 Park Square, Milton Park, Abingdon, Oxon, OX14 4RN, UK

and by Routledge
711 Third Avenue, New York, NY 10017, USA

Routledge is an imprint of the Taylor & Francis Group, an informa business

© 2016 Pedagogy, Culture and Society

All rights reserved. No part of this book may be reprinted or reproduced or utilised in any form or by any electronic, mechanical, or other means, now known or hereafter invented, including photocopying and recording, or in any information storage or retrieval system, without permission in writing from the publishers.

Trademark notice: Product or corporate names may be trademarks or registered trademarks, and are used only for identification and explanation without intent to infringe.

British Library Cataloguing in Publication Data
A catalogue record for this book is available from the British Library

ISBN 13: 978-1-138-64811-1

Typeset in Times New Roman
by RefineCatch Limited, Bungay, Suffolk

Publisher's Note
The publisher accepts responsibility for any inconsistencies that may have arisen during the conversion of this book from journal articles to book chapters, namely the possible inclusion of journal terminology.

Disclaimer
Every effort has been made to contact copyright holders for their permission to reprint material in this book. The publishers would be grateful to hear from any copyright holder who is not here acknowledged and will undertake to rectify any errors or omissions in future editions of this book.

Contents

Citation Information vii
Notes on Contributors ix

Introduction – Journal as methodological archive: introduction to a cataloguing system for insecure knowledge 1
Claudia Lapping and Tamara Bibby

1. Interrupting the frame: reflective practice in the classroom and the consulting room 9
   Julie Walsh

2. Bringing up gender: academic abjection? 21
   Emily F. Henderson

3. Writing in a foreign language as a science of writing or *grammatology* 39
   Arturo Escandón

4. The enjoyment of space: the university campus in students' narratives and photography 61
   Angie Voela

5. Learning to fail and learning from failure – ideology at work in a mathematics classroom 79
   Hauke Straehler-Pohl and Alexandre Pais

6. Reconstructing memory through the archives: public pedagogy, citizenship and Letizia Battaglia's photographic record of mafia violence 97
   Paula M. Salvio

7. Psychoanalytic notes on the status of depression in curriculum affected by histories of loss 117
   Lisa Farley

8. Explorations in knowing: thinking psychosocially about legitimacy 137
   Anne Chappell, Paul Ernest, Geeta Ludhra and Heather Mendick

9. Going spiral? Phenomena of 'half-knowledge' in the experiential large group as temporary learning community 157
   John Adlam

Index 169

Citation Information

The following chapters were originally published in *Pedagogy, Culture & Society*, volume 22, issue 1 (March 2014). When citing this material, please use the original page numbering for each article, as follows:

Editorial
Journal as methodological archive: introduction to a cataloguing system for insecure knowledge
Claudia Lapping and Tamara Bibby
Pedagogy, Culture & Society, volume 22, issue 1 (March 2014), pp. 1–8

Chapter 1
Interrupting the frame: reflective practice in the classroom and the consulting room
Julie Walsh
Pedagogy, Culture & Society, volume 22, issue 1 (March 2014), pp. 9–20

Chapter 2
Bringing up gender: academic abjection?
Emily F. Henderson
Pedagogy, Culture & Society, volume 22, issue 1 (March 2014), pp. 21–38

Chapter 3
Writing in a foreign language as a science of writing or grammatology
Arturo Escandón
Pedagogy, Culture & Society, volume 22, issue 1 (March 2014), pp. 39–60

Chapter 4
The enjoyment of space: the university campus in students' narratives and photography
Angie Voela
Pedagogy, Culture & Society, volume 22, issue 1 (March 2014), pp. 61–78

Chapter 5
Learning to fail and learning from failure – ideology at work in a mathematics classroom
Hauke Straehler-Pohl and Alexandre Pais
Pedagogy, Culture & Society, volume 22, issue 1 (March 2014), pp. 79–96

CITATION INFORMATION

Chapter 7
Psychoanalytic notes on the status of depression in curriculum affected by histories of loss
Lisa Farley
Pedagogy, Culture & Society, volume 22, issue 1 (March 2014), pp. 117–136

Chapter 8
Explorations in knowing: thinking psychosocially about legitimacy
Anne Chappell, Paul Ernest, Geeta Ludhra and Heather Mendick
Pedagogy, Culture & Society, volume 22, issue 1 (March 2014), pp. 137–156

Chapter 9
Going spiral? Phenomena of 'half-knowledge' in the experiential large group as temporary learning community
John Adlam
Pedagogy, Culture & Society, volume 22, issue 1 (March 2014), pp. 157–168

For any permission-related enquiries please visit:
http://www.tandfonline.com/page/help/permissions

Notes on Contributors

John Adlam is Consultant Psychotherapist in Reflective Practice and Team Development with the South London and Maudsley Foundation NHS Trust, London, UK.

Tamara Bibby is a Senior Lecturer in the Department of Early Years and Primary Education at the Institute of Education, University College London, UK. She has a background in primary education and is particularly interested in psychosocial dimensions of student and teacher experiences of learning. She is currently completing an ESRC funded seminar project: 'Bridging the Structure/Agency Divide: Interdisciplinary Approaches to Disadvantage and Education'. She is author of *Education – An 'Impossible Profession'?: Psychoanalytic explorations of learning and classrooms* (Routledge, 2010); and of a recent journal article in *Psychoanalysis, Culture and Society*.

Anne Chappell is a Lecturer in undergraduate and postgraduate education programmes at the School of Sport and Education, Brunel University, London, UK. Her own research has focused on narrative and auto/biography, identities, learning and teaching, and education policy. Anne has contributed a number of books and articles to her field, including a chapter in *A Practical Guide to Teaching Physical Education in the Secondary School* (Routledge, 2013).

Paul Ernest is a Professor and Professional Fellow in Mathematics Education at the School of Sport and Education, Brunel University, London, UK. He is the author of works such as *The Philosophy of Mathematics Education* (1991), *An Introduction to Educational Research Methodology and Paradigms* (1994) and *Social Constructivism as a Philosophy of Mathematics* (1998).

Arturo Escandón is Professor in the Department of Spanish and Latin American Studies, Nanzan University, Japan. Artuo researches and teaches in the sociology of education and foreign language development. His most recent publications include, 'The pedagogies of second language acquistion: Combining cultural-historical and sociological traditions', in H Daniels (ed.), *Vygotsky and Sociology*, (Routledge, 2012).

Lisa Farley is Associate Professor in the Department of Education at York University, Toronto, Canada. Lisa has published widely in her field, including in journals such as *History and Memory*, *Curriculum Inquiry* and *American Imago*.

NOTES ON CONTRIBUTORS

Emily F. Henderson is a doctoral student in the Faculty of Polity and Society, Institute of Education, University of London, UK. Emily is author of the book, *Gender Pedagogy: Teaching, learning and tracing gender in higher education* (2014).

Claudia Lapping is a Senior Lecturer in the Department of Culture, Communication and Media at the Institute of Education, University College London, UK. Her main research interests are the sociology of knowledge, reflexivity and the use of psychoanalysis within empirical social research. She is author of *Psychoanalysis in Social Research: Shifting theories and reframing concepts* (Routledge, 2011); and of recent journal articles in *Psychoanalysis, Culture and Society* and *Qualitative Inquiry*.

Geeta Ludhra is a doctoral student and Lecturer in Primary Education at the School of Sport and Education, Brunel University, London, UK. Her research focuses on the education of South Asian girls. Geeta has contributed a number of articles to journals such as *Gender and Education*, *The International Journal of Learning* and *Perspectives in Education*.

Heather Mendick is a Reader in Education at Brunel University, London, UK. Her research focuses on gender and social class identities, the influence of popular culture and the ways in which individuals form relationships with mathematics and science. Heather recently co-edited the book, *Debates in Mathematics Education* (Routledge, 2014), and has contributed numerous other articles and book chapters to her field.

Alexandre Pais holds a post-doctoral position at Aalborg University, Denmark. His research focuses on mathematics education and philosophy. Alexandre has contributed a number of articles to his field, which have been published in journals such as *Educational Studies in Mathematics* and *For the Learning of Mathematics*.

Paula M. Salvio is Professor of Education at the College of Liberal Arts, Department of Education, University of New Hampshire, USA. Her research focuses on curriculum theory and psychoanalytic analyses of writing and reading practices in performance and film. Paula has authored and edited numerous books and articles, including *Love's Return: Psychoanalytic essays on childhood, teaching and learning* (Routledge, 2006).

Hauke Straehler-Pohl works in the Department of Educational Studies and Psychology, Freie Universität Berlin, Germany. Hauke specialises in mathematics education, discourse studies, conversation analysis and systemic functional linguistics. He has published in several journals, including the *British Journal of Sociology of Education* and *Educational Studies in Mathematics*.

Angie Voela is a Senior Lecturer in Psychosocial Studies at the University of East London, UK. Her teaching and research interests include psychoanalysis and philosophy, femininity and masculinity, and myth in contemporary culture. Angie has contributed numerous works to her field, including, 'In Search of Higg's Boson', in P. Bennett and J. McDougal (eds), *Barthes' Mythologies Today, Readings in Contemporary Culture* (Routledge, 2013).

Julie Walsh is Director of the Psychoanalysis Across the Disciplines Network at the University of Warwick, UK. Julie holds a doctorate in Psychoanalysis and Social Theory from the University of Cambridge, and is a practicing Psychoanalyst. Her most recent book is *Narcissism and Its Discontents* (2014).

INTRODUCTION

Journal as methodological archive: introduction to a cataloguing system for insecure knowledge

Claudia Lapping[a] and Tamara Bibby[b]

[a]Department of Culture, Communication and Media, Institute of Education, University College London, UK; [b]Department of Early Years and Primary Education, Institute of Education, University College London, UK

> "The social world is saturated with powerful formations of knowledge that colonise individual and institutional identities. Some knowledge emerges as legitimised and authoritative; other knowledge is resisted or repressed. Psychosocial approaches highlight the unstable basis of knowledge, learning and research; of knowing and not knowing. How do we come to formulate knowledge in the ways that we do? Are there other possible ways of knowing that are too difficult or unsettling for us to begin to explore? Do we need the authority of legitimised institutions and regularized methods to build secure knowledge? What might it mean to build *in*secure edifices of knowledge? How might we trouble notions of knowledge in processes of teaching, learning and research?"
>
> Call for papers for the Psychosocial Studies Network Conference, Institute of Education, London, 2012

This was the call for papers for the Psychosocial Studies Network Conference at the Institute of Education, in London, in December 2012. The conference brought people together over the course of two days to discuss works in progress, and to engage in activities, framed by these questions, and by the title, 'Knowing and Not Knowing: Thinking Psychosocially about Learning and Resistance to Learning'. This collection is a selection of papers developed from those brief texts, discussions and activities. It aims, perhaps, to conserve, but also inevitably destroys something of the experiences and memories of the participants. The question of conservation and destruction, and the role of a journal or edited collection as an archive that performs both these functions, is a useful point from which to introduce these papers, and the field of Psychosocial Studies.

A conceptualisation of the archive as a site of political authority, in its simultaneous action of conservation and exclusion, is elaborated by Derrida. In the opening pages of *Archive Fever* (1998), he traces aspects of the word 'archive', and its association both with the idea of commandment, '*this place* from which *order* is given' (1), and with the Greek *arkheion*: 'The residence of the superior magistrates, the *archons*, those who commanded'. He explains the role of the *archons* as both guardians and interpreters of official documents:

> On account of their publicly recognized authority, it is at their home, in that *place* which is their house (private house, family house, or employee's house), that official documents are filed. The archons are first of all the documents' guardians. They do not only ensure the physical security of what is deposited and of the substrate. They are also accorded the hermeneutic right and competence. They have the power to interpret the archives. Entrusted to such archons, these documents in effect speak the law: they recall the law and call on or impose the law. To be guarded thus, in the jurisdiction of this speaking the law, they needed at once a guardian and a localization. (1998, 2)

The role of the *archons* resonates with that of the editor, and the archive with that of an edited collection, as both a guardianship and a localization of papers. An academic journal or collection of papers can be understood as both the location of a certain kind of recognized authority in relation to methodological legitimacy; and as the position from which the papers that it houses are able either to speak a methodological law or, alternatively, to disrupt traditional notions of methodological coherence. The role of editor, we might say, gives us an opportunity to shift or reorder the methodological archive.

The archive, for Derrida, is not only the location of a commandment; it is also understood as a response to the death drive, a force of destruction or annihilation. The drive to conserve through the creation of the archive, what Derrida calls 'archive fever', is constituted in this possibility of annihilation (19). Does this perhaps help us to understand the journal, not just as a domicile of texts that recall a methodological law, but also a space that preserves the possibility of existence of certain methodological identities and practices? The archive, or journal, is a collection of documents that might enable or legitimize these identities; always, though, in some sense collected together from a position of existential vulnerability. There is thus a certain reciprocity between creativity and destruction.

In drawing attention to the archive as a site of documents that might support a possible ordering of legitimate existence, Derrida also describes the archive as a site of destruction and construction of memory. As Paula Salvio's paper in this collection points out: 'Derrida casts the archive as a site of amnesia precisely because it destroys memories in the very process of selecting (and hence excluding) what will be remembered'. More concretely, then, this edited collection might be understood as destroying and constructing a memory of the 2012 Psychosocial Studies Network Conference. The following sections introduce the cataloguing system of this methodological archive. The documents are organized to foreground selected methodological resonances that we have identified and defined, in accordance with our right and competence as temporary guardians of the archive.

Writing as representation or disorganization

The first section of the archive houses papers that contrast the representational and the desubjectivating functions of writing. Julie Walsh, Emily F. Henderson and Arturo Escandón, in very different pedagogic contexts, juxtapose practices of writing as representation, with writing as, potentially, an encounter with the very edges of being.

Reflecting on a difficult supervision with an undergraduate student, Walsh explores the different potentialities of writing and speaking, in teaching and in psychotherapy. She notes: 'There is something especially demanding [. . .] in asking a student to account for their written work after the event', and suggests:

> For some, the possibility of expressing oneself through the written word – where time can be taken to arrange and rearrange the order of one's words creating the impression of coherence, exactitude and purpose – is infinitely preferable to being constantly caught short in one's speech.

She explores ways in which the turn to texts or fragments of texts might mediate the anxiety-inducing pedagogic or psychotherapeutic encounter, but also notes the possibility that it is precisely the dynamic of anxiety or shame that produces the dislocation necessary to learning: 'Presumably when the subject is laid open, the prospect of a different freedom comes into play; one where the contours of the subject's very subjectivity may be re-imagined'.

The opposition Walsh constructs between writing as a coherent representation of self or world and being 'laid open' or 'caught short' is echoed in Henderson's account of a shift in her understanding of 'gender'. Henderson begins with a question about how to help students 'bring up' gender outside the context of a gender studies class. She gradually reformulates this through an engagement with Kristeva's conceptualization of abjection and the Derridean heliotropic metaphor, which undermines the figurative–literal binary through which metaphor has traditionally been understood. She thus troubles the way her initial question rested on an assumption that 'gender' has a knowable, literal referent; and, in an attempt to meet the 'obligations' of Kristeva's 'quest to trouble the clear waters of signification' she explores 'the potential of abjection as a *disorganizing* concept and mode of writing'. The final, perhaps more experimental or performative section of Henderson's paper can be read as an attempt *not* to avoid being caught short, or *not* to submit to the temptation to use writing to create the impression of either a coherent, 'clean' self or a coherent, 'clean' conception of gender.

Escandón sets out this same problematic in a reflection on his own teaching of Spanish writing to university students in Japan. For him, writing in a foreign language necessarily challenges our identities as nationally, culturally and socially positioned subjects. However, he argues, dominant foreign language pedagogies are based on a conception of language that leaves out the social and psychological dimensions of communication so 'the instructor can be happy abandoning the student in the fantasy island of the classroom where an imaginary foreign language is spoken; and the student can be happy about learning an imaginary foreign language'. In opposition to this, he offers Vygotsky's and Derrida's conceptions of language as the bases for contrasting pedagogies of subjective transformation. Vygotsky's approach supports an intensification of the representational function of language; while Derrida's reconceptualization of writing, like Kristeva's, is characterized by 'the break with the horizon of communication as the communication of consciousness or presences' (Derrida, cited in Escandón), and demands a more radical and terrifying confrontation with the abyss beyond the normative conditions of subjectivity.

Extimacy, space and ideology

The Lacanian notion of extimacy offers another way for us to tease open the boundaries of subjectivities or discourses. As Angie Voela explains, Lacan's neologism combines 'exteriority' and 'intimacy' in a concept that challenges both the idea that motivations or desires are something opaque and 'internal', and the assumption that discursive or subjective identities are transparent to themselves. Instead the concept of extimacy opens a space to consider ways in which unrepresented or unconscious aspects of subjects or discourses may be evident in spaces or practices that are apparently 'external' to them. The two documents in this section of the archive develop contrasting interpretations of the concept of extimacy: the first explores the subject's relation to space; the second, an educational ideology's relation to the concrete practices of the school.

Introducing her study of students' relation to space on their university campus, Voela suggests:

> Lacanians [. . .] accept that space is not merely the background of individuals' actions; space does things *for* individuals. It is therefore an 'outside' in direct communication with the 'inside'.

Voela invited students to take photographs of places on the campus that made them feel at home, and then asked them to talk about the pictures they had taken. Her account explores the way the students' more or less undirected accounts reveal what the space of the campus 'does' for them. She suggests that the photographic task provided an opportunity for them to notice themselves as both present and absent, available to others to view, in the way that they also used the space to observe others. Spaces on campus provided repetitive points of return that students sometimes invested with an idealized significance. At other times these spaces seemed to offer the possibility of a more wordless, 'un-express' relation to self that Voela, drawing on Lacan's conceptualization of the drive, interprets as an immediate enjoyment beyond the deferred, utilitarian objective of getting a degree.

Hauke Straehler-Pohl and Alexandre Pais examine the relation between the educational ideology of inclusion and equity, and instances of failure in mathematics classes observed in a school in an underprivileged neighbourhood. The 'supreme goal' in the field of mathematics education is 'mathematics for all' and, they point out:

> it is assumed that a quality mathematics education will allow people to become active participants in a world where mathematics informs and formats many of the decisions that influence our lives.

Thus, they argue, 'the ideological frame is set in such a way that failure cannot be attributed to anything other than individuals making the wrong choices': if the teacher had a more appropriate pedagogy or the student was more compliant, failure would not occur. In opposition to this, their analysis suggests that failure is not an unfortunate contingency, but rather stands in extimate relation to the official discourse. Just as space has an unconscious function, it 'does things' for the students in Voela's study, so Straehler-Pohl and Pais suggest that the actualization of failure in concrete schools – the ways in which failures are accounted for by teachers, and the ways they come to be attributed to the 'chosen' actions of individual students – 'does things' for official educational discourse. Their account traces the concrete processes of production of failure as individual contingency. It posits these instances as sitting in a relation of extimacy that operationalizes an ideology that in turn covers over the fact that the economic and political system has failure at its heart.

Loss, politics and archival memory

The problematic connecting the two documents in the third section of the archive relates to loss, memory and politics. This methodological space can be traced to Freud's initial and later conceptualization of melancholia, or depression. His earlier writing (1917) draws an analogy between the painful condition of melancholia, or depression, and the painful process of mourning for lost objects. His later work (1923) extends this to consider the human condition more generally as one defined by the losses imposed by the constraints and prohibitions of social life. Where his earlier theory suggests a need to separate from the lost object, his later work foregrounds the persistence of the lost object within the psyche, and its relation to societal norms. This conceptual nexus has proved hugely generative for contemporary work exploring the affective politics of social repression and exclusion: the need to recognize the way such losses leave a persistent, deeply painful mark on the psyche; but also to explore how melancholic processes might help to maintain and rearticulate the objects of social exclusion (Butler 1997). Which aspect of mourning or depression should we foreground: The productive energies that might constitute a reparative or reconstitutive political agency? Or the deadening inwardness that, rather than offering political potential, cuts off the relation to the external world? The documents offered by Paula Salvio and Lisa Farley mark out distinctive spaces for exploring the politics of loss.

Salvio's paper expands accounts of melancholia as a reparative politics in which rituals of grieving enable the mourner to re-evoke aspects of the lost object. Drawing on Derrida's conceptualization of the archive, she elaborates the significance of an external site from which memorials can be transformed into a form of public pedagogy. She develops this idea through the history of Letizia Battaglia's 'accidental' archive of mafia violence, a digital photographic record of mafia crime that has given life to memories and modes of citizenship denied by the Italian state. Salvio marks out the polyvalent role of Battaglia's archive: sustaining 'a search for lost or neglected objects'; re-constituting traumatic memories; and offering 'an existential sense of belonging and political union'. She develops this argument through an analysis of specific photographs of grieving women, tracing how they 'migrate, via digital and social media, into the discourses of contemporary anti-mafia activists'. She thus suggests ways in which digital technologies offer a new medium for archiving and politicizing memorials of grief.

Farley, in contrast, foregrounds arguments that melancholia 'forecloses creative potential' as it is 'more about the ego's desire to consume than it is about ethical regard for the object-loss in its own right'. She introduces Andre Green's conception of the 'dead mother': a theorisation of the psychical effects on the infant of the mother's withdrawal or quasi-death as result of depression. There is, for example, 'an inversion of the structure of care, for it is the child who is charged to secure the adult's survival'; so the child's separateness is forsaken in the attempt to keep the mother alive. Farley uses this as a way to explore intergenerational depression as potentially foreclosing learning in a pedagogical context. The depressed teacher, she argues, like Green's 'dead' mother, may be unable to engage creatively either with the curriculum or with their students, unable to recognize, give space to and nurture their otherness.

The housing of insecure edifices of knowledge

The final section of the book can be seen as a reflection on different kinds of archival spaces: fragile spaces of guardianship and 'hermeneutic right', from which it is possible to confer or deny a sense of legitimacy. Each of the documents found here cites the conference's call to destabilize the location and meaning of this right: 'Do we need the authority of legitimized institutions and regularized methods to build secure knowledge? What might it mean to build insecure edifices of knowledge?' This call provoked reflection on the importance of what we might name 'anti-archival' spaces: spaces that perhaps don't strive for permanence or security, instead valuing transience and nurturing scraps of difference. John Adlam theorizes such a space in his discussion of the experiential large group: a practice that brings a group of people together for a set period of time with a convener, but no agenda. Anne Chappell, Paul Ernest, Geeta Ludhra and Heather Mendick discuss the way that different spaces – their reading group, the university, other research groups, the conference and the field of psychosocial studies – offer the potential to house or to exclude methodologies that foreground ignorance, doubt and subjectivity.

Chappell et al., describe their shared but differing trajectories through institutionalized and less institutionalized spaces, and the different forms of housing these offer for the emotions aroused in the research process, for untried methodologies, and for multilayered and contradictory readings of data. They suggest that psychosocial and psychoanalytically informed approaches provide a means to trouble academic requirements for a methodological respectability that involves the suppression of anxiety and doubt. At the same time, though, they describe their ongoing uncertainty about their legitimacy as participants at the conference: 'engaging in psychosocial thinking without a psychoanalytic background'. Their concern here suggests the way subjective fantasies structure our perception and experience of different spaces; and the way, at some moments, their experience of psychosocial studies foregrounds exclusionary hierarchies of legitimacy within the field.

There is a similar recognition of this fantasmatic relation in Adlam's account of the experiential large group. He describes the anxiety provoked by an unstructured large group experience as a potential resistance to new knowledge, which can then become the object of study of the group. The experiential group thus acts as a 'temporary accommodation for unhoused minds' that interrupts secure regimes of knowledge to allow scraps of 'half-knowledge' to emerge. The group is then presented as an ephemeral space in which difficult, incomplete, transient and troubling knowledge might be nurtured. In concluding, though, he also notes:

> Both permanence and impermanence, rigidity and chaos, have equal status as fantasies to be explored, rather than as facts to be assumed *a priori*.

This observation puts into question our perception of law and legitimacy, authority, reason and temporality. Spaces that appear rigid are always also vulnerable; apparently ephemeral spaces house points of institutionalized security. Just as Derrida points to the threat of annihilation that brings the archive into being, Adlam suggests traces of permanence can be found in the disorienting space of the large group. Like Chappell et al., he thus troubles any easy assumptions about what might constitute an anti-archival space.

Finally, it is worth noting the same tension in the space of this book. As methodological archive, it is in a sense produced in a feverish response to the possibility of annihilation: a drive to conserve, and in the act of conservation, the construction of a space from which to speak a methodological law. Our delineation of sections, here, through the themes of writing, extimacy, loss and institutional space, momentarily fixes associations between papers, imposing strands of methodological unity. However, in so far as the documents share a resistance to normative orders of legitimacy and coherence, perhaps it would be better to offer them as a source of play, rather than of law. In the spirit of non-utility, we hope we have also given a sense here of the immediate, wordless pleasure these papers have given us, and of our gratitude that they have fallen to our temporary guardianship.

References

Butler, J. 1997. *The Psychic Life of Power*. California: Stanford University Press.

Derrida, J. 1998. *Archive Fever: A Freudian Impression.* Chicago and London: The University of Chicago Press.

Freud, S. 1917. "Mourning and Melancholia". In *The Complete Psychological Works of Sigmund Freud Volume X1 V*. London: The Hogarth Press and the Institute of Psychoanalysis. 1957: 243–257.

Freud, S. 1923. "The Ego and the Id, *The Standard Edition of the Complete Psychological Works of Sigmund Freud Volume X1X: The Ego and the Id and Other Works*". Vintage, The Hogarth Press and the Institute of Psychoanalysis. 2001: 3–66

Interrupting the frame: reflective practice in the classroom and the consulting room

Julie Walsh

Institute of Advanced Study/Department of Sociology, University of Warwick, Coventry, UK

> In this paper I consider some of the affinities between the teacher–student dynamic in academic supervision, and the therapist–patient dynamic in the therapeutic relation. Drawing on my own experiences, I identify several difficulties that pertain to these two settings. First, in the context of the classroom, I consider how the requirement to speak and the requirement to write call for different modes of engagement, and can provoke different types of anxiety. I explore the function of mediating texts as a way of engendering a critical distance from one's own speech acts. I then turn to Sigmund Freud's intriguing evocation of the quality of 'aloofness' as that which should colour the patient's engagement with the transference situation. I shall treat Freud's recommendation of aloofness as a mode of critical distance – and a type of impersonality – that can be put to work in the classroom as well as in the consulting room. Finally, I ask what happens when distance fails; when there seems to be no space for impersonal critique. One way of thinking about the failure of distance is through the lens of shame. Here I focus my thought on the contention that the scope for shaming is especially prominent in vocational settings that challenge and interrogate the subject's capacity to know.

Introduction

> I am sitting opposite a young man of 19 years of age. It's just the two of us. We've not met before. Let's call him Matthew. We've been in the room together for over 10 minutes now and we've not got started. Matthew cannot meet my gaze. I offer another possibility of a beginning: Matthew shrugs his shoulders and blushes ferociously. By anyone's standards this is not going so well. 'This is difficult stuff' I suggest, 'but we can think it through together'. Matthew is quietly shaking. What on earth is going through his head, and what is my responsibility here? 'If only this was therapy', I think to myself, 'that would be easier'.

My encounter with Matthew took place in the classroom rather than the consulting room. It was one incident among many that made me consider the affinities between the teacher–student dynamic in academic supervision, and the therapist–patient dynamic in the therapeutic relation. The question I was asking myself in this instance – *what is going on for Matthew?* – highlights the rather obvious fact that it is not only the second party in these pairings (i.e. the student or patient) who can feel exposed for her ignorance, and get caught up in the frustrations that ensue. I have taken the Psychosocial Studies Network's conference 'Knowing and Not Knowing: Thinking Psychosocially About Learning and Resistance to Learning' as an opportunity to develop my reflections on this theme in relation to my work as an early career academic and as a psychotherapist in training. I am not concerned here to advance a particular theoretical framework for my thoughts, but rather to identify in broad terms some of the affinities that I have experienced between these two frames of activity. As an exercise in reflective practice, then, this paper comments on my understanding of the ways in which modes of knowing and not-knowing create the unstable grounds for any educative and/or therapeutic encounter. As my opening illustration perhaps already suggests, the challenge of bearing – and bearing witness to – a not-knowing can prove most difficult to tolerate. I am interested in thinking about how the different fields in which I work serve this particular difficulty: Can not-knowing in the classroom be thought about in terms other than deficit? How is the relationship between knowledge and authority differently configured for the teacher and the therapist? How might the desire for knowledge be a help or a hindrance in the educative or therapeutic project? As a teacher and a therapist how can the unknown impact of my speech be thought about? In what ways are the dynamics of distance and intimacy co-fashioned in the educative and/or therapeutic encounter?

Drawing on my own experiences I have identified below three areas that have emerged as common ground between the classroom and the consulting room. I shall consider how the requirement to speak and the requirement to write call for different modes of engagement, and can provoke different types of anxiety. The demand made of students to orally defend their own written work can generate an unproductive level of self-consciousness in which the student appears trapped by her own language. Comparable situations in therapy sessions have given me cause to think about the value of a critical distance from one's own linguistic productions, and techniques for engendering such a distance; I shall explore the function of 'mediating texts' as one such example. I shall then turn to Sigmund Freud's intriguing evocation of the quality of 'aloofness' as that which should colour the patient's engagement with the transference situation. I shall treat Freud's recommendation of aloofness as a mode of critical distance – and a type of impersonality – that can be put to work in the classroom as well as in the consulting room. Finally, and in recognition of my opening vignette, I ask what happens when distance fails; when there seems to be no space for impersonal critique. One way of thinking about the failure of distance is through the lens of shame. Shame comes to the fore when the subject feels herself to have been seen too closely, or to have been exposed as being somehow out-of-place. Here I focus my thought on the contention that the scope for shaming is especially prominent in vocational settings that challenge and interrogate the subject's capacity to know. Taking on board Slavoj Žižek's (2008) provocation that shame is the inevitable affective consequence of being asked a question, I ask how the shaming of the teacher's or therapist's questions might function positively.

Writing and speaking

Staying with Matthew, the student for whom sitting with me in academic supervision appeared to be unbearable, I would like to try to account for the failure of the encounter. In supervision, Matthew and I were due to be talking about his essay on the topic of Freud's theories of sexuality. It would be unreasonable to presume that this topic can be picked up by all students with ease: as a teacher when I speak of psychosexual desire (and introduce the concepts of penis envy, polymorphous perversity, infantile sexuality, the Oedipus complex and the incest taboo, for example), I am asking a lot for my students to speak back to me in the same language. Had we been discussing the status of psychoanalysis as a science, say, Matthew and I may have had a more comfortable supervision. But perhaps not; perhaps it was simply the injunction to speak rather than speaking about sexuality that proved difficult. I've found that students can often write eloquently about a given topic but not necessarily speak about it, and I do not think that this is at all unique to the psychoanalytic subject matter. There is something especially demanding, I would suggest, in asking a student to account for their written work after the event, which is precisely the logic of the supervision system where students and supervisors meet one-on-one and take the student's essay as the catalyst for discussion. The written and spoken word are only loosely related, and it is not always the case that competency in the former is indexed to confidence in the latter. Students demonstrate this frequently through their discomfort, anxiety and confusion at the task of *saying again in speech* what they feel they have already said on the page. But it is precisely in the gap that opens up between these two modes of representation that the lesson itself gets started. Practically, from the perspective of certain educative goals, this gap or disconnect might lead to the student becoming more attentive to the requirements of academic writing (focussing on the clarity of her written expression, and the structure of her argument, for example). However, just as importantly, by scrutinising the distance between her so-called 'authorial intent' and a reader's reception of it, the student may come to a more experiential appreciation of the frustrations of language that psychoanalysis – some traditions more so than others – makes central to its theorising. The student may reflect: 'I don't recognise my meaning in these words'; 'these words do not represent me'; 'I cannot be identical with the words I use to represent myself'; 'I cannot know how my reader will interpret my words which are already distant from me'.

The tension between the written and spoken word can be considered from another angle: if students can resist speaking about their own writing, then a sort of parallel can happen in therapy when a patient expresses the desire to communicate with the analyst via email or letter outside the session. As I read it, the desire to subvert, or outwit, the 'talking cure' in this way could be indicative of the fantasy that there may be a way of being more true to oneself – of representing oneself more fully – if only the conditions of self-narration would allow it. For some, the possibility of expressing oneself through the written word – where time can be taken to arrange and rearrange the order of one's words creating the impression of coherence, exactitude and purpose – is infinitely preferable to being constantly caught short by one's speech. I am reminded of patients who begin their therapy by articulating the wish that it could proceed without words (can there be another way, I ask myself). Perhaps, then, there is something shared between the student who involves herself in the act of deconstructing her own written work, and the patient who undertakes the work of psychotherapy, if only because what is played out in both instances is the experience of being subject to the failures and frustrations of language: whereas the student might say 'I know what I mean, but I can't explain it', or 'when I wrote that I think I meant something else', or 'yes, it's what you said, that's what I meant, but you said it better', the patient is more likely to remain silent.

Mediating texts

Accepting that individual students may find the prospect of speaking (rather than writing) anxiety-inducing, the educational setting has all sorts of 'props' to defend against too much exposure; the central prop being the text itself. With the text comes the introduction of a third element that can intervene in the dyadic relation. In the case of my supervision with Matthew, I was able to say: 'let's turn to the text', where the *subtext* was perhaps: 'let's avert our eyes from each other and find some neutral ground'. Because the student and I now have some autonomous material to address (which exists in a relatively impersonal relation to both of us), one would hope that working directly on the text would immediately reduce the type of anxiety that can be experienced. In the classroom, then, the possibility of a mediating text is always close at hand. There is a parallel observation to be made here with the work of psychotherapy. When a patient comes along with her own text-fragment (whether it be dream material, or a chain of associations that arise in the session) she too is bringing something into the frame that has the potential to act in a mediating capacity. The introduction of this third element in a session may function in all sorts of ways (only one of which could be to alleviate anxiety), but the conditions for *going to work on the text* are, it strikes me, especially precarious. Most critically, in order to explore the text-fragment the patient must already possess the capacity to hold herself at some distance from it.

I am reminded here of one of Freud's discussions of the analytic requirement to manage the patient's 'transference neurosis'. In the third section of *Beyond the Pleasure Principle*, Freud (1920) gives a brief history of the ways in which psychoanalytic technique evolved within the time of his own theorising. He tells us that initially psychoanalytic technique had been an 'art of interpretation' where what was crucial was the analyst's communication of unconscious material to the patient. However, such conscious – we might say 'educative' – communication failed to have therapeutic impact, and so greater attention had to be paid to the patient's *resistances* to his unconscious material. The provocation of the patient's resistances brings into the frame the transference phenomenon, where it is the patient's performative engagement with her resistances (rather than her conscious acknowledgement of them) that ensures the continuing mobilisation of the treatment. As Freud explains it:

> The patient cannot remember the whole of what is repressed in him, and what he cannot remember may be precisely the essential part of it. Thus he acquires no sense of conviction of the correctness of the construction that has been communicated to him. He is obliged to *repeat* the repressed material as a contemporary experience instead of, as the physician would prefer to see, *remembering* it as something belonging to the past … The ratio between what is remembered and what is reproduced varies from case to case. The physician cannot as a rule spare his patient this phase of the treatment. He must get him to re-experience some portion of his forgotten life, but must see to it, on the other hand, that the patient retains some degree of aloofness, which will enable him, in spite of everything, to recognise that what appears to be reality is in fact only a reflection of a forgotten past. (Freud 1920, 18–19)

The most intriguing point that Freud raises in this passage, I would suggest, is the recommendation that the analyst cultivate the patient's 'aloofness' [*Überlegenheit*] in order that the peculiar power of the transference be seen for what it is (i.e. a repetition or 'reflection' of a past situation).[1] Rather than take aloofness in this context to mean a psychological disposition of superiority, which would surely be interpreted as another form of resistance to the material, I take Freud to be referring to the patient's capacity to distance herself from the transferential material. This is indeed a tall order: the patient is in the throws of the transference but is yet required to maintain sufficient distance (with the analyst's aid) to be able to appreciate the formal qualities of her emotional investments. Leaving to one side the taken-for-granted neutrality of the analyst, Freud's thought seems to be that a degree of distance on the patient's part is a prerequisite for any interpretative work to commence. Resuming my previous comparison, then, for the patient to be able to engage with her own text-fragment in such a way that allows the work of interpretation to be taken up, she must be both invested in the enactment, and able to appreciate its form. I am inclined to think that there is a sort of learning at stake in all of this; that sometimes part of the work is to invite simultaneous investment *and* detachment towards the 'text' in question; to encourage the subject (whether the subject of education and/or therapy) to aspire to a degree of 'aloofness' with regard to her own material; to encourage her in her capacity as 'reader' of her own material where the very act of reading requires a standing to one side; and, in so doing, to explore the possibility of an *impersonal* relation to the self. I would suggest that in my supervision with Matthew we did not manage to achieve this type of impersonal investment in the material that facilitates critical reading. Importantly, it is this failing that opens the door to shame. However, there is a paradox to be anticipated here (and pursued further below): whilst I would acknowledge that the persistence of a destructive and immobile mode of shame may account for my negative supervision experience with Matthew, I shall also reserve the possibility that the very same shame-dynamics – those of proximity and distance; situatedness and dislocation – can work productively to mobilise the type of impersonality that I suggest is key to critical reflection, and that Freud suggested was necessary to the patient's handling of the transference.

What I have indicated so far is that the substantive topic in question – in this case psychoanalysis and sexuality – may be sufficiently difficult to create an awkward atmosphere in academic supervision, or to provoke a communicative impasse. Furthermore, there are innumerable factors relating to a particular student's psychobiography that are not for me to concern myself with too directly in the classroom. I remarked above that Matthew's apparent distress would have been easier for me to take on board had we been in a therapy context; but in supervision the force of his feelings were not the legitimate object of our discussion. The thought I would like to raise now is that these factors – the particular topic of discussion, and the student's idiosyncratic psychology – can be left to one side as we consider a more general difficulty that pertains to both the classroom and the consulting room.

Shame and the question form

In his *The Sublime Object of Ideology*, Slavoj Žižek ([1989] 2008) makes reference to a book by Aron Bodenheimer entitled *Why? On the Obscenity of Questioning* (*Warum?: Von der Obszönität des Fragens*; Bodenheimer [1984] 2011). Bodenheimer's thesis, Žižek explains, is that there is something obscene in the very act of asking a question, without regard to its content. It is the form of the question as such which is obscene: the question lays open, exposes, denudes its addressee, it invades his sphere of intimacy; this is why the basic, elementary reaction to a question is shame on the bodily level, blushing and lowering our eyes, like a child of whom we ask 'What were you doing?' (Žižek [1989] 2008, 202)

That a question can be felt as a violent imposition is evident in our everyday language practices, consider the following phrases: he was confronted by a barrage of questions; he was subject to an assault of questions; the interviewer saved his most penetrating question till last; he took a battering from the questioner. These mundane examples suggest that a question can insert itself with a force and an uninvited intimacy into the very core of the addressee. The question gets 'inside', so to speak; it insists on being received and hence provokes 'shame on the bodily level'. It is not quite that the question demands an actual *response* (although, as I mentioned above, the injunction to speak can no doubt be a cause of anxiety in itself), it is rather that the question demands a *reception*. The question does its obscene work in advance of – and irrespective of – the answer it elicits.

Žižek ([1989] 2008) holds that the act of 'questioning is the basic procedure for the totalitarian intersubjective relationship' (202) because the end goal is not the right answer, or in fact any answer, but rather 'a point at which the answer is not possible, where the word is lacking, where the subject is exposed in his impotence' (202). Hence 'totalitarian power is not a dogmatism which has all the answers; it is, on the contrary, the instance which has all the questions' (203). Clearly, Žižek's treatment of Bodenheimer's thesis on the obscenity of the question works in the service of his broader theoretical project. For the purposes of this paper, however, it is necessary only to engage with the claim that the question form is indecent because it seeks to reveal in the addressee a state of impotence and not-knowing. Can it really be the case, we might well ask, that all questions function in this way?

Indeed, the suggestion that the question operates in the service of obscenity and exposure may sit uneasily with those of us who rely on the practice of questioning (alongside listening and other practices of reflection) to perform our vocational identities. Therapists just as much as teachers (or social scientists for that matter) develop expertise in selecting the types of questions they use to engage their addressee. In doing so, no doubt, we also exercise caution with respect to those questions that might be received as destructive impingements on the subject; but Žižek's provocation here is that all questions are indecent so 'caution' is not quite the point. As a teacher and a therapist I have observed my own caution in this regard and retrospectively attributed it to something like care, or concern. But I am reminded of Philip Rieff's (1965, 158) helpful aphorism that 'care is the polite form of desire', and, accordingly, suggest that the question that is withheld in the name of concern or educative/therapeutic wisdom may also function to conceal the desire of the questioner. In which case the shame that inheres in the question form is immediately polyvalent: it is not simply that my question exposes you, for I too am exposed in the asking of it. And, to reiterate, we cannot escape this predicament simply by *taking care* because in crafting my question so as not to expose you, not only do I risk exposing myself (perhaps as someone with an inflated valuation of her own words), but I also risk putting shame into play with the inference that you could be made vulnerable by my less-than-carefully-worded question. The philosopher Alenka Zupančič highlights this possibility when she supplements Bodenheimer's argument by stressing that the obscenity of the question 'does not operate only on the level of exposing the other (the addressee of the question), but also on the level of exposing oneself' (Zupančič 2007, 162–3). However, if all this implies that shame is unavoidable in contexts where questions are asked, it also underscores just how unstable are our economies of knowledge and desire. Shame signals this instability; it communicates and compounds the subject's feelings of being 'caught out', or being seen too intimately by – and with – another. Zupančič glosses this point thus:

> Bodenheimer's definition of obscenity is that it takes place in the conditions where certain parts of my personality – parts that I normally hide from the others or from myself – are revealed directly and without me being prepared for it. I am being exposed without being able to prevent this. In the situation of obscenity, there is an act of exposure on the one side, and the effect of shame on the other. (Zupančič 2007 162)

With the rush of shame, that which would normally remain hidden or even unknown is, if only for a moment, revealed and made explicit. If we can envisage a productive potential in shame's two-way dynamic, it may be as a mechanism for thinking about how the precariousness of one's identity is always implicated in its relations with others.

In their recent work on shame and sexuality, Pajaczkowska and Ward propose that:

> …shame, the most painfully isolating of emotions, announces the presence of another, the person who shames us and the person before whom we are shamed, and as such it is one of the earliest social feelings … Shame exists in this double register of self-consciousness-with-others. (Pajaczkowska and Ward 2008, 1)

Because the presence of another is already at work in the moment of shame, isolation cannot be thought about in wholly oppositional terms to sociality. Shame's double register, in other words, implicates both isolation and sociality in the same instance. A further reason for shame's productivity, then, may be that it encourages us to consider the constant and volatile movement between isolation and sociality, including the shameful moments of their collapse into each other.

It is necessary to clarify that the social other does not need to be standing as a physical witness to the scene of shame; just as we can be caught out by our own questions, so too can we feel shame when there is nobody there to see us. Moreover, shame's double register calls into question the very idea of clearly marked boundaries between self and other. We might say that shame is all about boundary disputes: we feel shame when we fall short of ourselves, or when we overstep ourselves, or when another gets too close, or when another remains too distant to recognise us as we want to be seen. Shame keeps the antagonisms of isolation and sociality, distance and proximity, and situatedness and dislocation in conversation (the phenomenon of vicarious or contagious shame indicates just how mobile shame can be). Common to all shame scenarios, though, is the fact that the space of the self that the subject seeks to preserve is in some way trespassed. If we follow Žižek's account then this is felt as a breach or a rupture – i.e. the subject is 'laid open', 'exposed', 'denuded' and 'invaded' – but it is by no means established that this violation is entirely negative (or even unpleasurable). Presumably when the subject is laid open, the prospect of a different freedom comes into play; one where the contours of the subject's very subjectivity may be reimagined. Likewise, if we take the dislocation or 'out-of-placeness' that so often marks the shamed subject we can anticipate certain pleasures in being temporarily estranged (or released) from the resources and convictions that hold a particular self-conception in place. A further way in which shame is productive, then, is in its challenge to the idea that we can be secure in our sense of proprietorship; that we can declare the boundaries of our self-identity to be fixed and stable; and that we can know just what belongs where, or as the over-defended therapist might wish to assert 'that's your stuff, not my stuff'. To put it somewhat differently, we could say that the shameful act of trespass invites us to reconsider our property rights.

Conclusion

We can return now, by way of a conclusion, to my supervision with Matthew. Although I cannot know with certainty that our experiences of the hour we spent together were commensurate, I reflected afterwards on the ways in which a two-way mode of shame may have been created in our supervision. As I intimated above, the shame of shame rebounds: perhaps Matthew read my concern for him as condescension, which presumably would have compounded his self-consciousness; and from my perspective, the possibility that I was even formally responsible for what I took to be a profound discomfort on Matthew's part no doubt heightened my own sense of shame. But critically, in the supervision hour at least, the shame that was operative between us did not get put to good work. Faced with Matthew's silence, I used more language; I explicated the texts we were supposed to be discussing and I asked more questions. In therapy no doubt I would have let the silence stand, uninterrupted. Irrespective of how speculative or tactful my questions were, if we follow the thesis put forward by Bodenheimer and developed by Žižek and Zupančič, then they always had the potential to be received by my addressee as obscene impositions. With their rude proximity, questions threaten the subject's capacity to maintain the type of distance – or aloof impersonality – that is of value both to a learning encounter and to the work of therapy. Distance is diminished at the moment when the question impinges on the subject's space of self. And with this act of trespass, the question infers the possibility that there is another who knows the boundaries of the addressee better than she does; perhaps also, that there is another who is closer to her desire than she is. This inference wounds the ego and risks a defensive withdrawal. But, in principle at least, the breach of the ego is also a release. After all, if, momentarily, the subject has been caught out and feels less than herself, then she is also provoked into reimaging the familiar boundaries of her ego because, unexpectedly, there is another on the scene to account for (i.e. shame is always a 'self-consciousness-with-others'). Moreover, when a question penetrates, and the subject sees the other at a more intimate proximity, the shame she feels ceases to belong exclusively to her because the other who has transgressed on to the place of her desires is, by virtue of this act, obliged to share it with her.

We can think again of Freud's recognition of the importance of managing the transference. In the transference the 'correct' allocation of boundaries between self and other – and between multiple and past selves and others – is a necessary impossibility. For the transference to be set in motion, subject positions have to be, temporarily at least, 'laid open'. The therapeutic relationship is one in which a degree of trespassing on to the grounds of the other is central to the work. What is also central is a degree of not-knowing; if the transference is almost unbearable for the patient, as Freud seems to recognise, then it is because a secure knowledge of who (and what) the other is is unattainable. Such unattainability is, of course, enhanced by the therapist's conscious cultivation of transferred – or displaced – material, but it is also symptomatic of social relations beyond the consulting room. If there is a shame in this, there is also a pleasure. When Freud advises that the therapist cultivate in the patient a quality of 'aloofness' in order that the patient can 'recognise that what appears to be reality is in fact only a reflection of a forgotten past…', he points us to a paradox; the quality of distanced appreciation – or aloof impersonality – emerges from the intimate pains of transference love.

Note
1. I explore further the signification of 'aloof' in this passage in an article co-authored with Barry Sheils entitled 'Tragedy and transference in D.M. Thomas's *The White Hotel*' (Sheils and Walsh 2013).

References
Bodenheimer, A. R. 2011 [1984]. *Warum?: Von Der Obszönität Des Fragens*. Reclam: Ditzingen.
Freud, S. 1920. "Beyond the Pleasure Principle." In *The Standard Edition of the Complete Psychological Works of Sigmund Freud*. vol. 18, edited by J. Strachey and A. Freud, 1–64. London: Hogarth Press and Institute for Psychoanalysis.
Pajaczkowska, C., and I. Ward. 2008. *Shame and Sexuality: Psychoanalysis and Visual Culture*. London: Routledge.
Rieff, P. 1965. *Freud: The Mind of the Moralist*. London: University Paperbacks (Methuen).
Sheils, B., and J. Walsh. 2013. "Tragedy and Transference in D. M. Thomas's the White Hotel." *Psychoanalysis and History* 15 (1): 69–89.
Žižek, S. 2008 [1989]. *The Sublime Object of Ideology*. London: Verso.
Zupančič, A. 2007. "Lying on the Couch: Psychoanalysis and the Question of the Lie." In *Cultures of Lying: Theories and Practice of Lying in Society. Literature, and Film*, edited by Mecke, J., 155–168. Berlin, Galda & Wilch Verlag.

Bringing up gender: academic abjection?

Emily F. Henderson

Faculty of Polity and Society, Institute of Education, University of London, London, UK

> The principal questions raised in this article are: what does it mean to bring up the topic of gender in a space where it is not known, and how can this moment of bringing up gender – or not bringing it up – be conceptualised? The article departs from the thoughts and questions that were provoked by an interview conducted with a Gender Studies student as part of a wider study; the personal experiences of the author and the theoretical interrogation of the issue of bringing up gender are also addressed as 'data'. The approach that I develop builds on and troubles other Social Scientists' uses of Julia Kristeva's theorisation of abjection in *Powers of Horror* (1980), and constructs a notion of qualitative analysis that uses Kristeva's conceptualisation of metaphor to relate theory to data. I attempt a use of the theory that accords with the textual representation of abjection in *Powers of Horror*. During the article, the notion of 'bringing up gender' evolves from a question of not knowing how to bring up gender, to not knowing how to bring up the never-knowable that is gender in the context of academic abjection. The aim of the article is to destabilise reflection on how gender 'knowledge' is – and can be – brought into relevance.

Upbringing

It is an all-too-familiar feeling in our professional lives (not to mention our personal contexts, if the two can be separated): we are surrounded by people we respect, or are supposed to respect, at a conference or in a class, for example, and suddenly our engagement is invaded by a searing heat and deafening noise. We become aware that something important is absent from the discussion, gender for example, and that realisation of relevance creates an insurmountable barrier between us and the ongoing discussion, which continues as if nothing has happened. Bile: all of the ways in which gender is pertinent to the discussion rise up in clamouring unison. Not only can we no longer concentrate on the discussion, but the heat, akin to nausea, spreads from our swirling innards to our hands and legs: do we raise a hand, walk out, stand up and start spewing…? We know that if we do any of these things, even if we take the sensible route and wait to be asked for a contribution, politely apologising for our comment in advance, we will have taken a position that will alter irrevocably both the tone of the discussion *and* the identity that we are seen as embodying. If we 'bring up' gender, we will render the undeniable physicality of gender present to a room whose order depended on the upheld illusion of an 'emotion-free zone', a 'site of pure rationality' (Leathwood and Hey 2009, 429). What repercussions will the action of 'bringing up gender' have? We risk being branded as feminist activists, as the one who always harps on about gender. If we stay silent and swallow the rising bile, on the other hand, we are enacting a betrayal of our political instincts. There is no available option for inaction: both intervening and remaining silent are actions. The challenge then takes the form of a decision-making process of if and when and how to intervene, and how to cool the heat and dampen the noise in order to re-engage with the ongoing discussion in a manner that makes this physical intervention of knowing most effective, least physically disruptive.

The expression 'to bring up' in English bears three contrasting but related meanings that come together in this discussion. Firstly, the notion of introducing a topic, in which 'gender' is raised as a relevant idea to an academic exchange. Secondly, 'to bring up' food, to vomit. This meaning maps via analogy on to the action of introducing 'gender' to a discussion: 'gender', signifier of the physical, the human, is 'vomited' into the domain of the cerebral. Finally, 'to bring up' a child, to raise, educate, form: when 'gender' is brought up, introduced, vomited, it is pre-formed and shaped within its embodied home, and emerges into the world of the lecture theatre in a form that is constructed by the speaker. I employ the linguistic dovetailing of these three meanings to magnify and interrogate the action of 'bringing up gender'.

The idea for this paper originates from a pair of interviews with a student on a Gender Studies Master's module that I conducted in 2011 for a study on the learning of 'gender' through personal reflection in the Gender Studies classroom (Henderson 2012). The student in question, Anisha (pseudonym), was taking the class as an optional module for the Master's programme on which she was enrolled in an English university. Anisha had never formally studied gender before, and was taking the course to follow up on a personal interest in the topic. In Anisha's case, as with others that I interviewed, the course was perceived as having had a transformational effect on her, and it had led her to re-read her personal narrative, her home community and upbringing, as gendered. Anisha recounted a process of learning that moved from not knowing gender, or at least of not knowing gender well enough ('gender-unaware[ness]'), to developing an analytical gender lens, termed 'gender awareness' or, in a more nuanced form, 'gender sensitivity' (Leach 2003, 22). This lens permitted her to identify where gender could or should have been discussed in other Master's modules or educational settings in which she was involved. However, through further discussion with Anisha during our two interviews, I became aware that, whilst an acquired gender lens may seem to represent the 'job done' of a Gender Studies course, this learning objective leaves the student ill-equipped to decide how to act upon – bring up or swallow – the moment of 'nausea' when gender presents itself as relevant. The aim of this paper is to magnify the moment of 'nausea', to interrogate the action of 'bringing up' gender, in order to develop an understanding of 'bringing up' that could encourage students and academics alike to interrogate their own positions of knowing or not knowing gender, of bringing up or swallowing.

The interrogation takes the form of an analytical process that I shape in the second section, 'Bringing up', from a primary reading of Kristeva's *Powers of Horror* (Kristeva 1983).[1] A substantial proportion of this article is dedicated to the development of an analytical method that circles around the concept of 'the abject' that Kristeva develops in *Powers of Horror*. The justification for this is twofold. Firstly, I consider that this moment of 'bringing up', whilst only lasting a few seconds in the event, is an epicentre for the political capacity – and incapacity – of the concept of gender. As such, close textual engagement with theory is required for the development of an analytical method that seeks to magnify the emotions and processes of signification that surround this otherwise perfunctory occurrence. Secondly, I aim to contribute to the tradition of applying Kristeva's notion of the abject to the fieldwork contexts of social and educational sciences. This tradition encompasses topics as various as racism, sexism and homophobia (Young 1990), ageing mothers (Bousfield 2000), the working classes and Aboriginality (Kenway, Kraack, and Hickey-Moody 2006), alcohol consumption in young people (Nairn et al. 2006), television makeover programmes (Ringrose and Walkerdine 2008), skin-improvement products (Kenway and Bullen 2011), and, in the field of education studies, learning about gender in a social concepts class (Moffat 2004), boffin and geek identities (Francis 2009; Mendick and Francis 2011), bullying and social exclusion (Sondergaard 2012), and new teachers' identity formation (Somerville and Rennie 2012). The method of application in these studies, with the exception of Iris Marion Young's (1990) essay, is to set out the conceptual matrix of abjection, and to seek the equivalent points of the field to map on to the conceptual matrix. I problematise this mode of application further through the rest of the article, but at this stage I am merely hinting at the possibility of a more developed mode of application: one that engages with the textual and signification processes that are often neglected by Social Scientists in Kristeva's theorisation of abjection. Through a precise exploration of contrasting conceptualisations of metaphor, I aim to craft a methodological use of abjection that pushes, and is pushed by, my data (Jackson and

Mazzei 2012), and that complements Sara Ahmed's (2012) and Vanessa Andreotti's (2013) conceptualisations of similar moments in connection with diversity and postcolonialism. 'Academic abjection' thus serves both as a conceptualisation of a situation of knowing and not knowing, and as a mode of writing research.

I begin by bringing up the 'data' that serve as materials for analysis in this paper. The next section, 'Brought up', contains excerpts from the transcript of the interviews with Anisha, where gender is conceptualised as known but swallowed. In this section, I present the data, and open the article's discussion space for the bringing up of abjection. In the following section, 'Bringing up', I address modes of application for Kristeva's theorisation of abjection, and, in an engagement with the literary criticism that addresses *Powers of Horror*, as well as the clues that Kristeva gives in her text, I suggest a mode of application that listens to the 'roguish data' (Mazzei 2007, 55) of bringing up gender. In the final section, 'Bringing up gender', I apply the analytical mode of abjection to the data that were presented in 'Brought up', in an attempt to magnify the importance of 'knowhow' for bringing up gender. I conclude with some comments on further questions that the paper raises, and an evaluation of the usefulness of abjection as an analytical mode.

Brought up

I now present some interview text that I am bringing up as 'data'. These data have provoked me to find a theoretical lens that will allow me to explore them, and their resonances in my own lived and observed experiences, in greater detail. In presenting the data, I offer my first analysis: that of selecting and (re-)writing. Although I am presenting the interview as data, rather than as theoretical analysis, of course the interview emerges ready-theorised in 'descriptive' form. I appeal to the reader to empathise, by bringing my own presence as interviewer and writer into relief against the eroded content of the questions and answers of the interview. I do not pretend to supply fresh data: that which I present as relevant to bringing up has always already been brought up by me, introduced and vomited in the form that I have chosen. As such, I introduce Anisha and her words as relevant to my questions of bringing up and abjection. In the subsequent section of the article, I move on to establish an analytical framework to address the questions that my portrayal of the data bring up.

When I interviewed Anisha, she was in the first term of the second year of her two-year Master's programme. She was attending the interdisciplinary Gender Studies module that was the focus of my study as the only optional module in what was otherwise a highly programmed and practical Master's qualification. She told me she had chosen this module because gender had always been an interest of hers, but also because this interest had flourished in the educational context of London in which she had found herself; Anisha had been raised in a tight-knit immigrant community in a 'very conservative state' of the United States, in which 'it was basically you're male or female and that's it, there's no fluidity' (Anisha's words). I interviewed her twice in 2011 in the space of a month, for about an hour each time, and we discussed her experiences of the Gender Studies module, as well as how these experiences were feeding into and out of her other Master's courses, her own teaching and her experiences in general. I used an 'interview guide' (Cohen et al. 2011, 413) rather than structured questions, but in the second interview I employed some structured questions that related to themes raised in the first interview. On several occasions during the interviews, Anisha referred to the way that her new, more formal understanding of gender had made her see things in a new way. It was clear that the Gender Studies module represented a contrast to her other modules, and that her newly refined gender lens had travelled across into her other classroom contexts, but that she was not bringing up the findings revealed by this lens in these classrooms. I found myself identifying with all of the reasons she gave for not bringing up gender in her other classes, and found these reasons articulated in ways I had not formulated or interrogated for myself, but simultaneously I did not identify with Anisha's desire to keep her gender analyses to herself. Furthermore, the Gender Studies teacher in me became dissatisfied with my own lack of justifications or strategies as to when and how gender should be brought up.

Anisha was clear about the factors that would render a discussion space hospitable for gender to be brought up: the teacher would have to have planned for a discussion of this sort, and would need background knowledge in gender. Furthermore, Anisha herself would need a firmer grasp of the concepts, and her peers would also need some background knowledge. What she seemed to be describing as a space where gender could be brought up in a way that would not be perceived as a disruption or confrontation was, in fact, a Gender Studies classroom. Anisha planned to include gender topics in her own teaching, but could not impose the issue on to her teachers' lesson plans. When I asked her to think more about why she felt unable to bring up gender, she explained:

> maybe if I bring it up then ... the students might not know how to respond to me and so I might feel like it's just something kind of thrown out there but it's just like an elephant on the table I guess ... I don't want it to be something that makes others uncomfortable or feeling awkward.

This statement was a key element in my conceptualisation of the brought up topic of gender as abject, of the bringing up as academic abjection. In this response, Anisha posits gender as external to herself, as 'thrown out there', as external to everybody, as 'an elephant on the table'. However, she also situates herself in relation to the topic, in that 'the students' would have to 'respond to [her]' about this brought up gender, and they 'might not know how'; she would be responsible for their 'uncomfortable' or 'awkward' feelings. As I go on to discuss, the dialectic between an inside and outside, where this binary is both shored up and undermined, exceeded, is a core element of Kristeva's theory of abjection, and furthermore it is this problematised binary that serves as a launch pad for the many social theorists who structure their analyses according to the conceptual layout of abjection. My first reaction was also to apply one such conceptual layout to Anisha's words; my version of the situation at this stage was that bringing up gender is like vomiting on a clean floor, where the resulting mess is both seen as belonging to and external to Anisha, both inappropriately superimposed on to and yet now part of the clean floor of abstract academic discussion. The presence of this mess, that is neither fully an abstract concept nor a personal, private matter, introduces uncertainty to the classroom as to how the 'speaking bodies' (Becker-Leckrone 2005, 24) that are present in the academic discussion should be understood. I found this initial conceptualisation quite pleasing and descriptive, until I engaged in a more thorough reading of *Powers of Horror* and the corpus of critical literature that surrounds it. I realised that applying the theory in this way was in some vital ways contrary to Kristeva's textual project: the neatness of mapping theory directly on to the 'field' (in this case 'bringing up gender') runs against Kristeva's quest to trouble the clear waters of signification. Moreover, where abjection is used to *organise* and *structure* the field, the resultant writing, in asserting the potency of abjection as an analytical lens, paradoxically damages the potential of abjection as a *dis*organising concept and mode of writing, as 'not a thing but a potentiality' (Becker-Leckrone 2005, 33). I now offer an account of how the theory of abjection could be construed as a *dis*organising concept that troubles and extends this initial understanding of bringing up gender.

Bringing up

Bringing up Kristeva's theory of abjection is in itself a choice of introducing, raising, regurgitating. I could begin by describing some of the uses of abjection that I listed in the introduction, or I could paraphrase some of the authoritative voices who present and interpret Kristeva's texts for us, or I could attempt my own explanation of the text. Lacking certainty with regards to the purpose of any of these received routes, I begin with a question: *To what extent is writing about abjection writing abjection?* In asking this question, I hope to have circumvented the necessity of confidently stating, 'Abjection is…'. The reason for this circumnavigation is that abjection relates to our acquisition of language and our status as subjects, in that it calls to a realm of doubt where signifier does not match neatly on to signified, where we have not yet tried to make sense of the world in a language that has already made sense of us (Lechte 1990, chap. 6; Schippers 2011, chap. 1; Smith 1996, chap. 4). To un-ironically explain abjection in terms of what it 'is' is an action of fixing, of matching signifier with signified, in conjunction with the very theoretical term that forbids us from doing so with certainty. Kristeva's own anaphoric use of 'abjection "is"' sends the reader into a disorientating, disjunctive set of definitions that make a mockery of the syntax of definition.

The uses that are made of Kristeva's theory often take an un-ironic 'abjection "is"' approach, in that they work from an explanation of abjection that is given by a literary critic, often the summary and citation which Judith Butler includes in *Gender Trouble* (Butler 1999, 181), or they take guidance from one or more of the 'abjection "is"' statements that proliferate in *Powers of Horror*. This analytical practice then consists in elucidating the key features of abjection and making analogies between these features and aspects of the field of study. An example of this type of analysis can be found in the Nairn et al. (2006) study on young people who do not drink alcohol. At one stage of this article, the authors quote one of Kristeva's 'definitions': 'Kristeva (1983, 4) notes that 'It is thus not lack of cleanliness or health that causes abjection but what disturbs identity, system, order. What does not respect borders, positions, rules. The in-between, the ambiguous, the composite' (297). They then seek 'borders, positions, rules' and where 'system, order' are 'disturb[ed]' in their field. Alcohol thus becomes the 'disturb[ing]' agent for these young non-drinkers, where alcohol has an abjecting effect on their friends, who become 'different people' (297), 'abject, out-of-control bod[ies]' (299) when they drink. I am far from implying that this constitutes a redundant use of abjection. This technique of seeking analogies between theoretical expressions and aspects of the field is useful in this case for developing conceptualisations of alcohol consumption beyond essentialised or simplified versions that construct alcohol and drinkers as separate entities. In this study, the use of abjection theory as an analogy for alcohol consumption *dis*organises the separated entities of alcohol consumption into a series of contiguous separations and combinations (the drunk person from their normal self, the drink from the state of drunkenness), and so produces a more complex understanding of the field.

However, this application of abjection falls short of capitalising on the 'potentiality' of abjection; it builds on a conceptual neatness that is derived from the single definition of abjection that is cited, and the result is a separation between the researcher(s' text) and the state of abjection. This act of separation amounts to following the processes of meaning-making that Kristeva in fact aims to disrupt: in this study of alcohol and abjection, the authors are able to demarcate abjection in their field without being troubled by the processes of abjection working on them or their written representation of the field. Yet Kristeva implicates the authorial, 'analyst (intellectual)' voice (Smith 1996, 154), as well as the reader's eye, in the chaos that is usually reserved for the researched field. Whilst this and other similar applications of abjection to the researched field may lead to the productive *dis*organisation of the field in question, they do not emulate the 'discursive method' (Becker-Leckrone 2005, 35) of Kristeva's text, which is arguably a compulsory facet of the theory, in that the text 'performs and inspires the crisis of place that it describes' (35). Anna Smith (1996, 158) writes of 'a reading experience which may … lead us to the very edge of our identity as speaking being': this is the text of data analysis that I tentatively seek to establish.

With the exception of Iris Marion Young (1990, 210), who explicitly plays with the subject position 'I' in her essay on abjection, and Dorte Marie Sondergaard (2012, 355), who explains that she deliberately 'detaches [abjection] from concrete persons', social and cultural theorists who make use of abjection do not tend to discuss the linguistic properties and – dare I say – obligations of the concept. In the literary criticism on *Powers of Horror*, however, Kristeva's style comes under regular scrutiny. There is some disagreement as to what Kristeva is trying to do or show with the text that sets out 'her very least reassuring and most notoriously difficult theoretical concept' (Becker-Leckrone 2005, 20). For Juliet Flower MacCannell (2003), Kristeva is waging 'a hopeless guerilla warfare' (71) against 'the prison-house of language' (92), and her messy text is the evidence of this struggle against the order and structure of linguistic expression. Kelly Oliver (1993, 105) reads the 'oscillation between poetry and dense theory' in Kristeva's text as 'an oscillation between assigning the semiotic priority and assigning the symbolic priority': where does Kristeva let the structures of language order her thoughts, and where does the speaking, feeling body interrupt the smooth 'written' flow? Whilst the reasoning for – and success of – Kristeva's textual project vary according to different critics, there is a degree of accord between them that Kristeva's text in some way 'is … abject' (Oliver 1993, 104), 'produce[s] abjection' (Smith 1996, 155), '"incarnates" abjection in its very rhythms and contours' (Becker-Leckrone 2005, 37). How then to write abjection into data analysis?

One way I have found to access the abjection in my relationship with 'field' and 'text' is to appeal to Kristeva's comments on metaphor, which reside in the same realm as Jacques Derrida's 'White Mythology' ('La mythologie blanche') (Derrida 1972; Derrida and Moore 1974) and Paul Ricoeur's *The Rule of Metaphor* (*La métaphore vive*) (Ricoeur 1975; Ricoeur and Czerny 1986). Ricoeur and Derrida both destabilise the definition of metaphor that involves a comparison between a literal object and a figurative, or non-literal object, where the linking of the two objects brings about an enhanced or altered understanding of the literal object. In the metaphorical statement, 'the classroom is a prison', for example, the classroom would be understood as the literal object that is being described by the metaphorical term, 'prison'. The attributes of a prison, such as enclosed space, surveillance, punishment, are brought to an understanding of the classroom via this metaphorical link. These attributes come to mind because the metaphorical link draws attention to the attributes of the literal object which may be shared with the metaphorical term but which are only explicitly drawn out in this comparison. In Ricoeur's and Derrida's accounts of metaphor, however, the binary of literal and non-literal is undermined by the relentless querying of language as ever being literal as such. How can a unit of language that is always in a relationship of *re*presentation with the object to which it refers, ever literally *be* that object, without some degree of figurative authoring? The reader of these accounts is forced to rethink her relationship with language, in that she becomes simultaneously unsure of the possibility of figurative language and convinced by its importance (Henderson, 2014).

Kristeva's treatment of metaphor, in the chapter of *Powers of Horror* entitled 'Something to be afraid of', relates to the destabilisation of the literal–figurative binary that Ricoeur and Derrida effect. Kristeva conceptualises phobia as the 'métaphore manquée du manque' (PoH 46 Fr.). This phrase is translated as 'abortive metaphor of want' (PoH 35 Eng.), which removes the anaphora of 'manque', or 'lack'/'miss', in noun and adjective form, and so detracts from the alliterative circularity and ambiguity of the phrase. Perhaps 'métaphore manquée' can best be understood in conjunction with the French expression for 'tomboy', 'garçon manqué', where the implication is that the girl is both recognised as boy and other than boy (a boy that lacks), less than boy (a missed boy, in the sense of a missed shot). 'Métaphore manquée' thus could be said to constitute *both* a recognisable metaphor, with a literal object and figurative object, *and* a metaphor that misses its mark, that is lacking in some vital way.

This simultaneous state does not feel very possible; it is compounded by further exploration of 'manque', or 'lack'. 'Lack' indicates Kristeva's conceptualisation of phobia as being associated, via an object of fear, with lack (of an object), with the 'unnameable ... absence at the origin of language' (Lechte 1990, 160). Metaphors 'ought to' contain a metaphorical term and a literal referent, but this metaphor exceeds and falls short of these requirements: we have three terms, fear, phobic object, non-object. The phobic object is the metaphorical term for the literal referent fear, in that fear is signified by the phobic object, but the metaphor has 'missed' ('manquée') its mark. Fear itself is bound up in a metaphorical relationship with the lack of an object that recalls the pre-linguistic state where subjects and objects had not yet come into play, and which, after language acquisition, only emerges in abjection. Phobia is a 'metaphor of want [manque] as such' (PoH 35 Eng., 46 Fr.); linguistically, 'want' or 'lack' ask for an object (grammatical rules oblige us to say we want or lack *something*), but 'want as such' uncomfortably rejects the need for an object (the 'as such' takes the place of the *something*, but is also not actually an object). This understanding of metaphor is comparable with Derrida's 'heliotropic metaphors', where 'one of the terms ... implicated in the substitution ... cannot be known in its literal form' (Derrida 1972, 299), but it also goes beyond this formulation, in that (at least) one of terms cannot be known at all, because it 'is' 'something else, ... some non-thing, ... something unknowable' (PoH 42 Eng., 53 Fr.). The phobic object is 'a metaphor that is the anaphora of nothing' (PoH 42 Eng., 53 Fr.): the discernible object in this situation is paired in a metaphor with two – or no – referents: fear and/or a 'non-thing'. As the metaphor circles from the metaphorical term to the (referent/s) and back again, 'the traces of the frailty of the subject's signifying system' are exposed (PoH 35 Eng., 46 Fr.): metaphor makes it possible to understand phobia, but, in the process, metaphor must abandon its place as a trope in 'verbal rhetoric' (PoH 35 Eng., 46 Fr.) and enter a realm of affect and non-fixity.

In the 'abjection "is"' application of the theory, as set out in the alcohol study example, the relationship of field ('bringing up gender') to theory (abjection) could be described as a relationship between an unproblematised literal referent and metaphorical term, a 'smooth, regulated production of ... stable meanings' (Gross 1990, 82). If, to return to the question posed at the start of this section, writing about abjection *is* writing abjection, the relationship between field and theory should bear some experience of abjection's 'iffy state' (Dimen 2005, 5) that is inscribed in the text as the reminder of the 'impure chaos out of which is was formed' (Gross 1990, 90). This relationship could take the form of the metaphor that has been shaken to its core by Kristeva's conceptualisation of phobia. We could see the field (the phobic object, 'bringing up gender') as a metaphor for the (non-)referent that is, or is not, abjection (non-)theory. What if, in the relationship between the 'bringing up gender' and abjection theory, the 'bringing up gender' can only be metaphorical, and abjection takes the place of the literal referent? What if, following on from this, abjection theory can only be literal if it signifies the impossibility of anything ever being literal? Working from the perspective that 'bringing up gender' *is not* abjection, I now return to the discussion of 'bringing up gender' and the 'data'.

Bringing up gender: 'métaphore manquée du manque'?

So long as identity is absent, rubbish is not dangerous. (Douglas 1966, 160)

This is a sentence from *Purity and Danger*, the work by Mary Douglas that at least in part inspired Kristeva's theory of abjection. Here it represents the understanding of the question of 'bringing up gender' that I have been working with so far, where 'gender' is signified by 'rubbish'. In the 'abjection "is"' mode of interpretation that I first used on the 'bringing up gender' scenario, I now come to realise that I perceived gender as only dangerous when it is known by one and generally not known, when it is brought into a context with multiple academic identities who deny (by repressing and repulsing) the danger of gender. In this section, I explore the repercussions of this initial understanding for my analysis of 'bringing up gender', which are a neglect of that which is brought up: gender. In reconsidering the position of gender in the key question of this article, I come to perceive 'rubbish' as always already 'dangerous' to the system of signification that designates it as such. Thus the one who brings gender up must not only face abjection by those present, but must also deal with the abjecting process of putting gender into words with which it cannot be known. I now address these points in more detail, before returning to the 'data'.

When I first began to conceptualise the moment of bringing up gender, I now realise that I drew up a binary schema of inside and outside: I asked, what happens when gender bubbles up inside, *and then* how does it sometimes come to boil over into the room? I paired these two states with two different states of knowing: the boiling inside was associated with knowing gender, and I connected the boiling over (or deciding when and how to boil over) with knowing how to bring up gender. The allegory with which I began this paper situated bringing up gender in a matrix of nausea. It was my intention to *dis*organise my field (bringing up gender) and written text with this allegory, which was in fact operating at some level as an organising principle. I assumed that the 'gender' of 'bringing up gender' was known, and that 'bringing up' was the unknown.

In battling to understand the 'bringing up', I had drawn up a fieldwork mirror of abjection. In this mirror, the concept of gender emerges as vomit, as the 'elephant on the table' that is then external to and yet part of the one who brought it up. Because the vomit/gender brings the physical into the cerebral, the speaking body into the realm of the 'ultra-protected signifier' (PoH 49 Eng., 60–61 Fr.), it provokes revulsion for the speaking body in the other, gender unaware, people present. This reaction of disgust is the manifestation of abjection, where abjection acts as a 'safeguard[]' against the '[n]ot me. Not that. But not nothing either' which, 'if I acknowledge it, annihilates me' (PoH 2 Eng., 10 Fr.). In other words, the reaction of disgust and embarrassment that the vomit/gender provokes is a protective mechanism that prevents the academic subject ('me') having to face up to the fragility of the divide between the cloistered object of academic discourse and the non-object that surges up from the speaking being. And this upbringing recalls a time when neither object nor 'me' were defined as such: admitting to the 'relevance' of vomit/gender (and so the body) to the room would crush the necessary barrier between academic discourse and the bodies that produce it. To preserve the barrier, the vomit/gender remains attached to the speaking body that brought it up, and the repulsion that led to the bringing up in the first place is converted into general repulsion for the one who tried to impose the relevance of that which would destroy relevance itself.

I have fleshed out this conceptualisation of bringing up gender as vomiting, as abjection, in order to move beyond what is undoubtedly an 'abjection "is"' mode of analysis; I now make that move by engaging with the 'gender' part of 'bringing up gender' in a way that is provoked by my engagement with the theory of abjection. In the 'abjection "is"' mode, vomiting and abjection serve as metaphorical terms for the literal referent of 'bringing up gender'. The effect of this use of abjection is to equate the theoretical application of the 'abjection "is"' mode to an understanding of gender as 'gender "is"', where it is presumed to be possible to give a simple definition of gender. Gender certainly suffers from – and delights in – the same problematic of definition as abjection. The anaphora of 'Gender is…' in Judith Butler's (1999) *Gender Trouble*, which is arguably the text of reference for Gender Studies (as well as a common point of access to abjection for gender researchers), strikingly resembles Kristeva's ludic struggle with situating abjection in a schema of definition. I have argued that the concept of gender 'is' a heliotropic metaphor, because it can only be 'known' through its uses, rather than through a literal referent, an '"x" is gender' (Henderson, 2014). If we then apply Kristeva's 'métaphore manquée du manque' to the concept of gender, gender takes the place of the 'non-object', the '[n]ot me. Not that. But not nothing either', and so comes to signify the 'vortex of summons and repulsion' (PoH 1 Eng., 9 Fr.) of abjection, 'the place where I am not and which permits me to be' (PoH 3 Eng., 11 Fr.).

This notion of not knowing but being known by gender could constitute one interpretation of the linguistic expression surrounding the advent of Gender Studies and the currency of the term in feminist scholarship. Whereas 'woman' was/is perceived to have a literal referent as its political lynchpin, 'gender' was/is conceptualised as a liminal, mysterious force, an 'encroachment' and a 'smother[ing]' force (Zmroczek and Duchen 1989, 18), a 'thick cloud on the horizon of Women's Studies' (Klein 1991, 81), a 'lur[ing]' (Evans 1991, 73), 'dangerous' 'dressing-up-box version of reality' (72). 'Gender' becomes the (impossible) literal referent in these accounts, and the metaphorical terms that are used to 'bring up' gender in turn signify 'non-objects'. Here we see something of the 'métaphore manquée du manque', where the terms of the metaphor are caught in a circling motion between the desire for a literal referent and the fascinating suspicion that there may be no-thing as such. Played as either the literal referent or as the metaphorical term, or both, gender inevitably gestures to a lack of fixity and certainty in the terms that we require to understand our … gender.

How then does this renewed focus on gender affect our understanding of 'bringing up gender', and the obliquely developing thoughts on the 'data'? In the expanded 'abjection "is"' interpretation of the situation, I focussed on the fear of bringing up gender *where it is not known*. In this case, fear is conceptualised as provoked by the predicted reception of gender having been brought up. Thus the way in which gender is brought up is shaped by the potential reactions to the upbringing, and the cost–benefit analysis of bringing up (being abjected) versus swallowing (self-abjecting). Having explored gender as 'métaphore manquée du manque', I can now identify a 'métaphore manquée' in my gender/vomit application: Kristeva reminds us that '[u]rine, blood, sperm, excrement turn up in order to reassure a subject that is lacking its "own and clean self" ["son propre"]' (PoH 53 Eng., 65 Fr.). In this instance, I was gliding over the lack of 'my own and clean' notion of gender; the vomit analogy allowed me to sidestep an interrogation of that which is brought up. If knowing gender is impossible, how can it be brought up? Furthermore, if '[g]ender is there before consent' (Britzman 2010, 635), then everybody 'knows' gender, at least in the sense of abjecting its speaking subject. In starting this paper in a space of limbo between 'knowing' and 'bringing up' gender, I missed the discussion of what it means to put gender into words when we can never know 'it' with words. If I relinquish the hold on the question of 'bringing up gender' that vomit/gender gave me, and embrace a position where abjection cannot help me to organise gender, what is the effect on the 'data'?

Gender

'[G]ender is always a doing, though not a doing by a subject who might be said to preexist the deed' (Butler 1999, 34): gender is 'just something kind of thrown out there' (Anisha); '[t]here are hurt feelings and pedagogical failures' (Britzman 2010, 633). *Gender is heat, akin to nausea, that spreads from our innards to our hands and legs; we can no longer concentrate on the discussion.* Gender is 'the madness of trying to speak about it' (Britzman 2010, 634), 'something that makes others uncomfortable or feeling awkward' (Anisha). *Gender is a searing heat and deafening noise that invades our engagement.* 'Gender is a complexity whose totality is permanently deferred, never fully what it is at any given juncture in time' (Butler 1999, 22), 'a proto-writing and … a language of fear' (PoH 38 Eng., 49 Fr.), 'a very heavy topic [that] differs from culture to culture and from context to context and and [pause] yeah' (Anisha). 'It seems like one of those those taboo subjects' (Anisha): 'anyone at all can become gay, especially me' (Young 1990, 209). *Gender is an all-too-familiar feeling in our professional lives (not to mention our personal contexts, if the two can be separated).*

Bringing up gender

Bringing up gender is 'turn[ing] away with irrational disgust' (Young 1990, 209), is asking, *do I raise a hand, walk out, stand up and start spewing…?*

Asking, '[Can I] just kind of like raise it in the middle of something [when] I want to [even though] ... it's not really been planned[?]' (Anisha). *Bringing up gender is the decision-making process of if and when and how to intervene.* '[Bringing up g]ender is ... a set of repeated acts within a highly regulatory frame that congeal over time to produce the appearance of a substance, of a natural sort of being' (Butler 1999, 45). Bringing up gender is 'breaking up ['that shell of ultra-protected signifier'] to the point of desemantization, to the point of reverberating only as notes, music, "pure signifier"' (PoH 49 Eng., 60–61 Fr.). *Bringing up gender is taking a position that will alter irrevocably both the tone of the discussion and the identity that we are seen as embodying*; bringing up gender is 'incarnating what it signifies rather than merely referring to it' (Becker-Leckrone 2005, 35). Bringing up gender is 'meaningless, repulsive in an irrational, unrepresentable way' (Young 1990, 207), hence 'the madness involved in conveying gender to the other' (Britzman 2010, 635). *Bringing up gender is how to cool the heat and dampen the noise in order to re-engage with the ongoing discussion in a manner that makes this physical intervention of knowing most effective, least physically disruptive.* Bringing up gender is putting 'an elephant on the table' (Anisha); 'diversity workers have to put stuff "on the table"' (Ahmed 2012, 30). Bringing up gender is 'kind of a killjoy' (Andreotti 2013).

Academic abjection

Academic abjection is having no available option for inaction: both intervening and remaining silent are actions. Academic abjection is a 'stranger experience', or 'an experience of becoming noticeable, of not passing through or passing by' (Ahmed 2012, 3): 'the students might not know how to respond to me' (Anisha). Academic abjection 'is usually expressed in retching, vomiting, spasms, choking' (Gross 1990, 89), is 'people starting to twitch', 'blood boil[ing]', 'he became red' (Andreotti 2013). *Academic abjection is doing any of these things, even taking the sensible route where we wait to be asked for a contribution, politely apologising for our comment in advance*: it is 'the anaphora of nothing' (PoH 42 Eng., 53 Fr.). Academic abjection 'requires some mode of control of exclusion to keep it at a safe distance from the symbolic and its orderly proceedings' (Gross 1990, 93); *academic abjection is staying silent and swallowing the rising bile: we enact a betrayal.* Academic abjection is 'border anxiety' (Young 1990, 209), where '[p]eople's own anxieties about their own vulnerability are displaced onto those whose positions they fear' (Kenway, Kraack, and Hickey-Moody 2006, 125). 'Uncleanness or dirt[, academic abjection] is that which must not be included if a pattern is to be maintained' (Douglas 1966, 44). Academic 'abjection ... has to do with performing in, and simultaneously forming, the social context on which one depends' (Sondergaard 2012,

369). Academic abjection is 'how emotions of fear and hatred stick to certain bodies' (Ahmed 2012, 2). *Academic abjection is being surrounded by people we respect, or are supposed to respect, at a conference or in a class.*

Academic abjection

> If, in our lectures, we reduce gender to behaviour and social attributes, we lose contact with the emotional situation of gender's overabundance of meanings, conflicts and disavowals. (Britzman 2010, 644)

I could extend this comment by Deborah Britzman to cover both bringing up (or swallowing): when we bring up gender, we have to try to explain gender as explicable, and so we try to render it knowable. In an academic setting where gender is not explicitly known, it is known in the sense that no one wants to know it. Gender has no relevance in this setting. In order to make gender relevant, we have to bring it up (introduce it, vomit it, raise it) as if it were already knowable. However, we can never know gender as such; gender already knows us before we try to know 'it' in language. When we are thinking (if the heat and noise, the nausea, can be termed thinking) about whether or not and how to bring up gender, there are no other words in which to metaphorise or literalise gender. Gender helps to *dis*organise the illusion of the smooth surface of academic discussion, but it also *dis*organises our linguistic expression: where gender is known in the sense that no one wants to know it, it is difficult to bring it up as an unknowable not-thing, as a potentiality, especially when we know that bringing it up means bringing up our own insides so as not to bring up their insides. Bringing up gender involves tacitly acknowledging academic abjection. Through my exploration of and reaction to Anisha's comments on bringing up gender, I have come to realise that a pedagogy of gender would benefit from the deliberate consideration of, on the one hand, the processes of coming to know gender, and, on the other hand, the actions of making gender relevant. If we do not engage in these reflections for ourselves as teachers and with our students, we are imparting knowledge without equipping students – or ourselves – to use it outside the bounds of its 'home' classroom.

It has been a struggle to create a textual representation of 'bringing up gender', to portray the 'overabundance of meanings, conflicts and disavowals' of this complex moment, within the form of an academic article, without creating an unreadable text. Kristeva's conceptualisation – and textualisation – of abjection, and of metaphor within the context of abjection, have constituted the *dis*organising concept of this paper. They have operated with some success, in that they destabilised my initial attempt to organise 'bringing up gender'. In trying to adhere to the 'obligations' of the theory, I was obliged to re-think the role of 'gender' in 'bringing up gender'. I also found that Kristeva's development of metaphor beyond a rhetorical trope obliged me to re-think the relationship between 'data' and 'theory'. Whilst I cannot promise to have written abjection, I have attempted to produce a reading experience that puts you 'literally beside [your]self' (PoH 1 Eng., 9 Fr.).

Acknowledgements
The author would like to thank Claudia Lapping and Tamara Bibby for their invitation to contribute to this special issue, and for their helpful comments. In addition, thanks to Anisha (pseudonym) for her participation in this research. Finally, thanks to those who strive to create spaces for gender to be discussed.

Note
1. In this article, I cite page numbers from both the 1983 French edition, *Pouvoirs de l'horreur* (Kristeva 1983), and the 1982 English translation, *Powers of Horror* by Leon S. Roudiez, to facilitate access to the original, text references for these texts take the form of: (PoH *n* Eng., *n* Fr.)

References
Ahmed, S. 2012. *On Being Included: Racism and Diversity in Institutional Life*. Durham, N.C.: Duke University Press.
Andreotti, V. 2013. "Seminar: 'Poststructural and Postcolonial Epistemic Demands and Possibilities in Education (Washing the Dishes in the Kitchen and/or Dancing in the Living Room)." Paper Presented at at the DERC (Development Education Research Centre) Seminar Series, Institute of Education, University of London.
Becker-Leckrone, M. 2005. *Julia Kristeva and Literary Theory*. Basingstoke: Palgrave Macmillan.
Bousfield, C. 2000. "The Abject Space: Its Gifts and Complaints." *Journal of Gender Studies* 9 (3): 329–346.
Britzman, D. P. 2010. "On the Madness of Lecturing on Gender: A Psychoanalytic Discussion." *Gender and Education* 22 (6): 633–646.
Butler, J. 1999. *Gender Trouble : Feminism and the Subversion of Identity*. 10th anniversary ed. New York; London: Routledge.
Cohen, L., L. Manion, K. Morrison, R. Bell, and G. Mcculloch. 2011. *Research Methods in Education*. 7th ed. London: Routledge.
Derrida, J. 1972. *Marges De La Philosophie*. Collection "Critique". Paris: Éditions de Minuit.
Derrida, J., and F. C. T. Moore. 1974. "White Mythology: Metaphor in the Text of Philosophy." *New Literary History* 6 (1): 5–74.
Dimen, M. 2005. "Sexuality and Suffering, or the Eew! Factor." *Studies in Gender and Sexuality* 6 (1): 1–18.
Douglas, M. 1966. *Purity and Danger: An Analysis of Concepts of Pollution and Taboo*. London: Routledge and Kegan Paul.

Evans, M. 1991. The Problem of Gender for Women's Studies. *In out of the Margins: Women's Studies in the Nineties*, edited by J. Aaron and S. Walby, vi 244. London: Falmer Press.
Francis, B. 2009. "The Role of the Boffin as Abject Other in Gendered Performances of School Achievement." *The Sociological Review* 57 (4): 645–669.
Gross, E. 1990. "The Body of Signification." In *Abjection, Melancholia and Love: The Work of Julia Kristeva*, edited by J. Fletcher and A. Benjamin, 80–103. London: Routledge.
Henderson, E. F. 2012. *Tracing 'gender' through Presence: An Invitation to Explore the Learned and Learning of Gender Studies*. Master's of Research in Social and Educational Research: Institute of Education, University of London.
Henderson, E. F. 2014. "Poststructuralist Metaphor Analysis Through the 'Gender' Lens: Challenges and Conceptualizations." *Qualitative Inquiry* 20 (3): 332–340.
Jackson, A. Y., and L. A. Mazzei. 2012. *Thinking with Theory in Qualitative Research : Viewing Data across Multiple Perspectives*. London, New York, N.Y: Routledge.
Kenway, J., and E. Bullen. 2011. "Skin Pedagogies and Abject Bodies." *Sport, Education and Society* 16 (3): 279–294.
Kenway, J., A. Kraack, and A. Hickey-Moody. 2006. *Masculinity beyond the Metropolis*. Basingstoke: Palgrave Macmillan.
Klein, R. D. 1991. "Passion and Politics in Women's Studies in the Nineties." *Women's Studies International Forum* 14 (3): 125–134.
Kristeva, J. 1982. *Powers of horror: An essay on abjection*. New York: Columbia University Press.
Kristeva, J. 1983. *Pouvoirs De l'horreur: Essai Sur l'abjection*. Collection Tel Quel. Paris: Éditions du Seuil.
Leach, F. E. 2003. *Practising Gender Analysis in Education*. Oxford: Oxfam.
Leathwood, C., and V. Hey. 2009. "Gender/ed Discourses and Emotional Sub-Texts: Theorising Emotion in Uk Higher Education." *Teaching in Higher Education* 14 (4): 429–440.
Lechte, J. 1990. *Julia Kristeva*. London: Routledge.
MacCannell, J. F. 2003. "Kristeva's Horror" (First Published 1986). In *The Kristeva Critical Reader*, edited by J. Lechte and M. Zournazi, 69–97. Edinburgh: Edinburgh University Press.
Mazzei, L. A. 2007. *Inhabited Silence in Qualitative Research : Putting Poststructural Theory to Work*. Counterpoints (New York, N.Y.) 318. New York, NY; Oxford: Peter Lang.
Mendick, H., and B. Francis. 2011. "Boffin and Geek Identities: Abject or Privileged?" *Gender and Education* 24 (1): 15–24.
Moffat, K. 2004. "Beyond Male Denial and Female Shame: Learning about Gender in a Sociocultural Concepts Class." *Smith College Studies in Social Work* 74 (2): 243–256.
Nairn, K., J. Higgins, B. Thompson, M. Anderson, and N. Fu. 2006. "It's Just like the Teenage Stereotype, You Go out and Drink and stuff": Hearing from Young People Who don't Drink." *Journal of Youth Studies* 9 (3): 287–304.
Oliver, K. 1993. *Reading Kristeva: Unraveling the Double-Bind*. Bloomington, IN: Indiana University Press.
Ricoeur, P. 1975. *La métaphore Vive*. Paris: Editions du Seuil.
Ricoeur, P., and R. Czerny. 1986. *The Rule of Metaphor: Multi-Disciplinary Studies of the Creation of Meaning in Language*. London: Routledge & Kegan Paul.

Ringrose, J., and V. Walkerdine. 2008. "Regulating the Abject." *Feminist Media Studies* 8 (3): 227–246.

Schippers, B. 2011. *Julia Kristeva and Feminist Thought*. Edinburgh: Edinburgh University Press.

Smith, A. 1996. *Julia Kristeva : Readings of Exile and Estrangement*. Basingstoke: Macmillan.

Somerville, M., and J. Rennie. 2012. "Mobilising Community? Place, Identity Formation and New teachers' Learning." *Discourse: Studies in the Cultural Politics of Education* 33 (2): 193–206.

Søndergaard, D. M. 2012. "Bullying and Social Exclusion Anxiety in Schools." *British Journal of Sociology of Education* 33 (3): 355–372.

Young, I. M. 1990. "Abjection and Oppression: Dynamics of Unconscious Racism, Sexism and Homophobia." In *Crises in Continental Philosophy*, edited by A. B. Dallery, C. E. Scott and P. H. Roberts, 201–214. Albany, N.Y: State University of New York Press.

Zmoroczek, C., and C. Duchen. 1991. "What are those Women up to? Women's Studies and Feminist Research in the European Community." *In/Out of the Margins: Women's Studies in the Nineties*, edited by J. Aaron and S. Walby, 11–29. London: Falmer Press.

Writing in a foreign language as a science of writing or *grammatology*

Arturo Escandón

Department of Spanish and Latin American Studies, Nanzan University, Nagoya, Japan

> The present paper explores the issue of writing in a foreign language as a pedagogic process that may produce a radical subjective transformation. Drawing on Bernstein's notions of the *pedagogic device* and *discursive gap*, the paper explores the epistemic make-up of language and the way it has been normalised by academic and educational institutions as a reified notion that discourages an understanding of it as the very formation of subjects, social contexts and pedagogic identities. Based on a principle of complementarity, the study proposes the deployment of pedagogies that draw on both Derrida's science of writing or *grammatology*, and the dialectical approach of Vygotsky, in which writing is viewed as a representation of oral speech, capable of objectivising semiosis. The author draws on his experience as a language instructor in Japan, carrying the baggage of his self-imposed exile, to contextualise those pedagogies in relation to the positions subjects take (resistance, avoidance, commitment) and opportunities for subjective emancipation. In the end, the author suggests that Derrida's anti-epistemologic approach offers new ways of addressing the issue of subjective domination and emancipation.

Introduction

> Written speech is the algebra of speech. (Vygotsky 1987, 203)

> ...the destruction of discourse is not simply an erasing neutralisation. It multiplies words, precipitates them one against the other, engulfs them too, in an endless and baseless substitution whose only rule is the sovereign affirmation of the play outside meaning. Not a reserve or a withdrawal, not the infinite murmur of a blank speech erasing the traces of classical discourse, but a kind of potlatch of signs that burns, consumes and wastes words in the gay affirmation of death: a sacrifice and a challenge. (Derrida 2001, 347)

The aim of the present paper is to explore the issue of *writing in a foreign language* or *producing written discourse in a foreign language* as a pedagogic process that may further a radical transformation of all subjects involved in the pedagogic relation, whether they are learners or instructors. I argue that pedagogies of writing have a better chance of producing deep subjective transformations if educators approach the subject as *both* a *science of writing*, in Derrida's terms, i.e. as a deconstruction of knowledge and science, and in a more traditional linguistic sense, i.e. as a representation of oral speech.

I will analyse this process in terms of both language's epistemic make-up and the complexities posed by its instruction and learning. I will focus my analysis on the teaching of *Written Spanish*, drawing mainly on my experience as a language instructor of *Spanish Writing* for the past four years at the tertiary level in Japan. The argumentations I give are interested and biased, as they are based on my lifelong experience as a native speaker of Spanish, born and raised in Chile but of Spanish extraction, and learner of foreign languages. *My* English – the language in which I am writing the present article – is my third spoken language after French but it is unquestionably the language in which I conduct my (written) critical reflective practice. Learning English had for me an immense emancipatory effect. It was the language of my self-induced political and social exile in which I forged a new identity that kept me relatively distant from the atrocities of the Chilean dictatorship of the 1970s and 1980s. Eventually, English became the language through which I started to articulate more comprehensive critiques of the knowledge systems that I had come to know through Spanish and French. Thus, for me, language teaching has always been a serious business; I believe it has tremendous implications for the learner as the main vehicle to author him- or herself not only in times of political crisis, but of personal crisis as well. Therefore, for me writing has an emancipatory potential under certain pedagogic circumstances that I highlight below.

The paper is structured as follows. In the opening sections, I set out my position regarding the pedagogies of writing in relation to Derrida's notion of a *science of writing* or *grammatology*. Having that goal in mind I draw on different theoretical systems, especially on dialectical traditions (Hegel, Marx and Vygotsky) and on Bernstein's sociology of pedagogy. These systems coincide in certain aspects but also present divergent views and are subject to epistemic and theoretical contradictions. In my discussion of writing and subject transformation, I will defy several notions that place language and the pedagogies of foreign language, especially writing pedagogies, on safe ground and *normalise* their tenets, making them appear as unquestionable or unproblematic practices. Finally, I will give an account of the underpinnings of the pedagogies of writing in a foreign language according to the (contradictory) deconstructing principles already seen. I will describe a selection of practices that do not pretend to constitute an empirical body of work, as in a traditional research paper, but are rather an illustration of the underpinnings so that the reader can see them in action, so to speak, especially in light of the tremendous (social and linguistic) distance between Spanish and Japanese.

Writing as a representation of speech and writing as death

In order to situate ourselves with regard to writing and its pedagogies, let us start with a general analysis of the status that language is given and the particular role writing plays in foreign language study programmes.

I argue that writing classes are, in general, underrated in the pedagogical systems that deal with foreign language instruction. In fact, the very notion of *language* takes us back to the structuralist notion of a semiotic system devised by Saussure in his *Course in General Linguistics*, which not only inaugurated the modern linguistic vision of language as a system of signs that represent ideas, but gave writing the status of a mere representation of speech (Saussure 1959, 23). Saussure was not the first theoretician to treat writing as a representation of speech but he was one of the most influential forgers of the myth, as drawn on in the field of foreign language pedagogies.

The Japanese pedagogical system is not exempt from this problem. Writing does not occupy the place of a foundation course, along with grammar, translation and conversation courses. The positioning of writing as one of the last courses in the curriculum tells a tale in which its mastery is seen as disconnected from the rudiments of grammar, and as a logical step that follows the mastery of oral speech. The fact that writing is a highly reflexive activity, which in itself constitutes a grammar, is widely overlooked, helping to reproduce the idea, in Japan and elsewhere, that writing is a mere representation of oral speech.

Derrida's notion of *science of writing* or *grammatology* runs against this conception. For Derrida, writing is not a mere representation of speech but the means on which any science is based, that is, the foundation of knowledge. As Derrida points out:

> ...writing is not only an auxiliary means in the service of science – but first ... the condition of the possibility of ideal objects and therefore of scientific objectivity. Before being its object, writing is the condition of the *epistémè*. (Derrida 1997, 27)

Grammatology is a practical assault, first, on *logocentrism*, that is, on the belief that phonetic writing, and particularly alphabetic writing, is superior to other forms of written representation, and, second, on the systematic repression of writing practised by metaphysics, 'from the pre-Socratics to

Heidegger', which has 'always assigned the origin of truth in general to the logos' (Derrida 1997, 3), particularly the logos contained in oral, full speech.

We will return to Derrida's grammatology after we introduce the theories behind the current dominant conception of language and writing and its links with the dialectical tradition and Hegel's standpoint, which for Derrida, as we will see, occupies an ambivalent position.

The interested prevalence of Saussurean structuralism

Let us go back to the normative notion of language and how this contributes to the shaping and *normalisation* of pedagogic practices. The dominating idea, reflected in the name given to the main field of research into foreign language teaching and learning, Second Language Acquisition (SLA), is that learners *acquire* language and, therefore, *using* a foreign language amounts to an exercise in *translating* a communicative intention, without necessarily changing the communicating subjects. Let me give an example. If some speakers of Japanese successfully translate the words *kekkon* (marriage), *kazoku* (family) or *ikka* (clan or household) into Spanish and use them in an utterance without paying attention to what the terms connote in Spanish society, they are operating with a principle in which they assume the equivalence of the social and communicative contexts in Japan and Spain. They may be shocked and some disgusted by the fact that in Spain same-sex marriages are now commonplace and same-sex partners can legally adopt children; that women do not change their last names when they get married and do not become members of the husband's household, as is normally the case in Japan, and so on. In other words, simple terms like *family* or *husband* are part of a network of social relations that support dissimilar living conditions and rationales for organising society.

How did this conception of language get normalised? First, as I have already mentioned, we can trace the modern conception of language to Saussure's structuralist paradigm, which later influenced and set constraints on the cognitive-computational tradition, especially generative linguistics, one of the most influential theories of language of the last century. This paradigm helped to keep at bay competing notions of language, such as those of the dialectical tradition, which viewed it in its social dimension. Second, as we are going to see later, the structuralist paradigm was (and still is) subservient to the role that language pedagogies play in the educational system.

Let us see first how the SLA field still operates mainly under a Saussurean paradigm. In the *Course in General Linguistics*, Saussure (1959) establishes what at *prima facie* seems to be a doctrinal Hegelian distinction between *langue* (universal), *langage* (particular) and *parole* (individual) (*language–human speech–utterance*). For Saussure, language is a passive, receptive, collective and homogeneous system that comprises all manifestations of human speech. He stresses the point that human speech cannot be studied because it lacks unity. It is an imperfect and incomplete manifestation (9). Utterance, moreover, is the individual act, the actuality that establishes language (13). After setting up what I believe are Hegelian links, Saussure chooses the universal, language as the object of linguistics, that is, the most stable part of the triad (non-temporal being): the passive collection of the conventions adopted by society that enable individuals to exercise the faculty of speech. A science of language, argues Saussure, can only be built upon the exclusion of the other elements (15). But whilst Hegel (1975) in *Doctrine of the Notion* cannot conceive of the Notion, the universal, without instantiation in particular individuals (temporal process), for Hegelian dialectics is based upon the non-identity at any given time of the universal, the particular and the individual, Saussure in contrast leaves human speech (particular) and utterance (individual) out of language, effectively decapitating Hegel's dialectic. This amounts to leaving human institutions such as the school, the corporation, the church, the union or the family, and the speech acts produced by actual individuals that are grouped under those institutions, with their own needs and motives, out of the equation. As a unit of analysis, Saussure's option implies that researchers and educators working with that notion of language will leave out by default the social milieu which shapes and is shaped by language, and the psychological dimension of communication. The attempts to incorporate that milieu and language's psychological dimension will always be perceived as extraneous, artificial, accessory or forced under such a paradigm. Thus, when Saussure postulates *langue* as the object of linguistics he is consciously opting for the study of an abstract (and arbitrary) system. Most foreign language pedagogies deployed in the SLA field do not recognise that the social context, including its institutions, is itself constructed through language. As Johnson points out, the social setting of the dominant SLA pedagogies is described *a priori* as a stable context in which meanings are fixed non-negotiable entities (Johnson 2004, 85–99).

Discursive gap

The historical formation of the linguistic field is not the only circumstance that has helped in normalising a reified notion of language. The Saussurean paradigm also plays a subservient role to the particular works of what Bernstein (2000) calls the *pedagogic device*, through which actual discourse (in this instance, realisations of language) is transformed into an imaginary (pedagogical) discourse. Instructors and students alike seem to operate with a conception of (their own and the target) language as a *principle-based generator* of mathematic propositions and with the notion of mental *semantic normativity*, that is, meanings as stable entities that people store somewhere in their minds. The pedagogic device operates with internal rules that control or regulate the pedagogic communication that the device makes possible. In our case, the device is constraining the potential of language to produce subjective change by appropriating sciences and pedagogies of language ancillary to the idea of a non-evolutionary subject.

But what exactly is the pedagogic device? Bernstein views pedagogy as operating on a transformation principle (pedagogic discourse) through which the *what*, roughly translated as the academic content, and the *how*, that is, 'the theory of instruction' (Bernstein 2000, 34), are continuously *recontextualised* and evaluated to reinforce its aims. Put more blatantly, pedagogic institutions choose and appropriate actual discourses from several production fields, package them as imaginary school subjects, transmit them as imaginary discourses and evaluate the transmission's performance. Distributive rules (based on social class differentials), though, will allow a few subjects to produce actual discourse and access the actual field of production.

By distributive rules, Bernstein (2000) understands the distinction of two classes of knowledge, the 'thinkable class and the unthinkable class … one class of knowledge that is esoteric and one that is mundane' (29). These two classes of knowledge have different forms of abstraction that relate 'the material world and the immaterial world' (29), which are regulated by the division of labour and the particular relation between meanings and their material base. Therefore, if the ongoing accumulation of instances of language constitutes the material base (unrepresentable in its totality), different modes of abstraction provide us with alternative theories of language, which will serve the interests of different social groups. In other words, Bernstein is referring to the regulation of power relations between social groups by means of distributing different forms of knowledge and creating, therefore, consciousness differentials, whether we understand these differentials as orientations to meaning or pedagogic identities.

The meanings which are not directly linked to a material base create a potential discursive gap. Put in a rather brutal way, there is knowledge to be taught, which ensures the reproduction of institutions and social relations, and there is knowledge to be produced, which has the potential to reshape institutions and social relations. For Bernstein,

> this potential gap or space … is the site for the unthinkable, the site of the impossible, and this site can clearly be both beneficial and dangerous at the same time … [it] is the meeting point of order and disorder, of coherence and incoherence. It is the crucial site of the *yet to be thought*. (Bernstein 2000, 30)

In our case, the structuralist and cognitivist notions of language are ancillary to pedagogies through which discourse, the social context and the social relations, are not interpellated and consequently no radical transformation of the (individual) subject is sought. Foreign language instruction, therefore, becomes a safe, non-evolutionary pedagogic subject. If language is a static object, its instruction does not presuppose the transformation of the student/instructor as subjects, as socially positioned individuals. Consequently, there is a strong call against the evolution of the subject, an interpellation for a non-evolutionary subjectivation, or for his or her controlled evolution under the subject's own terms (i.e. an interpellation for consensual subjectivation), which amounts to a certain commoditisation of foreign language education. Students may only engage in the instructional process up to a certain point without compromising their own values or world views, or those of the society that is enabling this process. Neither the student nor the instructor has to take up a radical position regarding language in order to close the gap between pedagogic discourse and the discourse produced in the actual field of production (i.e. language use): the instructor can be happy abandoning the student in the fantasy island of the classroom where an imaginary foreign language is spoken; and the student can be happy about learning an imaginary foreign language. Language then starts working as a commodity, an accessory that is acquired in the market.

The Bernsteinian approach not only allows us to understand the implications of the adoption of a broadly Saussurian paradigm within foreign language pedagogies, its fundamental stance is that discourse, understood here as socially situated language, is not external to the field of power, but constitutive of it. However, even though this makes clear that the subject is configured and transformed through discourse, Bernstein's sociology lacks insight into the exact process of formation and transformation of the subject. This is why Bernstein's sociology has been supplemented with the dialectical tradition (Daniels 2001; Escandon 2012) in an attempt to give an account of intrasubjective processes.

Subject transformation and the ideal of emancipation

Let us analyse now the dialectical tradition, as an alternative to the structuralist-based cognitivist approach, and see what analytical tools it has to offer that can incorporate both the social and psychological fabrics of language. What are this tradition's main tenets? First, it works with a socio-genetic framework of analysis and explanatory principle whereby the development of the subject through higher psychological functions and the emergence of consciousness are the outcome of social activity, especially language (see Leont'ev 1981, 56). In this framework, the development of higher psychological functions such as voluntary attention, logical memory and generalisation appear twice, first on the interpsychological level, and later on, on the intrapsychological level (Vygotsky 1978, 56). These functions are developed in order to accurately reproduce the features of the *world of things*, as Vygotsky indicates, whereas linguistic means target the communication of ideas in order to organise societal activity, including one's own behaviour. Vygotsky depicted development as if happening in a zone, i.e. the *zone of proximal development* (ZPD), which may be interpreted as an analytical metaphor that helps to represent 'the fusion of the individual and the social setting' (see Robbins 2003, 34). Development is therefore a function of language's socio-communicative and representational functions, or, put in terms of the ZPD, the dialectical relationship between the zone's upper (scientific/theoretical concepts) and lower reaches (spontaneous/everyday concepts).

However, the main concern of the dialectical tradition is the issue of human development and freedom. Social relations develop human beings so that they can become full participants in society. The aim is to have the individual appropriating the means to free him- or herself from arbitrary social conditions by generating new social relations (see Chaiklin 2012). So, for Vygotsky, *developing* a foreign language allows a breaking away from the cognitive dominance of the native language, contributing therefore to the emancipation of the individual:

> ...[the native] speech system stands between the newly learned language and the world of things ...This process of concept formation requires entirely different acts of thought, acts of thought which are associated with free movement in the concept system, with the generalization of previously developed generalizations, and with a more conscious and voluntary mode of operating on these concepts. (Vygotsky 1987, 180–181)

The speech trap of the dialectical tradition

Teaching a modern foreign language usually aims first at the mastery of that language's socio-communicative functions, yet instruction is highly reflective and demands, according to Vygotsky, processes similar to those required in the mastery of scientific concepts and *written speech* in the native language. Thus, Vygotsky (1987, 179) sees similarities in terms of the psychological processes required in mastering (1) writing in the native language, (2) scientific concepts in the native language, and (3) a foreign language.

However, the basic tenets of the dialectical tradition are problematic, if we try to assimilate them to Derrida's grammatology. First, the differentiation between higher functions and linguistic means may work in terms of describing intended objects of activity – higher psychological functions are developed in order to reproduce accurately the features of phenomena, whereas linguistic means target the communication of ideas to organise societal activity – but is ontologically compromised. This is because both the world of things and the subject are primarily constituted through language and, therefore, there is no way to determine where one ends and the other begins. In fact, higher psychological functions belong to a system that is already predetermined and normalised and carries with it a moral stance given by the linguistic means used to regulate social relationships. Developmental targets predate development. Suppose that an instructor is teaching the linguistic means linked with the pragmatics of Spanish spontaneity in certain conversational contexts, yet, whether instruction deals with the grammatical or pragmatic aspects of the linguistic means, the instructor's demand for spontaneity is paradoxical. The linguistic and social excess that constitutes spontaneity for subjects of Spanish cannot be captured by the representational function.

The second problem we face is that in the dialectical tradition, development depends ultimately upon the internalisation of speech. In the process of internalisation, speech is *abbreviated*. This not only applies to the development of a foreign language but also to the development of the scientific concepts in the native language. Writing occupies a conflictual role that is a product of what Jones (2009) calls the *segregationist linguistics* adopted by Vygotsky. For Jones, Vygotsky's model assumes a mythical, reified and de-personalised notion of linguistic activity in which 'an anonymous language system, predicated on the assumption of social conformity, is taken to be the precondition for any communicative act' (168). In other words, linguistic activity (whether external or internal) is an instantiation of an external depersonalised code. Drawing on Wertsch's interpretation of Vygotsky's notion of development as predicated on the '*principle of decontextualization of mediational means*' (Wertsch 1985, 33), Jones points out that written language is the ultimate decontextualised universal model to which external speech and, eventually, other shorter, condensed forms are compared. Decontextualisation is the process 'whereby the meaning of signs become less and less dependent on the unique spatiotemporal context in which they are used' (Wertsch 1985, 33). Thus speech, whether external, private or internal, is an instantiation of a universal that is contained in full written form. Abbreviation operates as a semantic and syntactic condensation of full written forms.

For Vygotsky, the aim of instruction is to rise from context-bound forms of functioning, such as those linked to the use of spontaneous concepts, whether they have an extra-linguistic or linguistic context, to decontextualised forms, such as those linked to the use of scientific concepts. For him, spontaneous concepts refer to an extra-linguistic or linguistic context, and are therefore context-tied and transitory, whereas scientific concepts refer to a network of conceptual relations and are therefore stable. For instance, if we take the word 'wall', it refers to an extra-linguistic context in which there is a wall, or to a linguistic context in which there is an imaginary wall, a wall that is no longer present or something resembling a wall or containing its properties. However, if we take the word 'circumference', we are no longer dealing with a linguistic or extra-linguistic referent but with a network of concepts such as 'centre', 'diameter' and 'radius', and a whole network of notions contained in

Euclidean geometry. Now, the exact shape of the wall, its colour, the material it is made of, and so on, may change, but this is not the case with the word 'circumference', which only admits the predicate size.

As Wertsch (1985) points out, in 'developing his account of the factors that contribute to predicativity, Vygotsky argued that the end points of a continuum that extends from minimal to maximal predicativity are represented by written language and inner speech, respectively' (123). The paradox is that the abbreviated forms are located in the opposite reach, in the realm of what Vygotsky called personal 'sense' and written language is located in the realm of objective 'meaning' (109), and yet, abbreviated forms enable the subject to produce operations of decontextualisation and generalisation.

How can we interpret these similar and yet conflicting views on language? On the one hand, we encounter similarities. Derrida's position vindicates, as a first step toward the deconstruction of Saussurean linguistics, the supremacy of the *script* against the metaphysical dominance of the oral. By the same token, speech, within the dialectical tradition, is an instantiation of writing, an idea that reverses Saussurean linguistics, which views writing as a mere representation of speech. On the other hand, the approaches could not be more different. Because of its systemic nature, the dialectical tradition holds that writing is the universal, de-contextualised, complete, perfect form, in opposition to the particular, context-tied, abbreviated, incomplete and imperfect forms of social and inner speech. In contrast, for Derrida, writing can be characterised as a process of incompletion, for it is subject to the processes of differing (spatial displacement) and deferring (time displacement), which Derrida formulated in the neologism *différance* (see Derrida 1982, 3–27, my emphasis). In writing there is a necessary (structural) effacement of the addressee and the context, and the effacement of meaning, for the meaning of a text is always in connection to the (endless and incomplete) system of texts (as a citation is only valuable because it is citing something else). This amounts to an ontological negativity that, although described by Hegel (1977) in his *Phenomenology of Spirit*, was nonetheless left out for the sake of attaining true knowledge (see Derrida 2001, 317–350).

The positions overlap if we recognise Vygotsky's view of language and psychological method are eminently historicist. Even if Vygotsky, as Jones points out, operates with a reified notion of language that implies the individual is overdetermined by the social structure, he introduces an intermediate position, that of the instantiation, wherein the social and personal dimensions of the subject dialectically meet. For Vygotsky, signs are relational processes that bridge personal sense and social meanings. Put in dialectical terms: concepts, objectivised mainly in signs, obey at once the logic of social or historical forces and individual consciousness or psyche. However, Derrida's approach to historicism is that of making evident the absurdity of the apparent completeness of meaning making, its humourless *travestissement*. If the historicism of Hegel (and Vygotsky) is one of presence, a belief in totality or repression of losses, Derrida's historicist method (i.e. writing) is one that goes beyond presence and absence by virtue of the displacing and dislocation of *différance*. Addressing Rousseau's suggestion that writing is the destruction of presence (e.g. whatever we write will potentially outlive us), Derrida points out:

> Rousseau knew that death is not the simple outside of life. Death by writing also inaugurates life. 'I can certainly say that I never began to live, until I looked upon myself as a dead man' (*Confessions*, Book 6 [p. 236] ... Death is the movement of differance to the extent that the movement is necessarily finite. This means that differance makes the opposition of presence and absence possible. (Derrida 1997, 143)

From restricted to general economy

Derrida's (2001, 327) view of writing, then, radically interpellates the dialectical tradition's treatment of true knowledge as systemic, i.e., 'the unity of process and system'. Let us have a look at the dialectical method. A word, or an utterance, under such a system, is interpreted as dependent on the sum-total of meanings given by the totality of utterances that configure the abstract space of linguistic meanings. Every new utterance is different from itself when it enters the system, because its introduction alters the sum totality of meaning of all utterances. Derrida's basic assumption is that the systemic totalities of structuralism, and by extension Hegelian metaphysics, are forms of *totalitarianism*, for they ignore that the systemic totality does not account for the meaning losses registered at the ontological foundation of the system. Derrida is referring to what Bataille called *restricted economies*, that is, the notion that all objects of a system and their relations are always meaningful, or that all expenditures are productive. In contrast, Bataille and Derrida work with a *general economy* model, that is, a system which acknowledges that non-productive expenditures always exist. Real life, Bataille (1991, 12) points out, 'knows nothing of purely productive expenditure; in actuality, it knows nothing of purely non-productive expenditure either'.

For Derrida, writing (and even speech), under such a Hegelian metaphysical framework, presents meaning losses that are unaccounted for. These losses are produced by the excesses that Bataille spoke of in his account of general economy (Bataille 1985, 1991), the excesses or expenditures of 'destruction, suppression, death and sacrifice' (Derrida 2001, 327), and by all phenomena that are not mediated, uncontrollable experiences such as nausea, pain, sickness, anguish, delusion, which are beyond or exceed language and therefore lie at the limit of knowledge.

There is a basic destruction underlying knowing something through meaning-making activity. Derrida views Hegel's ontological foundation on the sovereignty stance of the master–slave relation as an example of general economy, which acknowledges that meanings are lost. Simply put, the operation can be characterised as follows: those who are prepared to die, to risk their lives, accede to lordship, to freedom, recognition, and to knowledge, *sovereignty*. In order to know you have to jump into the vacuum, face death, dissolve your existence:

> The lord is the man who has had the strength to endure the anguish of death and to maintain the work of death. Such, according to Bataille, is the center of Hegelianism. The 'principal text' would be the one, in the *Preface* to the *Phenomenology*, which places knowledge 'at the height of death'. (Derrida 2001, 321)

Yet, this general economy principle of sovereignty, which in Vygotsky has its equivalent in the catharsis, that is, the resolution of a personal conflict and the revelation of a higher, more general human truth, the condition of real learning, is eventually rendered as restricted economy in the Hegelian metaphysics deployed by Vygotsky. It is as if the work of art ended up conveying a moral.

What is in conclusion the problem with Hegelian metaphysics? As Derrida points out:

> The blind spot of Hegelianism, *around* which can be organized the representation of meaning, is the point at which destruction, suppression, death and sacrifice constitute so irreversible an expenditure, so radical a negativity – here we would have to say an expenditure and a negativity *without reserve* – *that* they can no longer be determined as negativity in a process or a system. In discourse (the unity of process and system), negativity is always the underside and accomplice of positivity. Negativity cannot be spoken of, nor has it ever been except in this fabric of meaning. Now, the sovereign operation, the *point of nonreserve*, is neither positive nor negative. It cannot be inscribed in discourse, except by crossing out predicates or by practicing a contradictory superimpression that then exceeds the logic of philosophy. (Derrida 2001, 327)

This amounts to saying that in the dialectical tradition there is neither a theory, nor an account, of the unconscious, or the immediate, i.e. all phenomena that are not mediated by verbalisations are substituted, as a form of testimonial act, by a chain of cross-referenced signifiers. An instance of this can be seen when Vygotsky, drawing on John B. Watson, seems to correlate the unconscious with the lack of verbalisations of the earliest childhood (Vygotsky 1997, 121). This condition of the unmediated is summarised by Derrida (2001, 167) in a brief quote from Bataille (1954, 29): 'Silence is a word which is not a word, and breath an object which is not an object'. The word silence can never represent silence. The sign and sign systems betray the no-meaning nature of certain phenomena. Vygotsky (1997) suggests in contrast that the unconscious does not exist unless is mediated through a psychophysiological process (119), which in dialectical psychology is dominated by 'the system of reversible reflexes' (77), i.e. words, utterances.

Therefore, Derrida's method is to keep the old name of *writing* for a new concept that alludes to that which is not susceptible to conceptualisation. The core characteristics of writing are:

(1) the break with the horizon of communication as the communication of consciousness or presences, and as the linguistic or romantic transport of meaning;
(2) the subtraction of all writing from the semantic horizon or the hermeneutic horizon which, at least as a horizon of meaning, lets itself be punctured by writing;
(3) the necessity of, in a way, *separating* the concept of polysemia from the concept I have elsewhere named *dissemination*, which is also the concept of writing;
(4) the disqualification or the limit of the concept of the 'real' or 'linguistic' context, whose theoretical determination or empirical saturation are, strictly speaking, rendered impossible or insufficient by writing. (Derrida 1982, 316)

What do these nuclear characteristics entail? First, that writing is an attitude, a sovereign stance that is well beyond some utilitarian aim of attaining knowledge or knowing the truth. Second, that writing involves a deconstruction of the metaphysics of presence, and particularly of speech. Third, that writing is a new philosophical method that operates to produce a clash between opposite metaphysical categories, which constitutes the locus of *différance*. In the case of writing in a foreign language, we face first and foremost the opposition of two *different* or *dissimilar* meaning systems or what I would call *allelosemia*. And fourth, the rejection or suppression of normalised ideas of linguistic context, especially the conventional ideas of national contexts. Writing is the context.

The principle of complementarity

Overall, by discarding the inexplicable, the Hegelian position recycles sovereignty, negativity, into a system governed by presence, the presence that is at the foundations of metaphysics, of repression of the non-verbal and immediate that Derrida (1997) unveils in *Of Grammatology*. Bataille, in *Erotism*, encapsulates the dialectical tradition's stance: '…in Hegel's mind the immediate is bad' (Bataille 1986, 255). This also amounts to a form of simulacrum or repetitive representations of sacrifice: it tames the negativity of the sacrifice, true sovereignty, for the sake of attaining knowledge, and of sustaining a moral order (see Bataille 1993). More precisely, Derrida points out that

> The necessity of *logical* continuity is the decision or interpretative milieu of all Hegelian interpretations. In interpreting negativity as labor, in betting for discourse, meaning, history, etc., Hegel has bet against play, against chance. He has blinded himself to the possibility of his own bet, to the fact that the conscientious suspension of play (for example, the passage through the certitude of oneself and through lordship as the independence of self-consciousness) was itself a phase of play; and to the fact that play *includes* the work of meaning or the meaning of work, and includes them not in terms of *knowledge*, but in terms of *inscription*: meaning is a function of play, is inscribed in a certain place in the configuration of a meaningless play. (Derrida 2001, 329)

Here we have reached an epistemological dead end stemming from ontological differentials. On the one hand, we have the dialectical tradition with no account of meaning losses, the negative outcome of sovereign activity. In effect, the dialectical tradition reduces true sovereignty to lordship, transforming it into knowledge, providing order to the world, producing a moral stance that is based on reason. Thus, Vygotsky's attempts to use the deconstructing power of the alphabetic script as a means to inquire into sign systems, becoming a form of scientific inquiry, are condemned to be apprehended again by the systemic structure of the dialectical method, by the *positive* of presence, and of speech. What is for Derrida, on the other hand, the killer sovereign act? It is writing. Writing is the method of dismantling the metaphysics of presence, the negation of negativity, of death, a method of destructing the moral order of philosophy, the door that opens the way to chaos and to what Bernstein, as already seen, qualifies as the *unthinkable*, that place where knowledge shows its weaknesses. And yet, even if, from a philosophical point of view we are persuaded to adopt Derrida's deconstruction and the anti-epistemology of a general economy, as Plotnitsky (1994) does in *Complementarity*, we seem, within the domain of pedagogies, unable to get rid of restricted economies, at least until the learner has mastered metaphysics or tasted its limitations. The problem we face is that deconstruction is not a gratuitous task. Deconstruction has often been misinterpreted as a game, as a baseless and unmerited stance, akin to a brief irrational diversion. However, Derrida's approach requires disclosing discursive gaps. That can only be accomplished by way of mastering classic knowledge and sustaining a lengthy praxis. As Plotnitsky asserts, the 'dislocation created by a general economy is never a simple or uncritical dismissal of classical theories, but is instead their *rigorous suspension*' (11). So we are in pedagogic activity one step behind incorporating the genuine principle of complementarity proposed by Plotnisky. We need reason and philosophy in order to set up moral orientations, reproduce the social order and help subjects to take control over their lives, to help them to emancipate themselves within a given world, but also, if we have any chance of changing the social order, of overcoming the discursive gap, we need to act on deconstructing speech and truth, we need to take a sovereign stance.

I believe writing, especially writing in a foreign language, can provide a complementary move between these two reaches until learners are ready to embark on Derrida's anti-epistemological method by themselves and adopt a genuinely complementary stance.

Pedagogies of writing in a foreign language

I am proposing to operate with a principle of preliminary complementarity in which writing produces, on the one hand, a move toward objectivised semiosis or reason, that is, a Vygotskian move that interpellates phenomena and their analytical constructs, and on the other hand, a move toward destructive construction or *poiesis*. This is an epistemically compromised and contradictory position in which no integration is possible. In other words, all we have left is to work by complementing both moves until the classical theories are superseded by a general economy. In regards to pedagogies, this means that tasks will be given to produce independently one of these moves. Thus, there will be writing tasks aiming mainly at exploring the world of things and the categories deployed to give shape to that reality, or to analyse it; and there will be writing tasks aiming mainly at producing a sovereign stance. In the case of the latter, since this stance is precisely about a confrontation with non-meaning, it is impossible to control, interpret (and even evaluate) the product of these tasks, and therefore I will try to situate the texts within the pedagogical context but I will refrain from interpreting them. We will see now examples of both.

Reason and the intensification of language's representational function

Under the 'classical concept of writing' Derrida (1982) believes that a 'written sign … is not exhausted in the present of its inscription' (317) and, furthermore, 'carries with it a force of breaking with its context, that is, the set of presences which organize the moment of its inscription' (317). For Derrida, this 'force of breaking is not an accidental predicate, but the very structure of the written' (317). In fact, I argue, by focusing on writing instead of speaking in a foreign language, this intrinsic characteristic of writing helps to substantiate the fissures and cracks of pedagogic discourse, intensifying language's representational function. Let us see how this may operate in a language class.

An example of how the pedagogic device operates as a recontextualisation apparatus in foreign language pedagogies in Japan is given by Hashimoto's (2000) research on the Japanese politics of *internationalisation* through education. Hashimoto concludes that the Japanese government's discourse of promoting globalisation through the teaching of English is 'in reality only a different form of promotion of Japaneseness' (49). The teaching of foreign languages may produce the opposite to its apparent intended effect as students, far from adopting a new foreign identity, reassert their own Japanese identity no matter how alien to the local context the pedagogies being deployed may appear to be (e.g. pedagogies associated with the communicative approach or task-based instruction). What Hashimoto refers to is the fact that in conversation classes, students do not seem able to engage in discussing topics or issues because they do not seem to have anything to say. Reasserting their Japaneseness, in opposition to the identity of the speaker of the foreign language, may be a strategy to fill up a missing content (40–41). Students may be urged to state 'We the Japanese…' in circumstances where in the past they did not explicitly assume that identity, for the customary is implicit. Now, this sounds like the normal outcome of having students redefining their own assumptions and in fact reveals a form of subject development that is welcome but dangerous, if the process is left unfinished. This intermediary stage ignores or neglects *reason* and therefore is only equivalent to the move from a natural religion to a positivist one, that is, what was customary morality (e.g. the way of the Japanese, the way of the Spaniards, the way of the English), and therefore implicit, is now explicit and backed up by the authority deriving from the right to cultural determination. Yet, excluding reason from the rights that correspond to each and every one of the faculties of the human spirit is, as Hegel (1978, 141) points out, a system that abhors human beings, for it may condone injustice. What Hegel is saying is that in order to avoid the problem we have to set as a benchmark the ideal of absolute reason, that is, a systemic analysis of the constructs of *reality* is required in order to avoid arbitrariness. Well, writing is one way to avoid leaving subjects in the limbo of cultural relativism.

In my writing class, if students are given an essay to write about almost any topic, their first attempt reflects the development of an explicit national point of view, as Hashimoto pointed out. Thus, if the task is the analysis of the widespread use by the Japanese of the surgical mask in everyday life, the assumed point of view is that of 'We the Japanese', even if 'Japanese' are referred to in the third grammatical person, that is, 'They, the Japanese'. Most students argue that Japanese wear surgical masks in the public transport system, the school, the office, the street, etc., 'to prevent virus from spreading and to avoid getting hay fever', and 'many women use them too to hide their faces when they have not applied make-up'. This process may include setting an in-group/out-group distinction such as 'I believe *foreigners* do not have that idea' (notice the word 'foreigners' helps to reassert the point of view of the Japanese). Yet, very few students are ready to question the widespread uses of the surgical mask by Japanese society at large. It is only when they are asked to re-read what they have written and apply a *scientific point of view* that challenges the beliefs of the Japanese and their social practices that they start backing away from their in-group position. In the second draft, they start moving toward a more critical review of the use of the surgical mask. Some conclude: 'Japanese are always afraid of getting and making other people sick. However, their use of the surgical mask works more like a talisman against diseases than a real way of protecting themselves'. Others write that 'by wearing surgical masks in everyday situations people are signalling that they may not be able to perform well and therefore request some kind of respect for their personal space, especially in places in which there is a lack of personal space such as crowded trains'. The final review of the topic will comprise the transfer of the analytical apparatus to the analysis of societies other than the Japanese. Many conclude that no matter how developed a society may seem, they always create rituals which are at odds with mainstream science. In summary, they have moved away from the in-group/out-group binary logic. The adoption of the point of view of the cultural anthropologist or sociologist helps students develop this position and in my class I teach a few methods drawn from these disciplines, including participant observation, and we spend time analysing sociological reports on customary societal behaviour. Eventually, the argumentative requirements imposed by the essay as a genre will be recognised first and foremost as analytical tools that can be directed to analyse the constitution of the foreign identity, but that is better done through the introduction of scientific conceptual systems (see Vygotsky 1987; Hedegaard 2002).

I would suggest further that writing not only demands attention to the representational function of the foreign language and consequently a clear reflexive–intensive teaching and learning approach, but that this explicit reflexivity extends to those socio-communicative aspects of the foreign language such as the position of *speakers* or the context. In writing it is easier to track down a change in the grammatical voice that may signal the social positioning of the addressor. An essay that begins with an aseptic 'people wear surgical masks...' may later turn into 'we believe that wearing surgical masks...' The attention of the student can be easily brought to these aspects by virtue of the written sign. In certain written genres of what we could call objective writing such as the essay, the journalistic report or the thesis, the authorial voice tends to assume the position of a more knowledgeable subject, even if the discourse is exploratory. This may be at odds with the assumed communication apprehension of Japanese students and may operate as a call to overcome the barrier of status-related behaviour, which seems to be dominant in conversational contexts involving Japanese and non-Japanese speakers (see Lucas 1984; Kowner 2002) .

The problem is how to help students move away from their existing subject and assume a social position they have never experienced, even if it is through a sort of play or pretence. Can students situate themselves in an unknown social context that is explicitly transmitted, internalise and appropriate it, and make it their own?

The displacing power of writing in a foreign language comes precisely from its relative avoidance of the untamed socio-communicative dimension of the conversation class, which writing restricts to an imaginary author–reader relation.

Writing as poiesis

The idea behind tasks involving *poiesis* is to facilitate students in the adoption of a sovereign stance. Drawing on Fernández's (2012) pedagogies of microtexts, I have developed a few tasks, each one lasting at least three or four 90-minute sessions, in which intermediate students explore the structural limitations of script and representation in general, without a particular utilitarian aim in mind. The main activity is the writing of microtexts. The only requisite is that the text length cannot exceed 140 characters, the length of social networking microblogging messages known as tweets.

These texts may well fall under the aims Raymond Queneau and François Le Lionnais advanced in their literature workshop *Oulipo* (*Ouvroir de Littérature Potentielle*) in Paris in 1960. They believed that artistic invention and playfulness was linked to the imposition of rules or structural constraints (see Lescure 2003; Lapprand 1998). The microtext task compels the author to draw on other stable or widely known discursive forms such as locutions, short poems, and prosaic verse or prose such as aphorisms, citations or advertising.

The writing of microtexts, especially of poems, is something with strong connections to Japanese poetry. Students quickly make the task their own and start writing short texts. For instance, about love, they write[1]:

(1) '…And they lived happily ever after. The End.' Love, like in all tales, is only found in books.
(2) I want a handsome boy. Japanese boys are cowards.
(3) Love is what you find after the morning has broken.
(4) If the husband does not give enough money, the wife divorces him.

Some of them (microtexts 1, 2 and 4) could also be considered anti-poems, the kind of poetry proposed by Nicanor Parra, using humour, everyday language, and sometimes mathematical and algebraic signs to break away from the seriousness and conventions of classic forms (see Grossman 1975; Parra 2004). Thus, whilst there are some examples of what could be considered classic or romantic poems (microtext 3), most of the students' productions go against the conventions of traditional poetry.

Other microtexts reinterpret human experiences with objects that are found in everyday life, such as these two texts about vending machines:

(1) It is so sad when the cover does not completely open and my hand cannot reach the drink.
(2) She is waiting by the corner in order to make money. I go toward her to kill my thirst.

Some microtexts are incipient *calligrams*, that is, poems in which the script is arranged so as to create a visual image. The calligram is a kind of poetic art cultivated by Guillaume Apollinaire, Stéphane Mallarmé and Vicente Huidobro, among others. Because of their visual nature, reading them aloud would be a reductionist rendition, and most of the time an impossible task. An example of this is microtext 7, a representation of university life:

(1) For students, the week goes by like this: MONDAAAAAY, TUESDAAAAAY, WEDNESDAAAAAY, THURSDAAAAAY, FRIDAAAAAY, saturday and sunday.

It uses both visual (i.e. use of upper and lower case) and phonetic representations (i.e. extending the sound *a* in words referring to weekdays) in order to produce a hierarchical distinction between weekdays and weekend days.

In summary, there are many connections between Derrida's grammatology and the *Oulipo* (see Tufail 1999), calligrams, anti-poetry and other writing devices that are worth exploring (see Derrida and Attridge 1992). In order to achieve sovereignty in a pedagogic context, I would like to stress the necessity of setting up structural constraints or rules, to liberate writing from any utilitarian aim. It may be the product of my own bias, but my experience tells me that many students for the first time feel empowered to embark on a personal discovery journey rather than following someone else's steps. The sovereign stance creates an anti-pedagogising field. Sovereignty cannot be taught.

Conclusion

Where do we stand in regards to language, or its sociological rendition 'discourse', writing and subjective transformation? Well, it seems that writing in a foreign language may be central to any serious endeavour of transforming the subjects involved in the pedagogical process of learning a foreign language. Whether we choose Derrida's deconstructionist approach or the immanent critique method of the dialectical tradition – or even the complementary approach whereby we adopt both approaches at once – writing is at the base of both objectivised semiosis and poeisis. The question I find hard to answer is: who are we as educators to engage in this transformative process, taking into account that deconstruction operates as a form of radical liberation that brings human beings back to a standstill, an aesthetic and epistemic standstill where the modern ideals of 'progress' and 'truth' are cancelled? And, who are we as educators to assume a hierarchically higher position, to stand above learners, dominate them with the promise that, after they pay their dues, they will be able to make choices or change the world we have planned for them because we, at this particular time, know better?

Learners' resistances seem paradoxically blissful; they may bring back some form of equilibrium into the asymmetric instructor–student relationship. Are the students who resist learning a foreign language afraid of reconfiguring their social relations? Are they afraid of dissolving their *essential* national selves or identities that seem more feasible, given the structural constraints and affordances regulated by social class, by the discursive gap, by the administration of the unthinkable? Are they afraid of losing themselves in the chaos of the unthinkable? Or is it fair to say that their resistance is part of a more subtle standpoint aimed at dissolving the (fake) sovereign stance *imposed* by their – usually boring – masters?

Alternatively, are the students who are committed to learning a foreign language invested in losing themselves, as I was when I started learning English and took refuge from my own Chilean identity? What are committed language learners taking refuge from?

In summary, the more-knowledgeable–less-knowledgeable relation in Vygotsky's ZPD, for all it is worth in accounting for subjective transformations, does not seem able to capture the subtleties of domination and emancipation within the pedagogic relation. If we stand by Derrida, pedagogies that rely on the metaphysics of presence are just another set of fantasies or collective delusion, another form of taming the true sovereign stance that only emerges in the act of writing, which is beyond presence or negativity, but is still fundamentally an analytical process.

Note

1. Cited texts in Spanish have been produced by students who took my writing course in 2012. The texts were published at the end of that year under the condition that individual authors could not be identified. The English translation is mine.

References

Bataille, Georges. 1954. *L'expérience Intérieure, Collection Tel 23*. Paris: Gallimard.

Bataille, Georges. 1985. "The Critique of the Foundations of Hegelian Dialectic." In *Visions of Excess*, edited by A. Stoekl, 105–115. Minneapolis: University of Minnesota Press.

Bataille, Georges. 1986. *Erotism: Death & Sensuality. 1st City Lights*. San Francisco, CA: City Lights Books.
Bataille, Georges. 1991. *The Accursed Share: An Essay on General Economy*, vol. I. New York: Zone Books.
Bataille Georges. 1993. "Hegel, Death and Sacrifice." In *G. W. F. Hegel: Critical Assessments*, edited by R. Stern, 383–399. London: Routledge.
Bernstein, Basil. 2000. *Pedagogy, Symbolic Control and Identity: Theory Research Critique*. Revised ed. Oxford: Rowman and Littlefield.
Chaiklin, Seth. 2012. "Dialectics, Politics and Contemporary Cultural-Historical Research, Exemplified through Marx and Vygotsky." In *Vygotsky and Sociology*, edited by H. Daniels, 24–43. Abingdon: Routledge.
Daniels, Harry. 2001. "Bernstein and Activity Theory." In *Towards a Sociology of Pedagogy*, edited by Ana Morais, Isabel Neves, Brian Davies and Harry Daniels, 99–112. New York: Peter Lang.
Derrida, Jacques. 1982. *Margins of Philosophy*. Chicago: The University of Chicago Press.
Derrida Jacques. 1997. *Of Grammatology*. Translated and edited by G. C. Spivak. Baltimore; London: Johns Hopkins University Press.
Derrida, Jacques. 2001. *Writing and Difference*. London: Routledge.
Derrida, Jacques, and Derek Attridge. 1992. *Acts of Literature*. New York: Routledge.
Escandón, Arturo. 2012. "The Pedagogies of Second Language Acquistion: Combining Cultural-Historical and Sociological Traditions." In *Vygotsky and Sociology*, edited by H. Daniels, 211–232. London: Routledge.
Fernández Lázaro, Gisele. 2012. "La Escritura Creativa en el Aula De Español Como Lengua Extranjera: El Microrrelato." *Cuadernos CANELA* XXIV: 45–62.
Grossman, Edith. 1975. *The Antipoetry of Nicanor Parra*. New York: New York University Press.
Hashimoto, Kayoko. 2000. "'Internationalisation' is 'Japanisation': Japan's Foreign Language Education and National Identity." *Journal of Intercultural Studies* 21 (1): 39–51.
Hedegaard, Mariane. 2002. *Learning and Child Development: A Cultural-Historical Study*. Aarhus: Aarhus University Press.
Hegel, Georg Wilhem Friedrich. 1975. *Hegel's Logic*. Oxford: Clarendon Press.
Hegel, Georg Wilhem Friedrich. 1977. *Phenomenology of Spirit*. Translated by A. V. Miller. Oxford: Oxford University Press.
Hegel, Georg Wilhem Friedrich. 1978. *Escritos De Juventud*. Translated and edited by J. M. Ripalda. Madrid: Fondo de Cultura Económica, 2003.
Johnson, Marysia. 2004. *A Philosophy of Second Language Acquisition*. New Haven, CT: Yale University Press.
Jones, Peter. 2009. "From 'External' to 'Inner Speech' in Vygotsky: A Critical Appraisal and Fresh Perspectives." *Language & Communication* 29: 166–181.
Kowner, Rotem. 2002. "Japanese Communication in Intercultural Encounters: The Barrier of Status-Related Behavior." *International Journal of Intercultural Relations* 26 (4): 339–361.
Lapprand, Marc. 1998. *Poétique De L'oulipo*. Amsterdam: Faux Titre.
Leont'ev, Aleksei N. 1981. "The Problem of Activity in Psychology." In *The Concept of Activity in Soviet Psychology*, edited by J. V. Wertsch, 37–71. Armonk, NY: M.E. Sharpe.

Lescure, Jean. 2003. "Brief History of the Oulipo." In *The New Media Reader*, edited by N. Wardrip-Fruin and N. Montfort, 172–189. Cambridge, MA.: The MIT Press.

Lucas, Jenifer. 1984. "Communication Apprehension in the ESL Classroom: Getting Our Students to Talk." *Foreign Language Annals* 17 (6): 593–598.

Parra, Nicanor. 2004. *Antipoems: How to Look Better & Feel Great*. Trans. L. Werner. New York: New Directions Books.

Plotnitsky, Arkady. 1994. *Complementarity: Anti-Epistemology after Bohr and Derrida*. Durham: Duke University Press.

Robbins, Dorothy. 2003. *Vygotsky's and A.A. Leontiev's Semiotics and Psycholinguistics. Applications for Education, Second Language Acquisition, and Theories of Language. Contributions in Psychology* Number 44. Westport, Connecticut: Praeger.

Saussure, Ferdinand. 1959. *Course in General Linguistics*. Translated and edited by W. Baskin, C. Bally and A. Sechehaye. New York: Philosophical Library.

Tufail, Burhan. 1999. "Oulipian Grammatology: La Règle Du Jeu." In *The French Connections of Jacques Derrida*, edited by J. Wolfreys, J. Brannigan and R. Robbins, 119–134. Albany: State University of New York Press.

Vygotsky, Lev Seminovich. 1978. *Mind in Society: The Development of Higher Psychological Processes*, edited by M. Cole, V. John-Steiner, S. Scribner and E. Souberman. Cambridge, MA.: Harvard University Press.

Vygotsky, Lev Seminovich. 1987. "Thinking and Speech". In *The Collected Works of L. S. Vygotsky: Volume 1, Problems of General Psychology*, edited by R. W. Rieber and A. S. Carton, 39–285. New York: Plenum Press.

Vygotsky, Lev Seminovich. 1997. Mind, consciousness, the unconscious. *The Collected Works of L. S. Vygotsky. Vol. 3, Problems of the Theory and History of Psychology*, edited by R. W. Rieber and J. Wollock, 109–127. New York; London: Plenum.

Wertsch, James V. 1985. *Vygotsky and the Social Formation of Mind*. Cambridge, MA: Harvard University Press.

The enjoyment of space: the university campus in students' narratives and photography

Angie Voela

Psychosocial Studies, University of East London, London, UK

> In this paper I discuss how students use narratives and photography in order to represent their everyday engagement with the university space. I draw on the Lacanian notions of the Real and the drive, and suggest ways in which these notions can be used to develop a different approach to educational spaces, especially when photographic material is used in conjunction with interviews.

Introduction

The view that a sense of belonging in an educational setting enhances learning has gained ground in educational literature (see Sagan 2008; Temple and Barnett 2007). With that in mind, I invited undergraduate students from various programmes at the University of East London (UEL) to take part in a study that would explore belonging at the university's Docklands Campus. Students who agreed to participate, 25 in total, were asked to take photographs on their mobiles of places that made them feel at home, and, upon their return, discuss five of them in a short interview. Prior to the task, I introduced the terms 'belonging' and 'feeling at home' and gave the students a brief outline of the hypothesis I wished to explore.

Most students spoke with enthusiasm about the places they had photographed but hardly endorsed the idea of feeling 'at home' at university. How could one feel at home at a place associated with deadlines and pressure? 'Home' means relaxation, sofa, television or, in the case of most mature students, a different set of responsibilities. And what did belonging have to do with getting a degree? At the end of the interviews, however, several students spontaneously declared that they had very much enjoyed the experience of taking the photographs and talking about them. They commented enthusiastically that they had never looked at the campus *that* way, or noted that, although they did not quite know what to expect at first, they had enjoyed the experience of taking a look at their own routines and at being 'there', at the campus. Others, not knowing what to make of the experiment, asked me, with some hesitation, if the information they had given me was what I wanted.

As the hypothesis of belonging was not being confirmed, I began to rethink the significance of space for the students. Something was beginning to emerge: evidence of an enjoyment of space which was intersecting with the ordinary uses of the campus but remained quite distinct from it and emerged as a response – not to say reaction – to the idea of 'belonging', as I will explain below. This led me to look at the pictures with the 'sound off' (Kingsbury 2010) and at the interview data 'awry' (Proudfoot 2010), drawing on Lacanian psychoanalysis. Lacanians accept that meaning does not reside exclusively in what the speaking subject intentionally expresses through words. Meaning is also communicated through what is *not said*, circumvented, avoided or left out of an intended message. They therefore suggest that as researchers we should be mindful of what exceeds intentional communication. Lacanians also accept that space is not merely the background of individuals' actions; space does things *for* individuals. It is therefore an 'outside' in direct communication with the 'inside'. For that reason, practices of space can *mean* alongside and often instead of words, and constitute an invaluable body of evidence when it comes to understanding individual or collective behaviour. Lacanian psychoanalysis therefore invites us to look at both words and images *differently*.

In this paper I discuss the enjoyment of space in a Lacanian framework. I argue that the enjoyment of space in the university setting appears as 'additional' or 'other' to the main purpose of education, which is the acquisition of knowledge and a degree. While this purpose is achieved over a long period of time – usually three years – the enjoyment of space is more immediate and organised in daily or quasi-daily cycles involving repetition of movements and regular habits that often go unnoticed. 'Unnoticed', however, does not mean 'meaningless'. These 'unnoticed' trajectories can be gleaned when interview and photographic data are examined *differently*, through the lens of the drive. The notion of the drive is introduced below. As it is one of the most complex Lacanian notions, its introduction is preceded by a brief account of the three orders of existence, the Symbolic, the Imaginary and the Real. The drive mainly originates in the latter. Apart from drawing on the notion of the drive, this paper is organised around the relationship between the outside-space and the inside-subject. This relationship is known as 'extimacy' (see Evans 1996, 160) and is also introduced below.

The theoretical section is followed by a data presentation section labelled 'the spatial organisation of enjoyment', a term I borrow from Psychoanalytic Cultural Geography. However, my understanding of the spatial organisation of enjoyment and the use of the drive are different from those proposed in Cultural Geography. My understanding of the drive encompasses the notion of *montage*, which is particularly relevant to photography, and the notion of the *new subject*, which is developed by Lacan (1986) in the *Four Fundamental Concepts of Psychoanalysis* and accounts for the possible effects the recognition of the trajectory of the drive might have on the speaking subject. Thus, unlike cultural geographers who only posit the Real/drive as a theoretical perspective that allows them to make sense of spatial data, I also focus on what happens when students become aware of the very trajectory they follow and discuss in my presence.

A partial topography of the Docklands Campus

'Situated in a stunning waterfront setting' as the official UEL website announces, the Docklands Campus is a 2000 development across the canal from the City airport runway. The majority of students and staff arrive by the Docklands Light Railway (DLR) which, like the canal, forms the other notional boundary of the campus. Walking from the DLR towards the campus, one has East Building to the left and West Building to the right, separated by a square. The two buildings, which house lecture and seminar rooms and offices, are mainly used by social sciences students. The library is situated behind the West Building and has a canal view. A row of accommodation blocks, known as 'the drums' due to their cylindrical design, is situated in front of the above buildings. Other buildings on the campus, such as the Arts building, the Knowledge Dock adjacent to the library and the new Sports Dock were not mentioned by the students.

The Lacanian topology of subjectivity and its relation to space

In this section I begin by offering a general outline of the three Lacanian orders of existence, the Symbolic, the Imaginary and the Real. This is followed by an introduction of the notions of the drive and extimacy, and practical examples of their use.

*The three orders, the notion of enjoyment (*jouissance*) and the drive*

As Evans (1996, 131) points out, Lacan was keen on emphasising that existence is simultaneously played out on all three orders. However, their clinical and theoretical separation creates the necessary perspective for understanding the composite nature of experience. The Symbolic order encompasses the following: language, which implies mediation and representation; the Law, which refers to the hierarchical, designated and organised relations in which we are introduced as infants; ideology, moral principles and values; culture and society. The Symbolic order arises with the child's entry into language and its separation from the mother. It harks back to the child's rivalry with the father and subsequent acceptance of the latter's authority, known in psychoanalysis as the Oedipus complex.

Because it originates in the Oedipus complex, an experience which is repressed and no longer accessible to consciousness, the Symbolic order is also directly related to the unconscious, the repressed and inaccessible part of our existence. Thus, the Symbolic is characterised by a double otherness-alterity: the alterity of the subject as unknown to itself (unconscious), and the otherness of the social, mediated relations (see Bowie 1991, 88–121; Evans 1996, 133). Very often the Symbolic order is referred to as the big 'Other'.

The Imaginary is generally understood as the order of vision and images. It is also the order of responding to these images via process of identification. Wanting to be like others, for instance, copying their manners or trying to doing what they do, could be located in this order. Falling in love or the investment of others with emotion also belong to the Imaginary. Lacan locates the Freudian ego – a cluster of organised and relatively inflexible ideas about the self – on the order of the Imaginary and often considers the latter as an obstacle to accessing the truth of the unconscious (see Evans 1996, 82–83). Yet the function of the Imaginary is no less important for existence than that of the Symbolic: imagine a world with no influences from external images or from others, no passionate pursuit of goals, nothing to 'capture our imagination'.

The Real is the order of the unrepresented, or that which resists symbolisation and remains repressed or unassimilable, outside language and consciousness (Evans 1996, 160). Un-represented does not mean 'lost' but entails the possibility of 'returning' or surfacing in some manner. In very simple terms, the Real is important for its disruptive power. It is not a mere repository of traumatic events and repressed desires but a potential source of insight into experiences, practices, motivations, beliefs and actions. There also is another, more literal sense to the term Real: it refers to the simple, naked materiality of the external world (Evans 1996, 159–60). We will draw on its dual status below.

The relationship between the Symbolic and the Real is important and concerns concepts like enjoyment, the drive and extimacy, which are also used below. Lacan's argument is that the child's entry into the Symbolic and Language is a 'mixed blessing': on the one hand, the ability to speak and represent one's desires in language ensures the achievement of satisfaction; on the other, it entails the loss of a more immediate form of satisfaction known as *jouissance* (enjoyment). *Jouissance* refers to the baby's close relation to the maternal body, the latter representing the first object to be lost and henceforth to be designated as *object a*. Although this obscure notion of the *object a* might appear exaggerated, Lacan considers it vital when conveying the idea that the Symbolic order (Other) is never complete, autonomous, closed or impenetrable. Something from the Real (un-represented and akin to the *object a*) may always challenge it. At the same time, Lacan is keen on demonstrating that social, cultural and ideological phenomena have their routes in psychic reality.

Another concept that originates in the Real is the drive. The drive harks back to the Freudian notion of the death drive and the philosophical opposition between life and death. However, the drive that interests us here is a force; imagine it as irreducible and constant psychic energy. This drive is 'plugged' into the Symbolic order and receives satisfaction via symbolic objects and activities. However, it has its own object, the *object a* which, as we already know, can never be attained. The Lacanian drive therefore resembles a detour, a looping trajectory around a missing object. Lacan locates enjoyment (*jouissance*) in this pretty pointless looping motion, and again, recognises its significance for the potential subversion of the Symbolic. Lacanians systematically draw on the notion of the drive in order to explain a wider range of phenomena; for instance, why people persist in practices that may appear meaningless or incompatible with their expressed aims and intentions, or why they commit acts which appear to be unmotivated, detrimental to them or totally devoid of pleasure. What I wish to highlight at this point is the idea that an apparently superficial task can reveal another source of pleasure and motivation that is not properly valued from a Symbolic perspective alone. To put it rather bluntly, an educational system oriented towards success rates does not seem to make room for the value and enjoyment stemming from everyday experiences. Yet there is definitely *something else* arising when the lens of academic success is cast aside. Can we ignore it? Should we ignore it? The present paper does the very least: points at ways of registering its existence.

The notion of extimacy in Cultural Geography and applications of psychoanalytic theory

I continue this introduction by clarifying the proposition that space as outside is intimately linked to subjectivity as inside via the notion of extimacy. Although the proposition that space and the inner world interact seems fairly self-evident, it is 'innovative' in at least two senses. First, it challenges the opacity of the 'inner' world by proposing that what is often not fully known to the speaking subject itself – unrepresented, unconscious – can be conveyed by simple spatial practices. At the same time, it challenges the common (mis)conception that the thinking-reflexive agent is in command of external reality and space.

Kingsbury (2007) shows how ordinary everyday practices can express 'inner' subjectivity. He discusses the case of 'Support the Troops' magnets often displayed by residents of mid-American states in support of the war in Iraq. The practice, he notes, illustrates the *overdetermined* and *dynamic nature of space*. The magnets support a constellation of psychic pleasures and defences, including the exhibitionist thrill of displaying while driving one's political beliefs, receiving narcissistic gratification for seeing one's convictions 'summed up' in the form of a car magnet, and warding off of the anxiety of doing something different or even critiquing the war (Kingsbury 2007, 245). Thus, Kinsgbury concludes, the ribbon magnets do not simply stand in for people's support and beliefs; rather, people support and believe *through* the medium of the ribbon magnets. Subjectivity, therefore, does not take place only when an *agent* is actively doing something, but rather when another thing (person or object) is doing it *for* the agent (Kingsbury 2007, 247). In that sense, it is not conscious intentions but *the spatial organisation of enjoyment* that 'speaks' subjectivity itself.

The close relationship between the 'inside' and the 'outside' described above is known as *extimacy*. Extimacy (*extimité*) is Lacan's neologism derived by joining 'exteriority' and 'intimacy', and pointing at how psychoanalysis problematises the opposition between the inside and the outside (Evans 1996, 58–9), drawing on the notion of the Real both as unassimilable and as simple, naked materiality of the external world.

The spatial organisation of subjectivity and the Real can offer new insights into research questions and can have important methodological implications. Consider the case reported by Proudfoot (2010) and the difficulties he encountered when researching the national pride of Canadians of Italian extraction during the 2006 World Cup. Proudfoot reports being confronted with incomprehension, silence and even hostility from his interviewees when asking direct questions about their national allegiance or about their preference for watching matches at the cafés of the Italian quarter in Vancouver: 'People are cautious and resistant when they have to signify their enjoyment in interviews' (515), he notes. At the same time, he observed the abundance of non-discursive (Real) elements in the scene: the elation, the shouting, the chanting, and even the tears that overcame one man who tried to articulate his feelings after an Italian victory (511). Proudfoot also found that while fans were unlikely to account for how and why they enjoy football as Italians, they were eager to talk at length about the teams, their style of play and their tactics, 'in short how *they organised their enjoyment* in relation to sport' (515, emphasis added). He therefore started *looking awry*, situating the object of research (nationality and national pride) at the periphery of his questions, focusing instead on the organisation of enjoyment. Regarding the methodological importance of such a procedure he adds:

> What psychoanalysis can teach us methodologically is that *looking and speaking awry* are key to capturing the extra-discursive dimension of enjoyment in interviews. Questions about enjoyment must necessarily *focus on ritual rather than attempt to directly confront the Thing [object a]* – that is the fulcrum of the subject's real enjoyment – in this case, the nation. (Proudfoot 2010, 515, emphasis added)

I found Proudfoot's experience akin to mine and remember a similar sense of bemusement at the students' resistance to engage with the idea of 'belonging to a place'. The spatial organisation I develop below draws on this research but incorporates photography and substantial interviews and does not preclude a reflexive component that is missing from Proudfoot's account. My emphasis on the trajectory of the drive means that I also pay attention to the interviewee's own chance of grasping the trajectory of enjoyment and the importance of their itineraries as *other* to the main goals of education.

The circular trajectory of the drive, the *object a* and the notion of enjoyment are further illustrated by Kingsbury through the example of the pool bar in a Caribbean resort. Kingsbury (2010) shows how enjoyment arises out of ordinary interaction. Hotel staff at the pool bar performed their duties with eagerness: they engaged the customers in short conversation, joked, moved to the rhythm of the music and improvised lines, offering 'more than' the drinks or food verbally demanded by the customers. The customers were drawn into the allure of the inter-space (525) created by the staff's improvisations, the solicited gazes, the sounds, the rhythms and the patterns surrounding the service. Thus, places like the pool bar become spatial hotspots of enjoyment (527) where the *object a* (the elusive supplement to the standard holiday pleasure) emerges in an elliptical, extra-discursive way. Kingsbury reports that he was able to conceptualise the spatial organisation of enjoyment when he looked at the pool bar scene 'with the sound off', noticing its repetitive and 'aimless' regularity. The researcher comments: 'Any activity has the potential to turn into the gyre of the drive, insofar as the activity brings to the fore the extent to which people can achieve satisfaction by not achieving their aim: by not finding an empty chair, by waiting and waiting for that magical number to be called out' (529) – deriving enjoyment, we might add, by taking their eyes off a designated goal and the rational strategies underlying its systematic pursuit.

While I draw in the insights of Cultural Geography, my approach departs from them in significant ways. The theoretical platform for this departure is supplied by Lacan and concerns two further aspects of the drive. In *The Four Fundamental Concepts of Psychoanalysis*, Lacan (1986, 169) refers to the drive as *montage*. By way of illustration, he gives the example of a surrealist picture, the elements of which produce just another surrealist picture when rearranged. I argue that the students' photographs can be seen as such a surrealist assemblage when looked at from the point of view of the drive: as snapshots of the *Real* which challenge the speaking subject to consider the multiple overtones and the reverberations of space that always exceed the attempt to impose order to and rationalise the visual material. It seems to me that pictures, like a montage, can be assembled in a different order and always tell a story. This 'arbitrary' rearrangement, I think, could be part of enjoyment.

Also in *The Four Fundamental Concepts of Psychoanalysis*, Lacan (1986) explains that the drive achieves satisfaction as partial drive via different zones of the body, the eyes being one of them. The satisfaction of the relevant drive, the scopic drive, consists not only in 'seeing' but also in 'being seen' and attempting to produce the 'gaze' under which the subject finds itself. Lacan sums up the tripartite trajectory of the drive, drawing on Freud's use of the grammatical terms active, passive and middle voice: to see, to be seen and to give oneself to be seen. With this last movement, notes Lacan, *a new subject appears* (178, emphasis added). The subject is 'new' because it is not caught in the exchange of seeing and being seen alone, that is, in the imaginary dialectic of the gaze. With the completion of the trajectory and the third move, one encounters what it possibly means to reveal oneself to one's own and the other's gaze, perceiving oneself as subject. Proudfoot (2010, 513) wonders: 'what would the faces of these fans suggest if you could occupy the position of the screen and *gaze back* at their anguished faces?' – in other words, what would enjoyment *look like* to the subject itself? This, of course, is an unanswerable question, since *jouissance*/enjoyment does not have a representation. But photography as a mode of capturing space and enjoyment might provide an alternative perspective for making *that* look appear at the margins, along with its ontological significance. I have argued elsewhere (Voela 2013) that this self-scopic attempt invites the subject to fathom its position in a complex scene, not as a superior overlooking eye/I but as just another element. Here I want to propose that contemplating photographs of places that are significant to the speaking subject but ultimately marked by its absence (no one figures in the pictures they have taken) allows the interviewees to 'play' with the drive, to experience enjoyment but also explore its margins and ultimately contemplate the un-told aspect of 'being' and 'not being' there, in the university environment.

The spatial organisation of enjoyment in photographic data and interviews

Below I trace the spatial organisation of the students' enjoyment at the university campus. I look for patterns and extra-discursive inscriptions of enjoyment as they emerge in photographs and interviews. Photography in social sciences is mainly seen as symbolic, indexical or metaphorical of real activities, and photo-elicited interviews are mainly treated as evidence of the interviewees' reflexive capacity (Banks 2001; Bijoux and Myers 2006; Gauntlett and Holzwarth 2006; Moore et al. 2008; Pink 2011; Tinkler 2013). In this paper, however, I use photography as a means of registering the students' trajectories through space, their absence from the frame, as well as their ability to grasp that very absence. I therefore also look for the moments of contemplative understanding that emerge in the process. As I said above, I consider the photographic excursion to resemble the trajectory of the drive, an 'aimless' de-tour around a familiar territory, a full turn, the 'goal' and enjoyment of which lies beyond the primary aims of education. This full turn is completed at least twice: first, as the students go around the campus taking photographs, and second when they revisit some of these photographs in the interview. The double loop chimes with other trajectories evoked in their absence: countless daily routines inscribed in their presence/absence in the visual evidence.

By the same token, I do *not* interpret interviews to their full linguistic potential, though I am quite aware that explanations other than those I am offering here can be proposed. In combining interview data with photographs I am trying to extract an overall view of space. Perhaps my method should best be described as a kind of observation out of which emerges a composite picture of space, comprising of a theoretical idea (the detour of the drive), photographic evidence of routines and locations, and narrative testimonies of their significance. I would therefore invite the reader to approach the following section as such a composite observation.

Based on the photographs and the interviews, I have devised a system of *points of spatial orientation* around the campus, further divided into *points of reference*, such as the library and the main buildings, and *points of passage*, such as the entrance/exist to the campus and the canal walkway. I envisage the campus as a bounded and clearly defined space, *a scene* which contains and holds the student experience, and by extension, their enjoyment. Students attempted to make sense both of the parts of the scene and of the scene as a whole. At times they discovered the (imaginary) fascination the place exercised on them (examples given below), or reaffirmed the symbolic reasons for being there. At times they only encountered the question of their own presence and absence. This, I will argue below, suggests the ontological significance of the entire experience: something (Real, yet to be addressed and verbalised) appears between photography and the narrative; between notional space and real space; between (re)visting a familiar landscape and having to account for its significance. The extimacy of space, its overdetermined and dynamic nature, is revealed while looking awry at the everyday and the ordinary, allowing this *something else* to appear, beyond the Imaginary and the Symbolic.

Points of Imaginary reference: the library, the bookshop, the classroom

The students' comments on space vary from attempts to offer rational, 'clever' or 'original' explanations about the photographs, to reminiscing about good moments, to free-associating, to being genuinely surprised by their own responses and trying to associate the campus to other places and new challenges. The university is simultaneously personal and public, a place to stay for a while but also of transition and passing. Whatever its precise identity, participants had little difficulty in locating the places required. In K's words: 'I knew immediately where to go'.

Unsurprisingly, perhaps, the library, the bookshop and the lecture theatres – all associated with knowledge as the primary purpose of being at university – appeared regularly in the photographic evidence. While some students included such places as 'the obvious choice' and offered no further comments, others commented on the comfort of returning to them regularly:

> E: Even if I don't need any books, I just go to the library and have a mooch around.

This regular return for no 'apparent' reason, belies the significance of an 'empty' gesture and can be used as an example of extimacy: the regular return to the library might be understood as organising and supporting the student identity when learning is not pursued in relation to assignments. It holds in its domain the desire for knowledge. Regular visits to the library, therefore, afford the pleasure of pursuing one's dream beyond mere accreditation.

Other places were invested with Imaginary significance. One student showed me a picture of the campus bookshop, adding that this was the place where she met a person she had prayed for, a good friend with whom to share the educational experience. In this example the almost magical (Imaginary) fulfilment of a wish evokes the emergence of an *object a* (good friend as answer to prayer). Chance (*tyche*), Fink (1997, 93) explains, is re-finding an object known to the subject only in its attribute of goodness. Here, however, it can be noted that it is not *tyche* but the very persistent repetition of the visits to the bookshop that increase the chance of coming across a compatible friend. Whether this is recognised or not is a different matter. In both examples, I would suggest that the regular inclusion of spaces like the library and the bookshop into the students' routine was significant because it yielded enjoyment and structured it through repetition.

Watching others go by: shifts between the Imaginary and the Real

Watching others 'go by' in spaces like the café, the atrium and the square was an essential and stable component of the spatial organisation of enjoyment. Communal spaces support an exchange of gazes as a way of getting to see what others do and doing like them. Mature and non-traditional students often seek (visual) reassurance that they are 'doing the right thing' and 'behave like students'. Watching others and observing their manners offers that reassurance.

In some cases watching meshed with the desire to apply one's growing knowledge and powers of observation on to others. The Imaginary position of the surveying eye was assumed in that case:

M: Studying Psychosocial you become so much more observant, you become so much more analytic in ... a nice way ... Studying human behaviour, the reaction, the look on their face, and trying to image what they are thinking ... I wonder what this person is thinking, I wonder how they are.

Before long, however, the gaze re-turned upon the student herself:

M: So it [looking at people] makes me see that it's okay to look at *yourself* in different ways, to question yourself a little bit.

The desire to know what lies beneath the surface (face) reveals more than the Imaginary correspondence with the other. It might be possible to say that it hints at an elusive object: the precious object (*object a*) of education yet to be mastered, a wisdom that could penetrate inscrutable faces and superficial impressions. But what is more important is what emerges when the imaginary 'penetrating' gaze was re-turned upon the student herself, when she realised that it is *herself* that she needed to look at differently. At such moments we are reminded of Lacan's third move of the drive, the return upon the self of that elusive gaze which disengages the subject from the Imaginary capitation with the other. At that point, we can speculate, the disruptive influence of the Real emerged with the student's own inability to continue assuming the mastery of the all-knowing subject. Also, at that moment one learns – and enjoys – something important: by re-turning gaze and knowledge upon oneself, one begins to look at the whole world awry.

Points of passage: that bench – encounters with the Real?

There is a place at the campus which students cherish and claim as 'their own': a bench with a view to the water and the airstrip on the other side of the canal. This is a place where students obviously go to relax and spend a quiet moment. In the context of the spatial structure of enjoyment, however, this place acquired additional significance, as is shown in the examples below. In dealing with these examples, one needs to remember the layout of the specific locus: when seated at the bench one has one's back to the campus with a view to the canal, the airstrip of City Airport and the City skyscrapers at the far right end of the landscape.

Students returned regularly to the benches:

D: Now, there's a good place, to sit, look afar, and bring yourself back to [yourself].

Notice the slight semantic peculiarity in the above sentence: how does looking afar make one come back to their self? What kind of trajectory joins the far and the near, the internal and the external? The notion of extimacy that I have outlined is perhaps one way of accounting for this faltering, as a signal of the role of space in the constitution of subjectivity.

For another student the significance of the bench was hard to articulate:

> K: The bench ... that one, um ... exactly outside the library ... it's kind of opposite the spot that I would go to ... near the ... where ... what I call the come together again ... this is almost, kind of, Freudian ... kind of ... uh, um ... reminiscent to the Freudian chair.

Notice the factual error in the above excerpt; one would speak of Freud's couch, not chair. Minutes later, the student provided further associations on the word 'chair':

> The places ... I used them as, uh ... do you know when you have, um ... the naughty corner for certain areas and the child associates the things bad with that place and when they are bad, they associate it with that place ... so I kind of associate good things with those places ... so when I go there, I know that I will receive energy ... I receive rejuvenation ... I'll receive those good things that I need that I'm missing right now.

Reward and punishment, chair and sofa, good place and bad, isolation and participation in the academic life: the bench resonates with the Real, the unexpressed thoughts which surface as errors and the pieces of (psychoanalytic) knowledge which join forces with the very modern 'obligation' to examine the self regularly and give an account. These procedures are never accomplished or fully expressed. Yet going back *there* regularly, sitting at *that* bench arguably does all the above for the subject: space does things for the subject.

In another case, the solitude of the spot suggested something more 'actual' than other activities:

> S: So it's not so much about watching other people, it's just about sitting there and reflecting on my own thoughts I would say ... and watching the river ... watching the world but in ... an actual sense ... marvelling at the technology [refers to the aeroplanes] ... or marvelling at the water.

Lacan (1986) designates the Real and the *object a* as an excess of meaning, a 'more than' beyond symbolic meaning. This might be what 'watching in *an actual* sense' alludes to. At the same time, the place, the water and the cityscape evoke an opaque mirror, a surface which does not return a gaze or an image; an endless slow flow towards other places; a linear, ineluctable movement, different from the looping trajectory of coming back to the same place in the containing familiarity of the campus; a dividing line between the students and the affluent Other, the customers of the business airport on the other side of the canal.

Some places, like the bench at the waterfront, stand out for their evocative multiplicity. They seem to operate as crisis heterotopias (see Foucault 2000), *other* places which confound the speaking subject and to which only a profound, inarticulate bond can be avowed. They are places of passage and return, gravitational points at which the speaking subject encounters the limits of symbolic identity as well as the imaginary anticipation of a better life. Being there, seeking solitude, turning one's back to the campus and facing the world, resonate with the very materiality of the locus but never quite fully coincide with it. In that sense, regularly re-turning to *that place* can be understood as part of a ritual of trying to find an answer to 'how am I doing right now?' It does not yield concrete answers but at least 'structures' anxiety and allays fears. It is bound to the extimacy of space and forms part of the trajectory of the scopic activity at the very point at which it loops upon the subject itself. In a similar manner, the tour of the campus and the photographic task chimes with it, recalling for the subjects the same excess of meaning that lurks behind this everyday activity and every structured and purposeful activity in general.

Points of passage: full turn and the deferral of satisfaction

The final set of examples concerns another regularity; the full turn of arrival to and departure from the campus. This was the occasion that yielded the most obvious sense of enjoyment, along with a celebratory assertion of being there, making it every day and considering the regular repetition of the routine as an affirmation of one's perseverance. Crossing the bridge to UEL therefore was important, whether it was remembered as the symbolic first crossing into Higher Education, or the repetition of a routine activity.

This can be briefly illustrated in a comment from a mature student who did not have time to savour university life at leisure and for whom passing from the same points summed up the day's good work:

> P: The bridge leading to DLR ... Yes, I've done my work, you know, I've come to uni, I've achieved something, so, you know, I am going home now, this is a weight off your shoulders.

While the ultimate goal (degree achieved at the end of three years) was deferred, satisfaction was achieved by the trajectory of the day's work, the full, successful passage, the very fact of having reached the end/beginning of a short journey. This, I argue, might be interpreted as another example of the trajectory of the drive which attains satisfaction by not achieving its symbolic goal. In that sense, 'insignificant' material points of entry/exit signpost a clear picture of enjoyment which exceeds the 'academic' achievement but is just as important as the latter.

Methodological, ontological and ideological implications of the enjoyment of space

In the previous section I gave an overview of the organisation of spatial enjoyment as it emerged from the students' photographs and interviews. I argued that it can be represented as a trajectory or detour signposted with points of reference and points of passage, all of which illustrate the extimate relationship of subjectivity and space, and the enjoyment of space which allows the Real to shine through the Symbolic and Imaginary functions of education. I further argued that space 'does' things for the students, both as a concrete scene which contains and structures the educational experience and as an *other scene* which exceeds it. Below I make some methodological and theoretical suggestions, starting with the use of photography in psychoanalytic research.

As noted in the previous section, in Social Sciences photography is mainly interpreted with reference to the reflexive subject. At the same time, photo-elicitation is becoming increasingly popular because it promises 'more': more of the speaking subject; more of its voice; more autonomy to the interviewees (see Bijoux and Meyers 2006). We might want to pause and think: what is this 'more' that is being sought? And does not 'more', in that context, reveal the researcher's own desire to appropriate the other's enjoyment?

In the present research, photography was not used in order to affirm the presence of a reflexive subject or to reveal their pleasure (see Del Busso 2011) or even to confirm a research hypothesis. Its 'use' emerged from the evidence of the spatial organisation of enjoyment. We can account for the *ontological* significance of this activity by returning to the properties of the drive. As discussed in the theoretical section, the drive is comparable to a surrealist montage (Lacan 1986, 169). The photographic task resembles the *montage* of the drive: whichever way one arranges the pictures they make sense. Their meaning does not depend on a linear order, much in the same way as the students' enjoyment of space does not depend on visiting all the places at all times.

At the same time, photographs and interviews cut into one another. Students varied the length of their comments and the frequency of flicking from one picture to the next, sometimes coming back to one, sometimes skipping others, having taken *more* pictures than directed. It can therefore be argued that an account of space comprising photographs and narratives is itself a montage activity, an active assemblage structured around a drive-like repetition: taking the photographs and coming back to them. What do students indicate with that experience? I would suggest that the process reveals an inclination to looking awry. In the end, it was not the researcher that found out how to look awry, it was the students that 'learned' first and showed her the way. Yet 'learning' is hardly the right word as the drive cannot be 'educated'. The concept of the drive invites us to look at the *sense* (of space) that supports and ex-sists beyond *meaning*, causality and interpretation.

Lacan draws attention to the fact that the drive does not have a socially valid goal. If the goal and meaning of education are found in the Symbolic or the field of the Other, that is, in the importance of knowledge and the face value of a degree, then the enjoyment of space must be understood as radically in-different to those values. Verhaeghe shows how the drive undermines symbolic meaning when noting that from the point of view of the drive the opposites 'life' and 'death' are reduced to an arbitrary allotment of names in culture (Verhaeghe 2001, 93). By the same token, ordinary spatial relations appear subverted when looked at and spoken awry. In the students' examples, points of passage, like the bridge to the train platform and the bench by the canal, which are not related to the 'proper' functions of the institutional space, emerge as important. Again, what begins to emerge is a different approach to making sense of the place which defies salient points of reference. Whether one attempts to take a panoptic view of the campus or keeps coming back to a particular locus at regular intervals, the enjoyment of space is found in the regularity of the movement, in the very circularity of the trajectory of the drive. And certainly it is the failure to see and get everything under the scope of a panoptic gaze that allows for the implicit emergence of an *object a*, an elusive 'centre' around which the trajectory is inscribed. Thus, when all is said and done, neither the activity of looking nor the acquired academic knowledge can penetrate the surfaces of others; enjoyment is therefore found in the simple repetition of the activity. In that sense, students always re-find the pleasure of looking awry.

There is, however, a further implication in the enjoyment of space which is related to 'being there'. Drawing on the tri-partite movement of the drive (to see, to be seen, to give oneself to be seen), Lacan (1986, 178) notes that with the completion of the movement a new subject appears. As noted in the theory section, this concerns the subject that dis-engages itself from the mirror-imaginary capitation of the other and freely gives itself to the scopic gaze. This property of the drive, I argue, is conceptually very close to the reflexive subject of Sociology but also distinct from it, in the contemplation of the ontological importance of *presence and absence* which photography supports and inspires. It tends towards the limits of self-presence and the meaning of absence. University life is about 'being there'. At the same time, the pictures also capture 'absence' from the *scene* (I am not there, I am behind the lens, I am not included in this landscape). Together the two moves engender the realisation that the scene (the ensemble, the composite image of the chosen photographs and, by extension, university space) holds *me* in its gaze as much as I hold 'it' in my gaze. This change of perspective, this anamorphosis (Lacan 1986, 83) contains the subject. As Evans notes, topology is structure (Evans 1996, 208); it reworks rather than rethinks the Cartesian subject: *I am thinking where I am not, therefore I am where I am not thinking* (Lacan in Kingsbury 2007, 253). Failure to notice, to grasp the conditions of the subject's implication in its own world, is a failure of critical thought.

A final comment about the critical validity of the notion of the Real needs to be added at this point. The Lacanian notions of enjoyment and the drive form part of the critique of ideology and of the subject's mode of attachment to the Other. According to Lacan, the Other is open and inconsistent. In an attempt to form a stable identity the subject veils the knowledge of this openness/inconsistency. In analysis, the subject must accept it along with the fact that one's being is not fully justified by the big Other (see Žižek 1994, 113). In the psychoanalytic critique of ideology, the notion of the subject's relation to the Other leads to two complementary approaches: the former focuses on the deconstruction and symptomatic reading of ideology; the latter aims at exposing '*the kernel of enjoyment*', the mode of *jouissance* prefigured by a specific ideology and emerging in subjects' phantasies (see Žižek 1994, 125). Along the lines of revealing the kernel of enjoyment, I would suggest that the enjoyment of the university space, the encounter with presence and absence, and *being there* go beyond the commodity on offer, beyond the promise of constantly updated knowledge and of constantly improving surroundings. This piece of research therefore is not about providing more benches for solitary contemplation, or new cafeterias for more gazing at others. It is not about enhancing 'the student experience' either. It may be more helpful to think about it as *just* inviting students to consider another source of enjoyment, apart from the deferred enjoyment of getting *that* degree at the end of the three years. Lacanian topology amounts to 'the mobilization of a new spatial imaginary' (Kingsbury 2007, 251). In that sense, it might perhaps be useful to start thinking about the shape of the current *educational spatial imaginary* in general and consider what it says about education today. The eagerness of UEL students to engage with the task and the advent of new technologies (mobiles) which makes photography easy (see Harrison 2004) indicates that we should explore it further.

From a productive, utilitarian perspective (in terms of just getting that degree), the enjoyment of space is useless. Yet Baudrillard (2001, 44) shows how the useless is the bit of the *Real* that resists commodification and assimilation is an elastic Symbolic order which can contain, assimilate and obliterate difference. In Lacanian terms, the activity of photographing and talking about space – uselessness and real – exposes the kernel of enjoyment and reveals to the students a morsel of truth (*jouissance*) alienated in the Other – in the wider educational system. So when the students assert 'I am here' they are perhaps reclaiming that enjoyment for themselves, claiming it back from both my immediate research intentions and the anxiety of a future investment in themselves as holders of a degree. *I am here,* therefore, means: I enjoy my very presence, I reclaim the excess of my own Symbolic and Imaginary desire.

Acknowledgements

For the design of this research I drew on Dr Olivia Sagan's study of the uses of space by arts students at the University of the Arts, London. I wish to thank Raymond Campbell (PhD student), who conducted some of the interviews for the present study.

Funding

This research was funded by the UEL Small Grants Programme (2011–12).

References

Banks, M. 2001. *Visual Methods in Social Research*. London: Sage Press.
Baudrillard, J. 2001. *The Impossible Exchange*. London: Verso Press.
Bijoux, D., and J. Meyers. 2006. "Interviews, Solicited Diaries and Photography: 'new' Ways of Accessing Everyday Experiences of place." *Graduate Journal of Asia-Pacific Studies* 4 (1): 44–64.
Bowie, M. 1991. *Lacan*. London: Fontana Press.
Del Busso, L. 2011. "Using Photographs to Explore the Embodiment of Pleasure in Everyday Life." In *Visual Methods in Psychology: Using and Interpreting Images in Qualitative Research*, edited by P. Reavy, 43–54. London: Psychology Press.
Evans, D. 1996. *An Introductory Dictionary of Lacanian Psychoanalysis*. London: Routledge.
Fink, B. 1997. *The Lacanian Subject: Between Language and Jouissance*. Princeton: Princeton University Press.
Foucault, M. 2000. "Different Spaces." In *Aesthetics: The Essential Works of Foucault 1954–1984* vol. 2, edited by P. Rabinow, 175–186. London: Penguin Press.
Gauntlett, D., and P. Holzwarth. 2006. "Creative and Visual Methods for Exploring Identities." *Visual Studies* 21 (1): 82–91.
Harrison, B. 2004. "Snap Happy: Toward a Sociology of 'everyday' Photography." In *Seeing is Believing, Apraoches to Visual Research, Visual Methods in Social Research*, edited by C. Pole, 23–39. London: Elsevier.
Kingsbury, P. 2007. "The Extimacy of Space." *Social and Cultural Geography* 8 (2): 235–258.
Kingsbury, P. 2010. "Locating the Melody of the Drives." *The Professional Geographer* 62 (4): 519–533.
Lacan, J. 1986. *The Four Fundamental Concepts of Psychoanalysis*. London: Penguin Press.
Moore, G., B. Croxford, M. Adams, M. Refaee, T. Cox, and S. Sharples. 2008. "The Photo-Survey Research Method: Capturing Life in the City." *Visual Studies* 23 (1): 50–62.
Pink, S. 2011. "Amateur Photographic Practice, Collective Rep-Representation and the Constitution of Place." *Visual Studies* 26 (2): 92–101.

Proudfoot, J. 2010. "Interviewing Enjoyment, or the Limits of Discourse." *The Professional Geographer* 62 (4): 507–518.

Sagan, O. 2008. "Playgrounds, Studios and Hiding Places: Emotional Exchange in Creative Learning Spaces." *Art, Design and Communication in Higher Education* 6 (3): 173–186.

Temple, P., and R. Barnett. 2007. "Higher Education Space: Future Directions." *Planning for Higher Education* 36: 5–15.

Tinkler, P. 2013. *Using Photographs in Social and Historical Research*. London: Sage Press.

Verhaeghe, P. 2001. *Beyond Gender, from Subject to Drive*. New York: Other Press.

Voela, A. 2013. "Catastrophe Survived? the Failure of the Tragic in Moira Buffini's 'Welcome to Thebes'." *Somatechnics* 3 (1): 133–148.

Žižek, S. 1994. *The Sublime Object of Ideology*. London: Verso Press.

Learning to fail and learning from failure – ideology at work in a mathematics classroom

Hauke Straehler-Pohl[a] and Alexandre Pais[b]

[a]*Department of Educational Studies and Psychology, Freie Universität Berlin, Berlin, Germany;* [b]*Department of Learning and Philosophy, Aalborg University, Aalborg, Denmark*

> When actualised in a concrete school, the official discourse of inclusion and equity often encounters a series of obstacles that research strives to identify and address under the imperative to eliminate them. Through the exploration of classroom episodes, teacher interviews and field notes from a German secondary school, we take failure not as a correctable obstacle but as a symptom of the ideology at work in current educational practices. Symptoms, as Žižek (after Lacan) suggested, cannot be eliminated but always (re)emerge since they concern the impossibility of official discourses actualising themselves. We thus argue for a research agenda that learns from failure instead of research concerned with the possible successes that might prospectively be brought into existence, if just the 'right' theory was applied 'correctly'.

Introduction

International organisations (e.g. Organisation for Economic Co-operation and Development (OECD)), professional institutions (e.g. National Council of Teachers of Mathematics 2000) and researchers (see Atweh et al. 2011; Gellert, Jablonka, and Morgan 2010; Herbel-Eisenmann et al. 2012) posit mathematics education as a key element in the development of a socially just and equitable society. It is assumed that a quality mathematics education will allow people to become active participants in a world where mathematics informs and formats many of the decisions that influence our lives (Gellert and Jablonka 2007; Skovsmose 1994). As a result, the main task of mathematics education research has been the development of teaching and learning strategies that can provide a meaningful mathematics for all. Researchers typically see persistent failure in school mathematics as an occurrence contingent on a system that officially aims at equity and freedom (Baldino and Cabral 2006; Pais 2012; Pais and Valero 2012). As such, researchers are often interested in describing successful experiences, showing how learning obstacles can be overcome, instead of analysing episodes of failure (Gutiérrez 2010; Presmeg and Radford 2008; Sriraman and English 2010).

This propensity to report successful experiences partakes in an ideology that Lacan (2008) characterised as *evolutionism*: the belief in a supreme good, in a final goal of progress that guides its course from the very beginning. In the case of mathematics education, the supreme goal is 'mathematics for all', and research has focused on eliminating the obstacles standing in the way of this goal (Lundin 2012; Pais and Valero 2012). The goal itself is seldom questioned – notwithstanding the evidence that mathematics is not for all – and the discourse of equity ends up functioning as a *regulative ideal* rather than an empirically realisable event (Davis 2004). Research is then moved by a desire for what *ought-to-be* in opposition to what *is* (46), thus failing to recognise the concrete conditions of today's schooling. From this perspective, as explored elsewhere (Pais and Valero 2012), the problems encountered by teachers are not didactical in the sense of better ways to teach and learn mathematics, but political, regarding the economic and socio-political implications of schooling. This is especially true at a time when the official rhetoric of the curriculum – which emphasises the high goals of equity and global access – contrasts with the economic demands on education (competition, employability, pressure to succeed in global assessment, etc.). Indeed, insofar as mathematics education research has to address the problems of practitioners, it cannot afford to dismiss the real conditions of their work.

Against this background, we present a study of educational failure. We set our investigation in a secondary school that can be thought of as *marginalised* or *underprivileged*, and analyse two classroom episodes that led to students' exclusion from learning mathematics. If we followed the *evolutionistic* thesis, we would be expected to formulate strategies to overcome the problems that led to students' failure. These could be formulated in terms of teacher education (e.g. a different way of interacting with the students), the curriculum (e.g. more challenging tasks) or classroom organisation (e.g. project or group work instead of blackboard-centred and individual work). However, we will instead analyse the classroom episodes *as they are* since our interest is not in providing solutions for the problems of practice, but in pinpointing the ideological injunctions at work in the way teachers and students interact in the classroom. By analysing things as they are (instead of how they 'should' be), we seek to make visible the incongruence between the official discourse and the lived experiences of students and teachers.

We focus our analysis on the way students 'decide' to participate (or not) in the activities proposed by their teachers. We argue that the ideological frame is set in such a way that failure cannot be attributed to anything other than individuals making the wrong choices. However, as we shall see, these are false choices, since they lack a crucial precondition of choice: the freedom to choose. On the side of the student, we will show that, whether or not they 'choose' to participate in classroom activities, the outcome will be failure in school mathematics. On the side of the teacher, we will reveal the fallacy of the belief that she could have transformed failure into success by making choices that were more aligned to the regulative ideal of school mathematics. The analysis of the cases we present leads us to conclude that the production of failure is a structural problem, escaping the realm of an evolutionist mathematics education.

The necessity of failure and the ideology of research

As a point of departure for our analysis we claim that failure is an integral part of the economy of schooling (Bowles and Gintis 1977; Baldino and Cabral 2006; Lave and McDermott 2002; Pais 2012). We conceptualise schools as a *credit system*, which school mathematics is a part of (Vinner 1997) and which operates through *selection* and *accreditation*. Mathematics is thus posited as an economically valuable resource under the condition of scarceness. In order to load such economic value, an accreditation of mathematical competence requires a momentum of distinction. The value of the ones who fail is appropriated by the ones who pass as surplus-value. As failure is inherent in the logic of the credit system, it appears no longer as a contingent phenomenon, but can be posited as a *necessary* condition for schooling: 'in order to perpetuate the process of production/seizure of surplus value, a certain amount of failure is necessary' (Baldino 1998, 77). Therefore, 'failure of students means success of the institution' (Baldino and Cabral 2006, 34).

To acknowledge that failure is a necessity of current schooling is not easy for those who work in it. To be able to operate efficiently and become a productive cog in the machine of schooling, one needs to believe that the final goals for which we all strive are equity, social justice, inclusion and the like. The discrepancy between the regulative ideal, which exalts the supreme goals of democracy, and its actualisation in a life-world context is a central concern of *ideology critique* (Žižek 2008a). In the Lacan-Žižek axis, ideology is conceived as a defence against some traumatic real, a 'fantasy-screen' (Žižek 2008b, 7) focused on restoring order to a situation that otherwise seems chaotic or impossible. A fantasy provides a rationale for failure, that is, a meaningful way of dealing with a traumatic situation. Failure – without the screen of ideology – is chaotic, impossible, or even unbearable for an individual teacher, researcher or policy maker.

The fantasy-screen of ideology provides a rationale for these uncontrollable experiences. When confronted with the worldwide problem of failure in school mathematics and the societal demand for 'mathematics for all', research establishes an explanatory scheme within which an approach to the problem is proposed (Baldino and Cabral 2006; Pais 2012, 2013). Although the particular constellation of the fantasy narrative changes from one research thematic to another, the figure of 'failure' functions as that which simultaneously thwarts the realisation of the ideal goal of a universally meaningful mathematics and compels the articulation of an entire discourse concealing the necessity of failure itself (hence providing researchers a frame within which to develop their work). As such, experiences of failure function as symptoms (Žižek 2008a) of mathematics education. The exploration of these symptoms reveals the impotence of current educational systems to deal with exclusion.

To paraphrase Žižek (2008a, 161), when one is dealing with a universal principle, such as the high goals of equity and 'mathematics for all', one invariably assumes that it is possible to apply this principle to every particular element, so that the principle's empirical non-realisation – the fact that people continue to fail in school mathematics – is seen as a matter of contingent circumstances. A symptom, however, is an element which, while appearing as a contingency, is in fact essential to the universal principle that it breaches. In Žižek's words, it is an element in which:

– although the non-realisation of the universal principle in it appears to hinge on contingent circumstances – has to remain an exception, that is, the point of suspension of the universal principle: if the universal principle were to apply also to this point, the universal system itself would disintegrate. (Žižek 2008a, 161)

When it is claimed that everyone should be provided with a meaningful mathematics education, this official goal conceals the obscenity of a school system that year after year 'rightfully' excludes thousands of students from the possibility of pursuing higher studies or a place in the society of abundance. This happens under the official discourse of an inclusionary and democratic schooling. It is in this discrepancy between the official discourse and its (failed) actualisation that ideology is made operational. Within the official discourse, what is *necessary* is the abstract motto of 'mathematics for all', all the exceptions to this rule (the ones who fail) being seen as contingencies. However, in our analysis, what is *necessary* is precisely the existence of those who fail, the abstract proclamation being a purely contingent result of the frenetic activity of individuals (researchers, practitioners, politicians) who believe in it. Failure as a symptom indicates that the condition of impossibility of realising the goal is simultaneously its condition of possibility. The antagonistic character of social reality – the crude reality that in order for some to succeed others have to fail – is the *necessary* Real which needs to be concealed so that the illusion of productive research and equitable schooling can be kept. The figure of 'failure' – which encompasses the marginalised, the excluded, the truant – has to remain an exception; and the universality preached by the official discourse masks the symptomatic character of exclusion, the fact that the true universality at work in schooling is the need to produce failure.

One of the ways the system has of constructing exclusion as a contingent occurrence is to treat it as an individual choice. Apparently, students are confronted with the choice of participating in the official discourse by means of active engagement in the classroom activities. However, as we shall see, there are places where this is a false choice since, even when students choose to participate, their choice leads to exclusion. As Žižek (2006, 348) puts it, '[t]his appearance of choice, however, should not deceive us: it is the mode of appearance of its very opposite: of the absence of any real choice with regard to the fundamental structure of society'. In our case, this appearance of choice – to participate in classroom activities – disavows the absence of any real choice regarding the possibilities these students have of pursuing a valuable education. The system initiates students into blaming failure on their own choices for the sake of keeping the appearance of a free and equal school system.

The place and the layout of a free and equal school system

Traditionally, the German school system was organised federally and streamed students after primary school into three different school-types according to their supposedly 'innate' ability.[1] This streaming was done in different ways with teachers and/or parents being able to shade decisions based on a student's average marks. However, the three streams were organised hierarchically with only the highest stream providing access to an academic education.

According to the official rhetoric, the stratification of streams allowed the effective design of classes for students according to their different 'innate' abilities. While in practice 'ability' meant achievement in literacy, mathematics and science, it still lacks any scientific operationalisation or justification. Rather, it is grounded in a historically grown common sense of different 'forms of ability' (Rösner 2007). According to this common sense there is 'academic ability' as opposed to 'practical ability'. While the high stream supposedly optimised learning conditions for 'academically able' learners, the low stream provided an environment supposedly optimitised for 'practically able' learners. The middle stream appeared as a hybrid that supposedly nourished both forms of ability. The administrative moral imperative that assured that such stratification would not collide with the democratic principle of equity, but could operate within it, was that 'without consideration of rank and assets of parents, the educational pathway has to stay open *which accords with his or her ability*' (Kultusministerkonferenz, cited in Pietsch and Stubbe 2007, 428, emphasis added). Together with the common sense of different abilities, this moral imperative provided the rationale for maintaining the fantasy of a free and equal school system despite the explicitly selective and stratifying organisation of schooling in Germany. Thus, while the structure of the German school system might make it easier to expose the systematic occurrence of failure, the system still provides an ideological fantasy-screen that deceives the observer about the nature and role of failure.

The data

This paper is based on the re-analysis of data from the project 'Emergence of Disparity in Mathematics Classrooms' with which one of us was involved (Knipping et al. 2008). As this project had its main focus on the social interactions that discursively produce mathematical knowledge and consciousness, data collection was made mainly through *videography*. The mathematics classes in which we undertook our research were in one seventh grade (first year of secondary school) in Berlin, Germany, just after the summer holidays of 2009. Before the summer holidays, all the students in the research class had finished their primary schools with a recommendation that they attend the lowest of the three available ability-streams in secondary school. During the first three weeks of the school year, we captured all mathematics lessons (14) in one classroom using a camera recording a long shot. While two teachers were present most of the time, one of the two teachers was responsible for the organisation of the mathematics classes.[2] In addition, we carried out in-depth interviews with the teacher leading the class and took field notes. There were 14 students in the class. The students in this study can be considered underprivileged given the social segregation that results from where they live, their background as members of a cultural minority, having German as a second language and by the institutional selectivity of the German streaming school system. A considerable number of the students in the class had already had to repeat one or two school years in primary school. Eight of the 14 students had Sinti and Romani backgrounds; the remaining six students were second- or higher-generation descendants of Turkish and Arabic immigrants. None of the students spoke German as a first language.

The analysis we present here is different from that in the original project; rather than analyse students' or teachers' interactions, here we seek to pinpoint how ideology is operationalised through these interactions. Thus, when we undertake an interpretation of a teacher's or student's actions and speech, it is a *theoretical reading of a social reality*. We do not claim to 'truthfully' represent the psychic situation of any real existing human being, but rather posit their activity within – and as a symptom of – broader structural arrangements which we then theorise. Therefore, we deliberately chose key incidents that would allow us to explicate the theoretical significance that we attributed to the whole data corpus. In our cases, and within the Lacan-Žižek theorisation we are deploying here, these key incidents allows us to address the system's points of *extimacy* (Lacan 2008), that is, the features that are simultaneously part of the school system (all the episodes we analyse occurred in regular mathematics classes) and strange to this same system (since they report experiences of undesirable failure and are thus extrinsic to the broader educational discourse of equity and access for all). In other words, the failure we analyse through these key incidents is something strange to the system of equity in which schooling is based, yet it is at the heart of this same system.

The episodes and their (psychoanalytical) interpretation

Elsewhere we have described the pedagogy enacted in the classrooms we observed as one that 'in order not to overcharge – infantilizes students and – in order to enable classroom management – objectifies students … Learning in such mathematics classrooms' we suggested 'adds to the underprivileged conditions that these learners face' (Straehler-Pohl and Gellert 2011, 198). Classroom interactions were set up in such a way that, as observers, we could identify very few opportunities to acquire mathematical knowledge. A deeper analysis, using Bernstein's theory of pedagogic codes, revealed that the pedagogy in this classroom was almost completely free from the 'instructional discourse' (Bernstein 2000, 32) that creates specialised skills. What remained was an excessive 'regulative discourse' (32) that was concerned with the regulation of the students' position in the social order so that, in the end, 'students are locked into an identity of failed primary school mathematical knowers' (Straehler-Pohl 2012). Against this background, participating in the classroom activities seemed inevitably to lead students towards failure in learning mathematics. In the following analysis, we present the cases of two students who 'decided' not to participate in the activities in the way that the majority of their peers did. We then contrast these students' (non-)participation with the ideological positioning of the teacher. The case of these students, although seen by the teachers as contingent occurrences that might be overcome through sanctions such as expelling the students from the classroom, will then be analysed as symptoms of schooling.

The case of Melinda

Melinda's participation in the classroom was characterised by a total refusal of the teachers' authority (most of the time two teachers were present in class). At the beginning of the first mathematics class in this new school, each of the students was asked to complete the sentence, 'I am feeling ___, because ___'. Though still not acquainted with the second teacher, Melinda articulated the following: 'I am feeling bad because today we have class with this teacher [pointing at the second teacher]'. During the course of the mathematical activity (working '887 − 339' at the blackboard), Melinda spent quite some time talking to Mariella, her classmate, in a foreign language. This was mostly ignored by the teacher, although twice she calmly admonished her. When Mariella was asked to finish the task at the blackboard, Melinda shouted at Mariella: 'what are you doing bitch?' Although clearly stated and quite loud, this interruption remained unsanctioned. However, a few minutes later, Melinda 'collected' (teacher's word) her third, calmly spoken, admonishment and was excluded from the classroom for the rest of the day. The following day, the mathematics class took a similar course, resulting in Melinda again being excluded. On the third day, Melinda did not reappear: she had been expelled from school. As she was still of compulsory school-age she would have been directed towards another low-streamed school in the neighbourhood.

The case of Hatice

On the third day of the researcher's observations, Hatice, who was already known to the teachers as a truant, appeared in class for the first time. In class, Hatice was quietly doing the calculations demanded of her by the work sheet (such as '9700 − 300'). Hatice was among three students who succeeded in finishing their work sheets. The next time Hatice appeared in class, she completed three work sheets in 20 minutes including 186 'simple multiplication exercises'. The fourth sheet, one given to Hatice 'as a reinforcement' (teacher's words), stated at the top of the page that 'it is now getting harder and harder', and concluded at the bottom: 'when you have solved all the problems correctly − then you are the king of computations' (see Figure 1). When Hatice came back to her seat and started filling in the solutions on the work sheet, the second teacher asked her to 'read the instructions first'. However, there were no instructions for the first 54 calculations. Ignoring Hatice's confusion, the teacher commanded, 'read!' Hatice did not show up to any of the rest of the observed lessons.

Interpretation

Both Melinda's and Hatice's behaviour resulted in their physical exclusion from the class, either by expulsion or by truancy. Yet their actions were fundamentally different, if not opposite. Melinda seems to have staged her opposition *against* the institution of the school and its norms: she insisted on making use of her mother tongue, which is forbidden in class; on

It is getting harder and harder - number range up to 10.000. Watch the tens!

1. 4509 + 2 =	3490 + 20 =	8970 + 40 =
3804 + 7 =	7180 + 70 =	1990 + 50 =
7205 + 9 =	2570 + 90 =	5980 + 60 =
2. 3400 + 760 =	2780 + 45 =	3247 + 80 =
8900 + 480 =	1460 + 52 =	1199 + 20 =
7600 + 690 =	9690 + 69 =	7881 + 40 =
3. 2800 + 754 =	7997 + 4 =	5600 + 2800 =
6700 + 986 =	4995 + 9 =	4800 + 2400 =
8900 + 211 =	1999 + 8 =	1900 + 2700 =
4. 5000 − 50 =	3200 − 60 =	4200 − 400 =
8000 − 80 =	6100 − 90 =	7300 − 900 =
2000 − 10 =	9300 − 70 =	8100 − 600 =
5. 8000 − 8 =	5200 − 7 =	2482 − 6 =
2000 − 4 =	1700 − 4 =	8113 − 5 =
6000 − 5 =	9800 − 1 =	3685 − 9 =
6. 3200 − 23 =	8000 − 45 =	9010 − 40 =
4400 − 98 =	3000 − 21 =	6020 − 80 =
7900 − 11 =	5000 − 83 =	4030 − 60 =

7. Write all the exercises in the form of packages and compute them!

4000	4500	1740	2375	+	2	20	200
6000	5800	7690	9764	−	3	30	300

When you have solved all the tasks correctly - then you are the king of computations.

Figure 1. Worksheet (translated from German).

speaking whenever she wanted to; and finally she swore at a fellow student and did not respect the teacher's authority. Melinda thus operated in ways that teachers may believe justifies the way they organise their classes: effective learning is not possible because of students' bad behaviour and thus mathematics instruction has to be suspended in favour of social regulation. The teacher succeeded in constructing Melinda's resistance as a matter of her own choice. While the teacher stayed calm and delivered quiet admonishments as some sort of countdown that Melinda could have accepted ('three strikes and you're out'), she *decided* to ignore them. We can interpret the teacher's 'counting down' as a *false activity* (Žižek 2007, 26). Installing this countdown, the teacher does not act in order to change something (in particular the fact that students are not learning mathematics), but instead acts to prevent change: once Melinda was expelled from the classroom community, business could go on as usual. Melinda thus appeared to be a contingent individual obstacle; once all 'Melindas' have been expelled, mathematics learning will occur.

On the other hand, Hatice seems to stage her opposition *in line* with the official discourse of the institution of school. She remained quiet, worked effectively and solved her tasks correctly. However, this form of behaviour deviated so strongly from what the teachers expected of a student in her position that it ended up being not rewarded but rather reprimanded. The reason for the reprimand may lie in the resourcefulness shown by Hatice: through her behaviour she laid bare the teachers' ridiculously low expectations regarding the learning of mathematics, and, as a consequence, how irrelevant school was for her future. When the teacher prohibited Hatice from doing the activity quickly, it appears that her intention was not so much to disturb Hatice's participation, to inhibit her from achieving what was indeed expected from her, but to mask the fact that students like Hatice are not supposed to behave/succeed like this.

It would seem that students such as Hatice might have greater potential to do well in schools since, instead of aligning themselves with the implicit demand to fail, they follow the letter of the 'law' and, in Hatice's case, she actually performed well in the classroom. However, her industry *could* also reveal the contradictoriness and hopelessness of her situation and threaten the effectiveness of the organisation of classes. This threat did not go unnoticed by the teachers, who reacted by reprimanding Hatice for her behaviour. In the next section we problematise the role of the teachers. From the perspective of an evolutionistic thesis, the teachers' pedagogy could be seen as the primary *contingent obstacle* to a meaningful mathematics education, yet we will provide a deeper insight into the teacher's perspective in order to highlight how we see her activity, not as contingent, but as articulated by ideology.

The teacher's perspective

> In the break between the two math-lessons, Mrs Streller [the lead teacher] sits down at her desk and immediately starts talking ... To me, it sounds almost like a confession, the way she gets the frustration off her chest ... When she started working at this school thirty years ago at the age of twenty-six, she said, she came home crying regularly. This does not happen anymore. However, the reason is not that the situation has changed; the situation, she says, is getting steadily worse. But it has changed, because she herself has 'dulled'. She doesn't care anymore about a lot of things, as she learnt to ignore when students swear at her or others ... She sees herself rather as a social worker, as a substitute mother, actually anything rather than a transmitter of knowledge. Transmitting knowledge appears to be unwinnable anyway, she says ... Many of the students would not reach beyond the attainment of third-graders at the end of class nine. In this class, she estimates, maybe four or five students would manage to leave school with a low-stream graduation. (Hauke Straehler-Pohl, extract from field notes, 16 September 2009)

When I started, right after finishing my teaching degree, I really came home crying. I said to myself, you will never ever go there again; my teacher education was a waste. (Extract 1, interview with Mrs Streller, November 2009)

Then they [the experienced teachers] said to me: 'No, you can't do a dictation [in German class] like that. You have to write the text on the board, word by word and let them copy.' I said: 'Well, I can't write a dictation on the board. What kind of dictation is that?', 'Well, just do it ... and you will see', they said. And still [after trying], children were only getting [marks] fours, fives and sixes, even though the whole text was written on the board... (Extract 2, interview with Mrs Streller, November 2009)[3]

Well I do not necessarily always want to have only stress with my students, I want to experience some nice things. (Extract 3, interview with Mrs Streller, November 2009)

If I force them and even more and even more ... then they won't get it anyway. They become nervous and fed up with it, yes? Why should I do math after all then? It leads nowhere ... And then I would, if I was alone, I would say, well lets go into the playground for 10 minutes yes, and count flowers or collect 10 leaves or well yes, just to make a little change ... The disadvantage is, when there are two teachers in the room, you never know well would my colleague agree with that or does he think it's stupid?, because you ... also with colleagues, you have not chosen all of your colleagues. (Extract 4, interview with Mrs Streller, November 2009)

Interpretation

The image of the teacher (from the two incidents with the students) as a cold and punitive figure does not match either the teacher's reflective discourse (interview) or the researcher's impressions of the teacher's spontaneous discourse (field notes above). The teacher explicitly reported her emotional reactions when she was hit by the discrepancy between the idealised school ('everything you studied') and what was actually going on in her new workplace. This led her to revaluate her role as a teacher. She reported this experience as a serious threat (extract 1 and field notes) that required her to develop a phantasmic defence (becoming 'dull', field notes).

As previously mentioned, a fantasy provides a narrative for failure, one that covers over the traumatic experience of having to fail someone. When confronted with the failed union between the ideal and actual school, the teacher operates – or rather *partakes in* – an ideology that allows her to continue her work. We suggest that the community constituted by her more experienced colleagues played a crucial role in this process: they provided the ideological material that allowed her to fill the gap between the official discourse and the concrete conditions of schooling. This ideological material was not the official discourse of equity, but the underlying belief, shared by all members of the community, that the official discourse is indeed a *lie*. In order for the new teacher to be part of the community, the public rule (assuring equity through meaningful mathematics instruction) was not a sufficient means for identification. It had to be supplemented by a clandestine 'unwritten' rule that constituted the true 'spirit of the community':

> What 'holds together' a community most deeply is not so much identification with the Law that regulates the community's 'normal' everyday circuit, but rather *identification with a specific form of transgression of the Law, of the Law's suspension* (in psychoanalytical terms, with a specific form of *enjoyment*). (Žižek 2005, 55, emphasis in the original)

The way the new teacher found to cope with the gap between the Symbolic reality and the Real of schooling was by identifying herself with practices that she knew would not lead to the high goals of the Law. Identification with the community is always based upon some shared guilt or, more precisely, upon what Žižek (2005, 55) calls the *fetischistic disavowal of this guilt*: I know very well these students will never make it; nevertheless I keep acting as if they can. The teacher's fantasy of pursuing the superior aims of education enables her to repress the traumatic insight that all she is doing is actually working against these aims. Moreover, the teacher deals with the guilt resulting from having given up her desire (for a truly emancipatory education) through a philanthropic idealisation of herself as a 'substitute mother' (field notes) or an advocate for these poor children (extract 4). This humanistic position allows her to ideally construct herself in opposition to her colleagues (extract 4). This move, although perceived by the teacher as a 'step away from' from the ideology that she criticises in her colleagues, rather signals her total immersion in it:

> an ideological identification exerts a true hold on us precisely when we maintain an awareness that we are not fully identical to it, that there is a rich human person beneath it: 'not all is ideology, beneath the ideological mask, I am also a human person' is *the very form of ideology*, its 'practical efficiency'. (Žižek 2008a, 27, emphasis in the original)

Ideology is effective not because subjects consciously adhere to its values, but because they keep performing the external ideological ritual, in this case, promoting low-level activities among the students, using excessive regulatory strategies, etc., even as they publicly maintain a distance from its values.

Within the Lacan-Žižek axis, the attachment to something we know is 'wrong' can only be explained in terms of *jouissance*, or, in its anglicised form, *enjoyment*: although the ideology has been exposed, we do not change our behaviour because *we enjoy it*. As the teacher is aware, she has to find some pleasures in her job (extract 3). However, as it appears impossible to fulfil the desires framed by the official discourse of mathematics education, she has to find *jouissance* somewhere else. As mentioned in the quote from Žižek above, what a subject enjoys when deprived of a full identification with the Law is the transgression of this Law itself. This is the domain of the *superego* which 'emerges where the Law – the public Law, the Law articulated in the public discourse – fails; at this point of failure, the public Law is compelled to search for support in an *illegal* enjoyment' (Žižek 2005, 54, emphasis in the original). In this sense, superego is the 'obscene underside' that necessarily redoubles and accompanies the 'public' Law. It represents the true spirit of the community yet simultaneously violates the explicit rules of community life. While the symbolic Law provides meaning (based on the high goals of equity and inclusion), the superego provides enjoyment that serves as the unacknowledged support of meaning (56). An ideological edifice 'bribes' subjects into accepting renunciation by way of offering enjoyment. Concluding from the case studies, we posit the enjoyment of the teacher not in the official Law, but in the entire set of regulative measures that she puts forward to control the classroom. This happens even though, or rather, precisely because, these measures keep the students in a situation of imminent failure. The teacher sees these regulative measures as being for the students' own good, thus failing to acknowledge her own enjoyment in this ordeal.

The forced choice

Apparently the 'choice' that students face regarding school mathematics is between participating in the classroom activities and refusing to participate. However, the argument we present in this paper is that in certain mathematics classes, the choice is not an 'individual' choice between participation and non-participation, but between two modes of 'non-participation'. The first mode offers the choice of a straightforward non-participation by abandonment or exclusion from the school system. In the second mode, the alternative is to participate in classroom activities that contribute to an understanding of one's own ignorance of mathematics. This implies participating in one's own stigmatisation and exclusion from access to socially valued vocational and educational opportunities. Although the majority of students explicitly participated in the classroom activities, the narrow-mindedly mechanical and arbitrary activities guaranteed that the outcomes of this learning will not provide students with the skills and knowledge to open up further educational or vocational options. Thus, students' decisions to participate in classroom activities result in their non-participation in further education, in much the same way as the direct decision not to participate. As such, the choice is a false choice, since either way students are paving the way to their own exclusion from a consensually valued form of life. At best, students can postpone the materialisation of an already-determined exclusion.

At stake here is what Žižek (2008a, 38) calls the *choix forcé*, which directly concerns the relation of a subject to her or his community: 'every belonging to a society involves a paradoxical point at which the subject is ordered to embrace freely, as the result of his choice, what is anyway imposed on him' (36). In our case, what the school community indicated, both to the novice teacher and to the students, was that they had freedom to choose, but only on condition that they chose the right thing, that is, on the condition that they chose to operate between the official discourse and the obscene unwritten rules of the superego. The role of the unwritten rules was to restrain the field of choice by prohibiting the possibilities allowed for, guaranteed even, by the public Law (38). Taken together, the cases of Hatice and Melinda can be read as a message from the teachers to the other students that subtly undermined their freedom of choice and established the *choix forcé*. In the case of Melinda the message was: you are free to choose to participate in the activities or not. However, be sure that you will lose your membership of the community if you decide not to. In the case of Hatice the message was: even when you choose to participate, do it in the way that we expect you to, that is, play the role of the 'deficient' student who cannot go beyond ineffectual and stultifying tasks. In both cases, the students were forced to choose what had already been given to them.

Can things be different? As we discussed previously apropos the teacher, fantasy designates the unwritten framework that tells us how we are to understand the letter of the Law (Žižek 2008a, 38). In this sense, Hatice's behaviour (not accepting the unwritten rule of the community: behaving in an orderly manner and correctly solving the exercises set by the teachers) posed a threat to the teacher's fantasy. As Žižek points out, 'the truly subversive thing is not to disregard the explicit letter of the Law on behalf of the underlying fantasies, but to *stick to this letter against the fantasy which sustains it*' (38, emphasis in the original). However, as discussed above, a shared lie is an incomparably more effective bond for a group than the truth. What keeps the class together is not a sense of emancipation, of fulfilling the Law, but a shared sense of failure. This is how Hatice, by following the Law, excluded herself from the community. She literally treated the forced choice as a *true choice* suspending the phantasmic frame of unwritten rules which told her how to choose freely, and chose the impossible: to actually learn mathematics.

Perhaps the truly revolutionary act would be for students to behave like Hatice, to fully identify themselves with the public Law and demand a serious and rigorous mathematics education from their teachers. Žižek (2008a, 29) calls this gesture one of *overidentification*, which consists of taking the system more seriously than it takes itself. He explains that 'an ideological edifice can be undermined by a too-literal identification, which is why its successful functioning requires a minimal distance from its explicit rules' (29). A student like Melinda does not present any threat to the teacher. On the contrary, her behaviour justifies teachers' arguments that there are some students for whom pedagogic efforts are not worthwhile: *even though we know we deny our students a meaningful mathematical experience, we do it for their own good since they lack any sense of discipline*. A student such as Hatice, on the other hand, by erasing the minimal difference between the Law and its underside, presents a real threat to the teacher's libidinal economy. The only way the teacher has to deal with Hatice's act is through blind challenge: 'read it'!

Final remarks

As the title of our paper indicates, our aim was twofold. Firstly, through the exploration of classroom episodes we aimed to explore failure as a necessary feature of current schooling. A critique of ideology provided us with the means to undermine the fantasy-screen built around the issue of choice. This allowed us, secondly, to frame our analysis within a broader critique of a certain research approach to mathematics education that we characterise as evolutionistic. To do this we built on the assumption that the failure evident in the key incidents was not an empirical obstacle to the actualisation of the ideal, but a symptom of the functioning of the school system based in this ideal. The objective was to demonstrate how putting failure in its place – as a necessity of the system instead of a contingent obstacle – can improve our understanding of it (and its unequal distribution). We have thereby shown what we might gain if we dared to escape the regulative imperative of an optimistic evolutionism and make 'failure' itself the object of educational research.

Our analysis reveals the risks involved in considering educational failure as an unpleasant obstacle on the didactic road towards salvation. Describing things in terms of what *ought-to-be* instead of what *is* requires us to refrain from seeing failure in its totality, and to compartmentalise it into contingent variables that allow us to formulate narratives of modification for each variable. However, as we have shown, such an action ignores the life-world contexts of those involved and, thus, of those who necessarily would be involved in the *change* that research wants to bring about. By maintaining the demand to disregard totalities in favour of contingent variables, much educational research becomes what we have described above as a false activity: instead of unfolding a potential for a real change, it creates the conditions for things to remain the same. This happens by creating the imperative to research the *conditions for success* which creates a blind spot around the *conditions for failure*. A research agenda that could unfold this potential for change would need to take serious account of the stratification of failure and success inherent in the current meritocratic organisation of schools. Research would not only have to ask questions such as 'Why do students fail to succeed?' or 'Why do teachers fail to make students succeed?' or 'Why does teacher education fail to make teachers make students succeed?', etc., but juxtapose these questions with their antagonist: 'Why does school succeed by making students fail?'

The first essential step towards such a research agenda is to acknowledge the apparently pervasive function of school as a *credit system* (Baldino and Cabral 1998; Baldino 1998; Pais 2013; Vinner 1997). In order for such a credit system to work effectively within the official discourse of a democratic society, it needs to portray itself as a place where equal students meet freely and an 'invisible hand' guarantees that the competition of individuals' egos work for the common good. An analytic approach such as ours makes visible that merit in this credit system is possible only in relation to the demerit of others, i.e. the notion of personal merit is only possible as long as others fail. However, our analysis of the German school system, which abstains from efforts to disguise its functions of selection and accreditation, has shown that only accepting schools as credit systems does not suffice to undermine effectively such ideology. Our analysis has pointed to the more subtle ways in which ideology works by making individuals (mis)recognise their choices as their own, as free choices – especially when these choices imply failure. However, as we have seen in the cases of Melinda and Hatice, refusing to produce according to demand results in being barred from the school(ed) community. Thus, it becomes imperative that individuals read failure as the result of fair competition among equals and repress the traumatic truth that they fail so that others can succeed. Our theorisation has illustrated how schools need to obscure this 'truth' in order to retain their central role in maintaining apparently democratic and inclusive societies. Our analysis has shown the need for more research that focuses on the subtle ways in which this 'truth' is performed in the actual contexts of students and teachers. We claim that this kind of research is necessary to expose how failure is entangled within a meritocratic school system.

The reader may be left wondering to what extent our analysis has been a product of the contingent (and by now even historical) organisation of the German school system as an overtly streaming system. We would like to close our article with a question: Are less explicitly segregated school systems not just more effective in veiling the 'subversive supplement' of necessary failure and thus maintaining the fantasy of an exclusively democratic and inclusive endeavour?

Notes
1. The educational system is organised federally, each Bundesländ (province) having its own educational laws. In some provinces, the decision on to which school-stream a student is sent is based on the average marks in the final report cards; in some provinces, the classroom teacher gives an obligatory suggestion

(parents can just deviate downwards); in some Bundesländer, the classroom teacher gives an optional suggestion and the final decision is made by the parents.
2. Schools receive a budget of additional teacher resources, assigned according to variables such as the number of second-language learners, students with learning disabilities, etc. As almost all of the relevant variables were high at this school, the school could, in the majority of cases, afford to allocate two teachers to each class for the main subjects.
3. In Germany, marks are given on a scale from one to six with one being the best mark, five being a 'fail'. Giving a six is reserved for marking a 'complete' failure, such as a refusal to take part.

References

Atweh, B., M. Graven, W. Secada, and P. Valero eds. 2011. *Mapping Equity and Quality in Mathematics Education*. Dordrecht: Springer.

Baldino, R. 1998. "School and Surplus-Value: Contribution from a Third-World Country." In *Proceedings of the First International Conference on Mathematics Education and Society (MES1)*, edited by P. Gates, 73–81. Nottingham: Centre for the Study of Mathematics Education.

Baldino, R., and T. Cabral. 1998. "Lacan and the School's Credit System." In *Proceedings of 22nd Conference of the International Group for the Psychology of Mathematics Education (PME22)*. Vol. 2, edited by A. Olivier and K. Newstead, 56–63. Stellenbosch, South Africa: University of Stellenbosch.

Baldino, R., and T. Cabral. 2006. "Inclusion and Diversity from Hegel-Lacan Point of View: Do We Desire Our Desire for Change?" *International Journal of Science and Mathematics Education* 4: 19–43.

Bernstein, B. 2000. *Pedagogy, Symbolic Control and Identity: Theory, Research, Critique*. Rev ed. Lanham: Rowman & Littlefield.

Bowles, S., and H. Gintis. 1977. *Schooling in Capitalist America*. Educational Reform and the Contradictions of Economic Life. New York: Basic books.

Davis, Z. 2004. The Debt to Pleasure. the Subject and Knowledge in Pedagogic Discourse. In *Reading Bernstein, Researching Bernstein*, edited by J. Muller, B. Davies, A. Morais, 44–57. London: Routledge Falmer.

Gellert, U., and E. Jablonka. 2007. *Mathematization and Demathematization: Social, Philosophical and Educational Ramifications*. Rotterdam: Sense.

Gellert, U., E. Jablonka, C., Morgan. Eds. 2010. *Mathematics Education and Society. Proceedings of the Sixth International Mathematics Education Conference. 20th - 25th March 2010, Berlin, Germany*. Berlin: Freie Universität Berlin.

Gutiérrez, R. 2010. "The Sociopolitical Turn in Mathematics Education." *Journal for Research in Mathematics Education* 41: 1–32.

Herbel-Eisenmann, B., J. Choppin, D. Wagner, and D. Pimm. eds. 2012. *Equity in Discourse for Mathematics Education. Theories, Practices, and Policies*. Dordrecht: Springer.

Knipping, C., D. A. Reid, U. Gellertand E. Jablonka. 2008. The Emergence of Disparity in Mathematics Classrooms. In *Proceedings of the Fifth International Mathematics Education and Society Conference*, edited by, J. F. Matos, P. Valero and K. Yasukawa, 320–329. Lisbon: Centro de Investigação em Educação, Universidade de Lisboa.

Lacan, J. 2008. *The Ethics of Psychoanalysis: the Seminar of Jacques Lacan Book VII*. New York: Taylor and Francis. (Orig. pub. 1986)

Lave, J., and R. McDermott. 2002. *Estranged Learning. Outlines* 1: 19–48.
Lundin, S. 2012. "Hating School, Loving Mathematics: on the Ideological Function of Critique and Reform in Mathematics Education." *Educational Studies in Mathematics* 80 (1-2): 73–85.
National Council of Teachers of Mathematics (NCTM). 2000. *Principles and Standards for School Mathematics*. Reston, VA: NCTM.
Pais, A. 2012. "A Critical Approach to Equity in Mathematics Education." In *Opening the Cage: Critique and Politics of Mathematics Education*, edited by O. Skovsmose and B. Greer, 49–91. Rotterdam: Sense.
Pais, A.. 2013. *An Ideology Critique of the Use-Value of Mathematics. Educational Studies in Mathematics*. doi: 10.1007/s10649-013-9484-4.
Pais, A., and P. Valero. 2012. "Researching Research: Mathematics Education in the Political." *Educational Studies in Mathematics* 80 (1-2): 9–24.
Pietsch, M., and T. Stubbe. 2007. "Inequality in the Transition from Primary to Secondary School: School Choices and Educational Disparities in Germany." *European Educational Research Journal* 6 (4): 424–445.
Presmeg, N., and L. Radford. 2008. On Semiotics and Subjectivity: A Response to Tony Brown's "Signifying 'students', 'teachers', and 'mathematics': a Reading of a Special Issue". *Educational Studies in Mathematics*, 69, 265–276.
Rösner, E. 2007. *Hauptschule Am Ende. Ein Nachruf*. Münster: Waxmann.
Skovsmose, O. 1994. *Towards a Philosophy of Critical Mathematics Education*. Dordrecht: Kluwer.
Sriraman, B., and L. English. 2010. "Surveying Theories and Philosophies of Mathematics Education." In *Theories of Mathematics Education: Seeking New Frontiers*, edited by B. Sriraman and L. English. Heidelberg: Springer.
Straehler-Pohl, H. 2012. *Devaluing Knowledge: School Mathematics in a Context of Segregation*. Aix-en-Provence, France: Paper presented at the Seventh Basil Bernstein Symposium.
Straehler-Pohl, H., and U. Gellert. 2011. Learning Mathematics as a "Practically Able" Learner: an Instance of Institutional Denial of Access. *Quaderni Di Ricerca in Didattica / Mathematics (QRDM) Quaderno*, 22 (1): 195–199.
Vinner, S. 1997. From Intuition to Inhibition – Mathematics Education and Other Endangered Species. In *Proceedings of the 21th Conference of the International Group for Psychology of Mathematics Education (PME21)*, ed. E.Pehkonen Vol. 1, 63–78. Lahti, Finland.
Zizek, S. 2007. *How to Read Lacan*. New York: Norton & Company.
Žižek, S. 2005. *The Metastases of Enjoyment: Six Essays on Women and Causality*. London: Verso. (Orig. pub. 1995)
Žižek, S. 2006. *The Parallax View*. MIT Press.
Žižek, S. 2008a. *The Plague of Fantasies*. London: Verso (Orig. pub. 1997).
Žižek, S. 2008b. *The Ticklish Subject*. London: Verso. (Orig. pub. 1999).

Reconstructing memory through the archives: public pedagogy, citizenship and Letizia Battaglia's photographic record of mafia violence

Paula M. Salvio

College of Liberal Arts, Department of Education, University of New Hampshire, Durham, New Hampshire, USA

> This essay shuttles between the archive in its literal sense as a site of storage, and in its figurative senses as a migrating, foundational concept that is fused with affect and speaks of memory and forgetting, disavowal and betrayals. I maintain that a productive ground for theorising the archive as a site of radical public teaching can be found in the public pedagogical projects of anti-mafia activists currently working in Sicily. In the following pages, I focus on the photojournalism of Sicilian anti-mafia activist Letizia Battaglia. Bound up with traditions of social documentary and autobiography, Battaglia's collection of over 6000 photographs of the mafia's internal war in Sicily works as a moving, portable archive that takes place at the breakdown of memory and challenges the world to understand organised crime as far more than Sicily's 'local problem'. Drawing on the work of D.W. Winnicott, Masud Khan and Elisabeth Young-Bruehl, I argue that Battaglia's photographic archive creates a social protective shield that exemplifies how archives can psychically and physically protect communities who have suffered societal trauma by expanding the arc of remembering and, in turn, challenge the state repression of memory.

Introduction

What isn't an archive these days? ... In these memory-obsessed times – haunted by the demands of history, overwhelmed by the dizzying possibilities of new technologies – the archive presents itself as the ultimate horizon of experience. Ethically charged, politically saturated, such a horizon would seem to be all the more inescapable for remaining undefined. Where to draw the limits of the archive? How to define its basic terms?

(Rebecca Comay 2002, *Lost in the Archives,* 12)

> I felt it was my responsibility, as a part of the Sicilian people, to fight ... And so, with my camera, it turned into a madness, a desperate life where in a single day I might see five men killed, men with families. And, despite the horror of it all, I tried to maintain a minimum of poetry within me.
>
> (Letizia Battaglia, interview with Melissa Harris 1999, 15)

In his compelling portrait of organised crime, *Cosa Nostra: A History of the Sicilian Mafia*, historian John Dickie introduces a restricted 485-page document housed in Italy's Central State Archive in Rome. The document was submitted to the Ministry of the Interior in instalments between November 1898 and January 1900. Written by Palermo Chief of Police, Ermanno Sangiorgi, the report systematically describes the personal details of 218 mafia members, their initiation rites, business methods, how the mafia forged money, committed robberies, terrified and murdered witnesses. Perhaps most stunning, is that Sangiorgi's records corroborate, almost to the letter, the report given by informant Tommaso Buscetta to antimafia prosectuor Giovanni Falcone in the late 1980s. If Sangiorgi's papers had not come into the wrong hands, he might have exposed the mafia only a few decades after it emerged. Instead, the mafia has sustained generations of traffic in toxic waste, environmental destruction, heroin rackets and government-sanctioned assaults on Italian civil society (Dickie 2004, 101). Dickie identifies Sangiorgi's hand-written, brittle, yellowing record as a 'riveting illustration of Italy's long-standing failure to see the truth about the mafia (91).

If the emergence of the modern state charged the archive with housing material to generate social solidarity and to make national memories, the story of Sangiorgi's archived reports are a painful symptom of a nation's insistence, not to repress, but to deny a history of violence and corruption. In his Outline of Psycho-analysis, Freud distinguishes between repression and denial by way of one's relationship with the internal and external world. While repression is an important pathway of mental conflict that signals unbearable, shameful or difficult internal instinctual demands, denial (or disavowal), directed toward the outer world, is a process through which the ego defends against an intolerable external reality (Freud 1940, 195–207).

'Whenever we are in a position to study them', [disavowal and repression] writes Freud, 'they turn out to be half-measures, incomplete attempts at detachment from reality' (204). Thus while the Italian state may have disavowed the presence of systematic mafia infiltration into civil society, this disavowal cannot be contained. Not only does Dickie find in Rome's Central State Archive written evidence of the State's failure to protect its people, but he locates a destructive psychic disturbance and abuse of state power that, in the words of Christopher Bollas, 'trades in denial' by exploiting the human need to believe in State protection as it pursues its destructive end. Bollas describes such 'trading in denial' as an attack on the earliest and most profound of human relations and assumptions: the relation to the parent.

> Each state is a derivative of the parenting world that exists in the mind of its citizens, and a terrorist regime will exploit the unconscious relationship to obtain a denial of its terrors among the citizens, who will support the denial. (Bollas 2011, 173)

Italy is not alone in its refusal to recognise the truth about organised crime and its lasting and sorrowful global presence. Archives, for example, in Argentina, Chile, Uruguay and the United States house evidence of human rights violations tied to organised crime that raise important questions about contested memories and what happens when human rights violations are denied by citizens due to fear of retaliation, or when the perpetrators of such violations are protected by the many faces of impunity – political, judicial and cultural.[1] The traumatic legacy of Sangiorgi's document burns with the kind of fever Jacques Derrida has in mind in *Archive Fever*, a mal d' archive – an inability, according to Derrida, to recognise that the archive is 'irrealizable', that its structure is spectral, neither present nor absent 'in the flesh', neither visible nor invisible and most certainly not stable (Derrida 1996, 84). The archive is in fact positioned, according to Derrida, between absence and presence; an indeterminate entity that is persistent in its resistance to categorisation and in its destruction of memory. Derrida casts the archive as a site of amnesia precisely because it destroys memories in the very process of selecting (and hence excluding) what will be remembered. In response to the question, 'what is an archive?' Derrida responds:

> The archive, if this word or this figure can be stabilized so as to take on signification, will never be either memory or anamnesis as spontaneous, alive and internal experience. On the contrary: the archive takes place at the place of originary and structural breakdown of the said memory . . . (Derrida 1996, 11)

'There would be no archive desire', argues Derrida, '. . .without the possibility of a forgetfulness which does not limit itself to repression' (19). Stitched into this archival forgetfulness are desire, longing, anxiety and denial. Housed in the archive in Rome are secrets concealed by the state, artefacts of private betrayals, and unthinkable histories. Scholars, journalists, educators and activists such as Dickie, who burn with the desire to know, to make known and to unearth early evidence tied to present trauma, emerge on the other side of disavowal, reaching, as they do, beyond the stasis of the physical archive in order to represent half-spoken, traumatic memories that perhaps can never fully be understood or remembered.[2] Taking place at the structural breakdown of memory, this kind of archival work potentially creates, I argue, a social matrix which psychically and physically protects communities who have suffered societal trauma by expanding the arc of remembering. Let me explain.

In her study of cumulative societal trauma, Elisabeth Young-Bruehl uses the concept of a 'social protective shield' elaborated on by D.W. Winnicott (1958) and Khan (1963) in order to describe the social matrix protecting communities from a violent breach, rupture or break-in that compromises their health and psychic well-being. 'A social protective shield', she writes,

> could be defined as a relational network of people and institutions that grows up to enwrap basic social units – like families, but also states – in customs,

programs ... that prevent the unit's failure and remedy their ills medically and psychotherapeutically. Social shields of all sorts develop in societies as different needs and 'social ills' are discovered and addressed. (Young-Bruehl 2013, 45)

Social protective shields may develop spontaneously or from political movements that build on civic participation and emphasise human rights as we see, for example, with the mothers of the disappeared in Argentina and the United Nations (UN) Convention on the Rights of the Child.[3]

The Central State Archive in Rome houses documents, letters, ephemera– lost lives – that might otherwise be forgotten and can be read, following Derrida, as an illustration of how the archive occurs at the very moment when there is a structural breakdown in memory, when something traumatic has occurred, causing a kind of feverish sickness. In a restricted file protected from public access, Dickie discovers a malice in the archive. Wrapped up with documentation presumed to be lost or kept secret, Dickie breathes life into a story previously denied, a story that contains evidence of harm tied to traumatic, unthinkable societal experiences. In the act of recovering this story, Dickie also bears witness to the catastrophe of memory traces that call out to be re-worked and re-storied (Steedman 2001; Featherstone 2006, 591).

Dickie's work, however, is no longer that of a solitary or privileged scholar. Standing on the other side of state and national archives are the ever-expanding, capacious, globalising archives made possible through social and digital media, digital recording and storage technologies. The sheer volume of recordable archived materials and the possibilities these technologies present to ordinary residents call into question what constitutes 'legitimate knowledge', what can and should be archived, and opens up spaces for calling into question the security and the meaning of the nation-state (Featherstone 2006). The question posed by Rebecca Comay in my epigraph 'What isn't an archive these days?' is a pointed question – where does the archive begin and end? What is included and what is excluded? What happens when previously privileged materials such as the documents Dickie comes across in a restricted folder are made publically accessible? What is altered when, for example, the archive is housed in a photo-journalist's apartment? Or on Facebook? A blog? Or, when an archive is provided a GPS coordinate, an idea set forth by Elizabeth A. Povinelli and her colleagues in rural northwest Australia, so that it can be accessed only in a certain place with a specific piece of technology (Povinelli 2011, 149)? What can we learn from the archive – both literal and figurative? In what ways can the archive work as a social protective shield, most especially among communities working through the trauma of war, climate disasters and the terror of mafia-related crime?

This chapter shuttles between the 'archive' in its literal sense as a site of storage, and in its figurative senses as a migrating, foundational concept that is fused with affect and speaks of memory and forgetting, disavowal and betrayals. I argue that a productive ground for theorising the archive as a site of radical public teaching that sustains an engagement with difficult knowledge among contemporary communities traumatised by violence can be found in the public pedagogical projects of antimafia activists currently working in Sicily. In the following pages, I introduce the photojournalism of Sicilian antimafia activist Letizia Battaglia as an exemplary form of radical public pedagogy. Drawing on the early work of Henry Giroux and building on the work of Jennifer Sandlin, Brian Schultz and their colleagues, I use the concept of public pedagogy to refer to forms of public intellectualism and social activism taken up by individuals who are dedicated to cultural criticism as political action (see Sandlin et al. 2010; Britzman 2013).

Based on an analysis of interviews with Battaglia, on-line circulations of her images, her 2013 exhibit to celebrate International Women's Day and newspaper coverage of her work, I also argue that Battaglia's archive of photographs contributes to prompting a renewed cultural formation of the female speaking subject by creating, over time, a different narrative of female rebellion against the mafia. I consider the extent to which her archive challenges a culture that has, for too long, been suffused with death, martyrdom and suffered at the hands of what feminist philosopher Adrianna Cavarero (2000, 142) describes as 'the inadequacy of male justice'.

The moving emotional force found in Battaglia's archive of photographs of mafia violence, specifically of women, is the desire of what Cavarero (2000, 87) describes as 'the narratable self' that longs for and gives, 'receives and offers, here and now, an unrepeatable story in the form of a tale'. Cavarero inspires educators to enliven the stories housed in the archive. Not by imagining that one can objectively settle on how things were in a distant past. Rather, the material housed in the archive must be continually, ritualistically, re-storied through the work of narrative transformations that compose and re-order what communities find meaningful (Ihanus 2007, 122). With these ideas in mind, I focus on select photographs of Battaglia's that are reproduced digitally on various on-line antimafia social networking sites and that were exhibited in March 2013. I use these photographs to place in relief three pedagogical principles that might serve as a guide for educators interested in creating or working with archives that aim to represent marginalised histories or to challenge the lure to trade in denial in the face of difficult knowledge:

(1) Battaglia's archive of photographs sustains a search for lost or neglected objects, lost stories, subjugated knowledges and 'excluded socialities' (Povinelli 2011, 151).
(2) Battaglia's portable archive of photographs does not simply preserve a past, but re-elaborates and re-inscribes history in ways that expand, disturb and ultimately reconstitute traumatic memories so they can be worked through.
(3) Battaglia uses her photographic archive to create a 'social protective shield' that offers members of her community an existential sense of belonging, political union and a source of expression.

An 'Unintended Archive'

Married at 16 with the hope of establishing her freedom from what she describes as Sicily's 'macho society', Letizia Battaglia left her husband 19 years later, having realised that marriage left her feeling isolated, depressed and alone. 'I grew up first surrounded by a family that was afraid ... of a culture where things can happen to a young girl who was too free ... they kept me in the house.'

> My husband turned out to be worried about my safety ... so I still didn't have any freedom. For a few years, I couldn't go out alone, my husband was so fearful ... It was a culture of fear ... my parents, my husband – they were crushing me ... I fell ill. I was confused ... and then I had the luck to meet a splendid Freudian psychoanalyst in Palermo, Francesco Corrao, whom I will never forget. He told me ... 'You are strong ... You can rebuild your life and save yourself.' I went into psychoanalysis, and after two years I had the strength to leave my husband. (in Harris 1999, 12)

Soon after leaving her husband at a time when divorce was still illegal in Italy, Battaglia began to write for newspapers in order to support her three young daughters, first in Palermo and then in Milan.

In 1974, Battaglia was inspired by a theatre piece she saw in Venice, *Apocalypsis cum Figuris*, directed by Jerzy Growtowski, one of the most influential theatre directors of his time. Growtowski (1968, 78) was recognised for what he termed a 'theatre of participation' or 'Paratheatre' that, among other things, broke down the division between actor and audience. When first asked to join his ensemble, Battaglia refused. Months later, when asked again, she agreed to participate with the group. There Battaglia met Franco Zecchin, also a participant in Growtowski's ensemble at the time. They would become lovers and, over the next 19 years, political and artistic collaborators. He was 22, she was 40.

In 1975, after working for three years in Milan, Battaglia received an invitation from Vittorio Nistico to direct photography at the newspaper, *L'Ora*, Palermo's Communist daily newspaper. Under Nistico's leadership, *L'Ora* was known as the 'great school that defied the mafia'. The paper dedicated itself to investigative reporting, and, in the words of Giuliana Saladin, 'never tired of denouncing the scandal and cried out against the mafia that dominated public life in Sicily' (see Ruta 2013). Known for skilful reporting that refused to settle on reports from the police or official explanations distributed from the corridors of power, the work of photojournalists such as Battaglia and Zecchin would eventually mark a tradition of journalism as public service that stands starkly apart from the contemporary media conglomerates associated with the private empire of Silvio Berlusconi.

Battaglia recently described herself to journalist Carlo Ruta as knowing very little about the mafia during her early years at *L'Ora* (Ruta 2013): 'I was a girl of about 40, lively, generous with libertarian ideals and vaguely communist . . . but then drugs arrived and youth began to ruin their lives . . . I began to understand a little bit more.' In 1975, Battaglia began to photograph the convulsive mafia executions that erupted throughout the streets of Palermo. 'I was bare-handed except for my camera', recalls Battaglia,

> against them with all of their weapons. I took pictures of everything. Suddenly, I had an archive of blood. An archive of pain, of desperation, of terror, of young people on drugs, of young widows, of trials and arrests. There in my house, . . . surrounded by the dead, the murdered. It was like being in the middle of a revolution . . . (Battaglia, in Harris 1999, 15)

In the years following 1977, Palermo descended into what journalist Alexander Stille describes as 'the long night of one of the most bloody and tragic periods any European city has known since World War II' (Stille et al. 1999, 18). Between 1978 and 1992, approximately 1000 people were murdered or made to disappear as the mafia established a booming heroin industry that, by 1984, would bring Italy's hard-core addict population to more than 200,000 (Stille et al. 1999, 82). Battaglia, Zecchin and their assistants were present at every major crime scene throughout the city. In 1980, they were joined by Battaglia's 27-year-old daughter, Shobha. Together they covered the brutal murders of the chief of detectives, the head of the fugitives squad, three chief prosecutors, and Italy's two most important and beloved mafia prosecutors, Giovanni Falcone and Paulo Borsellino; in politics, the head of Sicily's leading opposition party, the head of the leading government party and two former mayors of Palermo. The Battaglias and Zecchin used what have now come to be iconic antimafia images to create antimafia exhibitions in schools and on streets where no one could avoid seeing them. In a 1999 interview for Aperature, Zecchin recalls that 'No one believed that photographs could be a weapon in the battle against the mafia.'

> Our idea was just to put up photographs everywhere . . . in piazzas, in schools, in the streets. In the decade from the late 1970's to the late 1980's, there was a veritable war against the mafia, and a serious escalation in violence . . . The mafia, which had always been so absolutely sure of its own power, did not expect that a bunch of photographs could have such a powerful effect. And the people of Palermo had their doubts – in fact at first they thought we were crazy. They had been living so long in a state of terror, and everyone was desperately afraid of naming names. (in Harris 1999, 13)

Over the course of 20 years, of which 18 were spent without even a zoom, only a wide-angle lens separating her from the death and degradation that surrounded the city, Battaglia documented every crime committed by the mafia on the streets of Palermo (http://www.artnet.com/artwork/426255717/425933685/letizia-battaglia-fotografie-1974-2013.html). Together with Zecchin, Battaglia created a photography school and gallery in an effort to introduce the world to the Sicilian mafia, tragedies understood at the time as marginal and exclusively local (Stille et al. 1999, 84). The role northern Italy and Europe at large played in mafia crime went unnoticed (see, for example, Mohanty 2005).[4] In the face of so much crime and its attendant poverty, it was never a question, recalls Battaglia in an interview with Melissa Harris, 'of making beautiful photographs. It was a question of standing up to these people and saying 'we are here and we are against you' (Harris 1999, 16).

For Battaglia, the photograph works as a means to engage the public pedagogically. Growtowski's influence can be felt in the way in which Battaglia used photography to create a direct encounter between the people of Palermo and the mafia. Recognised for his belief that the theatre should have a therapeutic function for people in present-day civilisation, Growtowski (1968, 22) argued that actors should co-create the event of theatre with its spectators – intimately, visibly, 'in direct confrontation with him and somehow 'instead of' him'. Growtowski suggests that the actor may at times find it necessary to make contact with difficult aspects of society on behalf of the spectator, so that, in turn, the spectator is able to recognise an aspect of society previously denied. The art of confrontation characterises Battaglia's public pedagogy insofar as she uses her camera to make contact with the criminal activities of the mafia and state political corruption. On behalf of the people of Palermo, she, Zecchin and their colleagues curated antimafia exhibitions in public spaces, apart from state control and without profit. Battaglia's photographs began to challenge students, shopkeepers and ordinary residents to recognise what for so long had previously been disavowed – that there was a mafia. Her photographic lessons, composed in black and white, interrupt the pull to deny the infiltration of organised crime into just about every sector of civic life in Palermo and the surrounding areas. In a 2013 interview I had with Marina DeCarlo, a former shipyard director in Palermo who resigned from her position due to the daily stress of mafia threats (DeCarlo was pressured to smuggle drugs into the cruise port of Palermo), she emphasised that 'yes, Battaglia's photographs woke up our city, but we knew deep inside there was a mafia'. Most important, her photographs provided evidence to the world that there was a mafia and it was not simply a 'Sicilian problem'.

Battaglia's photographs, exhibited in what I would describe as portable 'pop-up' spaces throughout the city, stand outside state control and describe the precarious conditions or what Giorgio Agamben designates as 'zones of indistinction' which produce 'states of exception' that render citizen rights irrelevant. These zones demonstrate, argues Agamben (2005), the ease with which governments can shift categories of people from those who have rights to those who do not. And while many residents of Palermo were ostensibly protected by a formal 'citizenship', their right to state protection from mafia violence as citizens was denied. The lives portrayed in Battaglia's photographic archive are seen as 'devoid of value' by the sovereign government. Battaglia used her wide-angle lens to re-frame, in the words of Dora Apel (2012, 9), 'the reality of the visible and bring into focus the invisible'. Moreover, her photography functions according to the critical principles laid out by Ariella Azoulay (2008, 9) in her study of photography's civil contract: 'to contest injuries to citizenship' in the form of 'photographic-complaints'.

In an interview with Melissa Harris, Battaglia expresses the acute sense of abandonment the people of Palermo felt in the face of the Italian state during this time.

> This war began in 1975, one against the other – in a 'civilized' society. War had broken out against the men and women of the institutions, war against the honest judges, politicians, policemen, and journalists. The biggest civil war that could happen in a city began, because the mafia had gone too far and the bloodshed extended beyond their own family vendettas. (Battaglia 1999, 15).

The 1976 photograph (Figure 1) of Vincenzo Battaglia's murder stands as a statement of horror that declares the extreme conditions in which the people of Palermo lived, confirming what so many viewers knew, but preferred to keep silent out of fear of retaliation from the mafia. At any moment a resident of the city could be murdered, caught in cross-fire, mistaken for some-one else or be used to set an example. These conditions of fear and denial structure the position of what Azoulay terms the 'civil addressee' or the viewer of the photograph.

For Figure 1, see: http://41.media.tumblr.com/235b02338c8b2d404dc984a78e154d6e/tumblr_mse07hNIYa1r60zrho4_1280.jpg

Figure 1. Palermo, 1976. Vincenzo Battaglia is killed in a dark alleyway. His wife desperately tried to help him, but was too late. Photograph by Letizia Battaglia.

Upon viewing the photograph, the 'civil addressee' is called upon to deviate from the side to which she may be wedded – that of silence or *omerta* (a code of silence) and address the emergency claims being made by taking action (Azoulay 2008, 201). This can produce a shift from looking at the emergency claims made in a photograph as a generalised statement of horror – in this case, 'the Sicilian misery' that does not implicate me – to a specific civilian discourse that provokes a shift in the viewer's awareness by altering how they routinely see a photograph and urges them to demand an intervention. Battaglia's photography shifts awareness, in part, by framing not only the direct victims of mafia crimes, but their families. Standing in an alleyway, barefoot, alone in her grief, her legs splattered in blood, a woman leans forward, as if in a desperate prayer, towards her dead husband's body. He was killed on his way to the bakery to buy cannoli. In the 1980 photograph (Figure 2), a woman, also barefoot, mistakenly believes that her son has been murdered. In the grip of imagined loss, falling into the arms of police and male bystanders, she seems to cry out on behalf of all women sentenced to silence and left unprotected by the state (Azoulay 2008, 302).

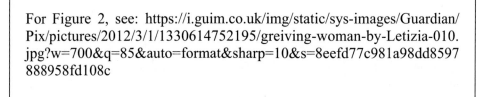

For Figure 2, see: https://i.guim.co.uk/img/static/sys-images/Guardian/Pix/pictures/2012/3/1/1330614752195/greiving-woman-by-Letizia-010.jpg?w=700&q=85&auto=format&sharp=10&s=8eefd77c981a98dd8597888958fd108c

Figure 2. Capaci, 8 August 1980. Three killers have murdered the owner of the Hotel Costa Smeralda. The woman believes the murdered man is her son. Photograph by Letizia Battaglia.

The trauma of mafia violence erupting throughout the city breached the shield of existential belonging, social care and service which Khan and Winnicott believed was so essential for a community's well-being (Young-Bruehl 2013, 46). Stille notes that

> when citizens' basic rights – to physical security, health care, housing, even a place in the cemetery – are turned into privileges that can be granted or refused, as they havebeen in Palermo since time immemorial, people tend to turn for help to extralegal authorities such as the mafia. (Stille et al. 1999, 91).

Such illegal turns – for example, to drug trafficking, tax evasion and black markets – can be understood as a traumatic response – transmitted to future generations – to a cumulative social erosion, deterioration and failure of the state to care for its people over time. A societal trauma, notes Young-Bruehl, inflicts harm on social relationships and this harm is compounded in the person and the society it harms (as well as in the perpetrators). These traumas accumulate, are passed on and interfere with thinking – including the kind of sound political judgement that is contingent upon freedom of mind, imagination, and a capacity to speculate about multiple causes of and outcomes to events (Young-Bruehl 2013, 41). Societal trauma undermines a thoughtful unity in which communities might flourish by cultivating a form of fundamentalism described by Young-Bruehl as

> embracing a pre-exiting thought system with a fundamental event that explains all of history, polarizing all humankind into all-good and all-bad. The thought system also plots an endpoint at which ultimate judgment is delivered by a forgiving or punishing deity, ruler of the macrocosm who is outside the macrocosm, transcendent. (Young-Bruehl 2013, 41)

Battaglia understands these conditions well and uses her photography to transform a negatively attained unity formed in the face of fear into a thoughtfully chosen, flourishing unity that inspires democratic life and creative living (Young-Bruehl 2013, 41). Battaglia's public pedagogy complicates the disavowal of societal trauma by inspiring, along with a range of grassroots Sicilian antimafia organisations, forms of social activism that can sustain a thoughtful unity in the face of unthinkable experiences through a combination of public work, organised resistance and artistic expression.

After 19 years in Palermo, Zecchin left to live in Paris. Letizia Battaglia continued to photograph, in black and white, the brutalities of mafia crime and her photographs have become part of a larger antimafia project organised by educators, activists, artists and social entrepreneurs to challenge the mafia and to cultivate democratic life, an ethical economy and civility in Sicily and Italy as a whole. Her collection of photographs continues to serve as an 'unintended archive' that documents a history of violence as well, I believe, as a desire for radical hope and renewal. The images of Battaglia are those, notes

For Figure 3, see: http://stantrybulski.com/wp-content/uploads/2014/03/Rosario-Schifani-police-widow.jpg

Figure 3.   May 1993. Rosaria Schifani. Photograph by Letizia Battaglia.

photographer Lorenzo Linthout, of a photographer who 'participates' and who witnesses the profound need for justice and beauty (in Harris 1999, 13). Her photographs are described by Antonio Negri as capturing the faces of men and women that 'speak to the heart . . . and their unresolved demand for humanity' (in Harris 1999, 12).

In the following section I move in closer to two photographs of women in Battaglia's archive that migrate, *via* digital and social media, into the discourses of contemporary antimafia activists. I use these photographs to explore the pedagogical and aesthetic practices Battaglia uses to 're-storie' a cultural record that creates shared political spaces of action for narrating the lives of persons ordinarily rendered non-existent by history. 'A life led in the absence of a space of exhibition leaves behind no life-story', argues Cavarero (2000, 58). Battaglia's photographic images, read as historical documents, make lives legible, present and insist on restoring civil relationships and forms of being together that imagine a future apart from violence and corruption. In Azoulay's terms, Battaglia's pedagogy utilises photography to support community and, 'as well' notes Apel, 'to build an oppositional public sphere so that people may, ultimately, act on the rights they do not have, and by enacting those rights, bring them into being' (Apel 2012, 8).

'Make your skepticism a lever for knowledge'
The iconic photograph of Rosaria Schifani (Figure 3), the 22-year-old widow of bodyguard Vito Schifani, was taken by Battaglia in May of 1993, one year after Rosaria's husband was assassinated with antimafia prosecutor Giovanni Falcone, his wife, Judge Francesca Morvillo and two other bodyguards in a car bomb explosion in Capaci. Over the last 20 years, this photograph has taken on the symbolic weight of a nation's grief and sustains memories of the upsurge of organised revolt against the mafia emerging at this time (Siebert 1999, 178). The photograph almost always invokes memories of Falcone's state funeral at the basilica in the San Domenico Church. And each year, on the anniversary of the assassination at Capaci, the photograph migrates across Facebook sites

and antimafia blogs and recalls the words of Rosaria Schifani standing at the podium in the San Domenico Church. Schifani continues to be remembered for spontaneously departing from a speech prepared with a Priest and moving an entire nation when she announced, with a lucid desperation, 'Without justice, I cannot die . . . There are mafiosi in here, too . . . too much blood, there's no love here, there's no love at all . . . I forgive you, but you have to kneel.' Her grief erupted, observes Renate Siebert,

> 'like night thoughts moving into the clear prayer of daylight . . . like breaking a taboo. . .' Standing at the podium, she expressed a longing for her husband in a physical way, she misses his beautiful legs. 'Nobody had the right to destroy his body. This is what I always think, simple as can be, without thinking about it at all in a clever way.' It is the pagan despair of someone with the painfully reached understanding that *never again* really means *never again*. (Siebert 1996, 26).

Over the last 20 years, this photograph continues to move from anti-mafia websites to magazines and newspapers, art exhibits and book jackets. Circulating around this photograph are narratives, letters and testimonies that speak of Schifani's courage to break the code of silence (*omerta*) and publicly address the mafia, to challenge state and church complicity in mafia violence as well as to refuse the position of female martyr.[5] In one of many letters written to Schifani soon after she spoke at Falcone's state funeral, Giovanna Giaconia, widow of Judge Cesare Terranova, murdered by the mafia on 25 September 1979 writes: 'What I really appreciated in your prayer at San Domenico was the mistrust woven into those words, "the state, the state." Well done, Rosaria, make your skepticism a lever for knowledge. And remember this is a state that signed a blank cheque for the mafia' (in Siebert 1996, 24).

The black and white portrait of Rosaria Schifani, half exposed by light, is considered one of the most important in Battaglia's archive. It has been described by photographer Lorenzo Linthout as 'a deathmask, split between light and shadow' (Siebert 1996, 22). Battaglia took this photograph at the home of Felice Cavallaro, for the cover of a 1993 biography he published of Rosaria. Her grief composed, her eyes closed, this photograph expresses the reclusive, guarded life that is forced on those who combat the veiled civil war that is the mafia (Siebert 1999, 121). Not only is the particular life of Rosaria Schifani represented in this photograph, but the digital, film and print-based circulation of this image suggests that it works as a powerful provocation for women who know intimately of mafia violence, to tell a story of their own, attesting to the power of Battaglia's photography to engender the reciprocity of storytelling and to work as a social protective shield by creating political union and existential belonging. The testimony and portrait evoke one another – taken together, they continue to inspire women to speak publicly, and to share their grief, anger and memories, practices that, in part, fuse the joint political activism that has, for generations, been taken up by women in the antimafia movement. In letters to Schifani written weeks after her husband's funeral,

Rita Bartoli, widow of the State prosecutor, Gaetano Costa, wrote, 'I advise you always to ask for justice because it is not pointless. And I advise you also to speak, to speak a great deal. Don't think only of forgiving. Ask, claim justice and speak most of all to those who live in this place' (Siebert 1996, 181). Another letter, written by Marina Pipitone after Schifani spoke at San Domenico reads:

> The words I heard you speak on TV, Rosaria are the same words I spoke then. I saw myself in your image. I saw myself as a very young woman, struck in the face by the monster. Be strong, Rosaria. And strengthen others because it really seems to me that you have it in you to give hope to people. (Marina Pipitone, widow of Michele Reina, Christian Democrat Party secretary in Palermo, quoted in Siebert 1996, 179)

And:

> Speak, speak, speak dear Rosaria. For years I stayed at home refusing to take part in meetings and debates. I didn't feel ready. Then one day I found myself in Bologna involved in a demonstration. I spoke. The words I said were simple. But they were effective. Word got around and from that day on I got invited all over the place, even to consulates abroad. I have even written a biography. (Giuseppina Zacco, widow of the Sicilian Communisty Party secretary, Pio La Torre, quoted in Siebert 1996, 180)

In a recent documentary about Rosaria Schifani directed by Fabio Vannini, *"Ho Vinto Io"* [*I Won!*], Schifani returns to Palermo after 20 years away. And while she describes how the support from the larger antimafia community taught her that grief can be turned into 'a springboard for collective pressure', for social change, she does not believe that the mafia will ever repent – 'they are', she states, 'in a death spiral, without hope' (Vannini 2012).

The re-elaborations (rielaborazioni)

On 23 May 1992, the day Schifani's husband Vito was murdered, hours before Falcone and Morvillo died along with their escorts, Antonio Montinaro and Dicillo Rocco, Battaglia stopped taking photographs of mafia massacres. In a recent interview about a European retrospective of her work in Venice, Battaglia recalls the shock she felt upon hearing of Falcone's death and her consequent refusal to take another photograph of the dead:

> I sat watching a documentary on the television with my mother, her hands in mine. I would usually to see him [Falcone] on a Sunday afternoon, but this time I was unable to do so. At a certain moment my programme was interrupted by the news that something had happened to Falcone on the motorway. We were unable to move for a few seconds, then panic hit me. . . . The only thing I could do was to telephone my studio and to warn Franco and Shoba. I wasn't about to go to the

motorway, in fact, I was never again to take photographs of the dead and all that goes with it. Eighteen years later, I realized that I had taken photographs of just about everything I could have done, in Palermo, for my then newspaper, *L'Ora* ... But most of all, I took pictures of misery, of dead bodies, of those being arrested, of bombs, of court cases, of litter, of the wounded, of fascists, of children, of women of demonstrations and of the humiliated ... on that fateful afternoon whilst holding my mother's white and soft hands, something inside me died and I took the decision to never take another photograph of another dead body, of any more pain and certainly of no more Mafiosi. Today, exactly twenty years later, I can only deplore my weakness or indolence or whatever you want to call it. It blocked my courage. It was my duty to resist, to take more photographs and to consign them to a future memory. These photos, which I never took, actually hurt me more than those that I did ... (interview with Lucio Ganci 2013)

After the murder of Falcone and then, weeks later, the murder of Paulo Borsellino, Battaglia ended her 20 years of photographing crime scenes. In the aftermath of these tragedies as well as the closing of *L'Ora*, Battaglia created her own publishing house and turned to politics full time (Stille et al. 1999, 91). In 2004, still feeling disgust at all Palermo had lost, she was examining a large photograph of a mother with her three poor children huddling together in a bed because of either cold or hunger. In that moment, Battaglia recalls feeling the need 'to destroy it' [the photograph]. 'That is', she explains, 'to make it into something else, I could give it a new life. So, from 2004 on were born *le Rielaborazioni* (the re-elaborations) and I started to turn my reportage shots into something different.' Battaglia contines to 're-storie' the old shots, by using them as background to something else. In front of a dead body, she inserts into the foreground what she describes as a positive image, such as a young woman, for example, to breath new life into it. The photograph 'Tre Donne' (Three Women; Figure 4), featured at the Workshop in Venice between 20 April and 18 May 2013 to celebrate International Women's Day, captures how Battaglia uses juxtaposition and montage to interfere with chronological planes, to look towards the future and to 're-storie' the violent history of Palermo. *Tre Donne* juxtaposes the lit portion of the portrait of Schifani, whose face is in the far background, against little more than a profile of the face of Francesco Laurana's stone bust of Eleonora of Aragon, which floats behind the face of Martha, Battaglia's 14-year-old granddaughter, as if to create historic resonances. What histories are cross-referenced in this portrait of three women? What pedagogical implications are inherent in Battaglia's re-workings?

'Spectral time' suggests that the past inhabits the present. 'The ghostliness of time', writes Nicoletta Di Ciolla, 'is not only enacted through the incursions of the past into the present, but also through infiltrations in the opposite direction: as the past casts a shadow on the present, the present similarly unfolds into the past' introducing education to a synchronic idea of history (Di Ciolla 2007, 40; Salvio 2009). Also called forth is Arendt's and Cavarero's concept of natality. Recall that in Battaglia's discussion of her re-elaborations, she

For Figure 4, see: http://41.media.tumblr.com/tumblr_lv754ewrZ71qcl8ymo1_1280.jpg

Figure 4. Tre Donne (Three Women). Photograph by Letizia Battaglia.

explains a moment, when feeling disgust at all that Palermo had lost, she realised she could transform the photograph of the mother and her hungry children into something else – 'I could give it [the photograph] a new life'. Her re-elaborations create, I believe, an 'imperishable memory' of loss and destruction that looks to birth and to life rather than to death as a central pedagogical category.

Called forth in these images are the unrepeatable and singular lives of Vito Schifani and Eleanora of Aragon. Also called forth are the unique lives of Rosaria Schifani and the young Martha. Cavarero uses the notion of uniqueness to indicate a person's irreplaceability. In each of these lives, in the unique response of each person to their historical and social particularities, is a concrete location for natality, a spot where newness can enter the world. Rather than premising her work on mortality and death, Battaglia joins Cavarero in turning to the category of birth and, in turn, departs from the narratives of martyrdom that are so prevalent in the antimafia imaginary (Puccio-Den 2008; Pickering-Iazzi 2010; Salvio 2012). The turn to new beginnings creates an ethos of hope and renewal that strengthens the 'social protective shield' through an act of imagination that invests an unthinkable past with a reparative promise. Winnicott (1958) might describe Battaglia's urge to juxtapose past images against present images as a 'spontaneous gesture' that offers access to lived experience in the present and is met by the people of Palermo with a sense of feeling alive.

Conclusion

Housed in Battaglia's apartment in Palermo is an 'unintended archive' of over 6000 photographs that exposed the corruption and anti-democratic practices of the state and challenged the world to understand organised crime as far more than Sicily's 'local problem'. The documentary practices of Battaglia draw on pedagogical and artistic traditions that, in the words of Apel (2012, 5), 'claim the frame for the rightless' by making her stance apparent, and by making visible the social and political conditions that make her photography possible. The spaces of violence and vulnerability captured by Battaglia over the course of 20 years continue to be in urgent need of representation. Contemporary antimafia activists, teachers and journalists who use narrative and photography such as journalist Roberto Saviano, and the citizen-writers of *Corrleone Dialogos*, have inherited from Battaglia a civil contract that Azoulay describes as being produced from documentary photography. This civil contract creates a new kind of citizenship that is based on spectator's relationships with and duty towards one another rather than to the state and creates a 'civic refuge' for those robbed of citizenship as well for those who, while citizens, are denied state protection. The photographic complaint, which can more easily migrate *via* digital technology, can produce grievances and claims that otherwise, argues Azoulay, would not be made and might not be so easily seen. Battaglia offers education important lessons in how the photographic archive can serve as a social protective shield for communities traumatised by organised crime. Her photographic archive continues to expand the arc of remembering by challenging the state repression of memory and its practice of 'trading in denial'.

Acknowledgements

I gratefully acknowledge Professor Burt Feintuch and the University of New Hampshire Center for the Humanities, and Dean Ken Fuld and the College of Liberal Arts for their generous support of this project. I also extend my gratitude to Franco Zecchin, Deborah Puccio-Den, Amy Boylan, Mike Middleton and Piero Garofalo for their scrupulous observations and perceptive advice.

Notes

1. For documentation of human rights violations that fail to be addressed by the state due to legal obstacles, see, for example, the Amnesty International reports on Uruguay, the United States and Argentina (see: http://www.amnesty.org/en).
2. One way to define a trauma is as an experience or series of experiences that is absolutely unthinkable. The unthinkable, at once persistently haunting, resists an integrated narrative or even an integrated neuronal memory. Often, traumatic memory is made manifest in compulsive thinking or, conversely, is denied, dissociated or disavowed (see Young-Bruehl 2013, 40–1).
3. The UN Convention on the Rights of the Child has secured signatures from all UN members except Somalia and the United States.

4. For an analysis of Northern Italy and Europe's role in the drug trade during this time, see *Modern Sociology: Globalization and Urban Sociology* by Mohanty (2005).
5. Schifani's position challenges that of the female martyr who trades political engagement for her life as we see, for example, in the public memories circulating around the memories of Rita Atria. As well, she represents a departure from the discourse of martyrdom so prevalent in the anti-mafia imaginary. For an astute analysis of this discourse, see the scholarship of Deborah Puccio-Denand Robin Pickering-Iazzi.

References

Agamben, Giorgio. 2005. *State of Exception*. Chicago, IL: University of Chicago Press.
Apel, Dora. 2012. *War Culture and the Contest of Images*. New Brunswick, NJ: Rutgers University Press.
Azoulay, Ariella. 2008. *The Civil Contract of Photography*. New York: Zone Books.
Bollas, Christopher. 2011. *The Christopher Bollas Reader*. New York: Routledge.
Britzman, Deborah. 2013. "Between Psychoanalysis and Pedagogy: Scenes of Rapprochement and Alienation." *Curriculum Inquiry*. 43 (1): 95–117.
Bertolino, Elisabetta, and Adriana Cavarero. 2008. "Beyond ontology and sexual difference: an interview with the Italian feminist philosopher Adriana Cavarero." *Differences: A Journal of Feminist Cultural Studies* 19 (1): 128–166.
Comay, Rebecca. 2002. *Lost in the Archives*. Editor. Toronto: Alphabet City Media.
De Ciolla, Nicoletta. 2007. 'Perfecting Females/ Pursuing Truths: Texts, Sub-Texts and Postmodern Genre-Crossing in Salvatori's, Noir, *Sublime Anima Di Donna.' Trends in Contemporary Italian Narrative: 1980–2007*. edited by, Gillian Ania and Anna Hallamore Caesar. Newcastle: Cambridge Scholars Publishing.
Derrida, J. 1996. *Archive Fever: A Freudian Impression* (trans. E. Prenowitz). Chicago, IL: University of Chicago Press.
Dickie, John. 2004. *Cosa Nostra: A History of the Sicilian Mafia*. London: Hodder and Stoughton.
Featherstone, M. 2006. "Archive." *Theory, Culture & Society*. Vol. 23: 591.
Freud, S. 1940. 'Outline of Psychoanalysis.' *The Standard Edition of the Complete Psychological Works of Sigmund Freud*, Volume XXIII. edited by, James Strachey, 141–216. London.
Ganci, Lucio. 2013. "Letizia Battaglia" Accessed December 9 http://www.demotix.com/ news/1857617/letizia-battaglia-photo-exibition#media-1857261
Growtowski, Jerzy. 1968. *Towards a Poor Theatre*. Denmark: Odin Teatret Forlag.
Harris, Melissa. 1999. *Passion, Justice, Freedom: Photographs of Sicily by Letizia Battaglia*, 1999. New York: Aperature.
Ihanus, Juhani. 2007. "The Archive and Psychoanalysis: Memories and Histories towards Futures." *International Forum of Psychoanalysis*. 16: 119–131.
Khan, Masud. 1963. *The Concept of Cumulative Trauma*, 1974. The Privacy of the Self. New York: International Universities Press.
Mohanty, G. S. 2005. *Modern Sociology: Globalization and Urban Sociology*. New York: Isha Books.
Pickering-Iazzi, Robin. 2010. '(En)Gendering Testimonial Bodies of Evidence and Italian Antimafia Culture: Rita Atria'. *Italian Culture* 28 (1): 21–37.
Povinelli, Elizabeth. 2011. " 'The Woman on the Other Side of the Wall: Archiving the Otherwise in Postcolonial Digital archives'." *Differences: A Journal of Feminist Cultural Studies*. 22 (1): 146–171.

Puccio-Den, Deborah. 2008. "The Sicilian Mafia: Transformation to a Global Evil." *Etnografica*. 12 (2): 377–386.

Ruta, Carlo. 2013. "L'Ora, the Mafia and Palermo." Accessed June 5, 2013. (http://www.liberainformazione.org/2013/06/05/lora-la-mafia-e-palermo/).

Salvio, Paula M. 2009. "Uncanny Exposures: A Study of the Wartime Photojournalism of Lee Miller." *Curriculum Inquiry*. 39 (4): 521–536.

Salvio, Paula M. 2012. " 'Eccentric subjects': Female Martyrs and the Antimafia Public Imaginary." *Italian Cultural Studies* 67 (3): 397–410(14).

Sandlin, Jennifer, B. Schultz, and J. Burdick (eds.). 2010. *Handbook of Public Pedagogy: Educating and Learning beyond Schooling*. New York: Routledge.

Siebert, Renate. 1996. *Secrets of Life and Death: Women and the Mafia*. New York: Verso Books.

Siebert, Renate. 1999. In *Passion, Justice, Freedom: Photographs of Sicily*, edited by Letizia Battaglia New York: Aperture Foundation.

Steedman, Carolyn. 2001. *Dust: The Archive and Cultural History*. New Brunswick, N.J.: Rutgers UP.

Stille, Alexander, Renate Siebert, Roberto Scarpinato, Leoluca Orlando, Simona Mafai, Melissa Harris, and Angela Casiglia Battaglia. 1999. In *Passion, Justice, Freedom: Photographs of Sicily by Letizia Battaglia*. New York: Aperture Foundation.

Vannini, Fabio. 2012. "*Ho Vinto Io*." Documentary film directed by Fabio Vannini. Produced by Cerioni. Music by Fabrizio Mancinelli. Rai Tre Radiotelevisione Italiana, Rome, Italy.

Winnicott, Donald W. 1958. *Collected Papers: Through Pediatrics to Psychoanalysis*. New York: Basic Books.

Young-Bruehl, Elisabeth. 2013. *The Clinic and the Context: Historical Essays*. London: Karnac.

Psychoanalytic notes on the status of depression in curriculum affected by histories of loss

Lisa Farley

York University, Toronto, Canada

> This paper examines debates about the meaning and value of depression in relationship to efforts to teach about, and learn from, historical loss. It is argued that depression is not solely an individual illness or biological aberration, but a trace and effect of facing the many and profound losses – of culture, language and life – that constitute history. And yet, where there is a tendency to privilege the negative affect of depression as a source of critical insight and remembrance, this paper turns to Andre Green's (1980) concept of 'the dead mother' to examine the inhibiting effects of depression in the context of the inter-generational relationship between parent and child, and arguably, the teacher and student as well. Using a case study from education, I suggest that depression, while indeed a painful trace of loss, can hinder the capacity to represent and so encounter the sadness, vulnerability and lost omnipotence that history leaves in its wake. I conclude with some thoughts on the conditions needed to narrate the meaning and effects of loss that negative affect alone embodies but cannot yet speak.

Psychoanalytically informed educational theory begins with a crucial assumption: that cognitive processes do not alone organise the work of learning and teaching, but are rather saturated in and constituted by a profoundly 'emotional situation' (Britzman 2009, xi). At stake is a theory of learning that acknowledges the ways that the very effort to know about the world rests on processes that are themselves largely unknown to us. Not to be confused with mistaken information or misunderstanding, psychoanalysis confronts education with 'another form of knowledge' that does not proceed from rational deliberation or understanding (Kristeva 2002, 40). Such knowledge, in the words of Julia Kristeva 'characterizes *fantasy*' and 'remains resistant to 'enlightenment' (40, original emphasis). Unconscious in its form, this is a knowledge that 'does not wish to be *familiar* with the real world through learning and adaptation to reality' (40, original emphasis). But as much as fantasy resists adaptation to reality, it is not the opposite of reality; the psychoanalytic insight here is that fantasy is a structuring agent through which we come to understand reality as meaningful in the first place.

As it comes into contact with education, psychoanalysis offers a language to consider how the fantasy formations of our earliest relationships shape the experience and representation of teaching and learning. Proponents of psychoanalysis posit a fulsome and at times difficult set of emotional conflicts that work underneath the more usual story of education as a conscious pursuit of knowledge. Some highlight the teacher's fantasy of rescuing a ruined world or a ruined student even at the risk of denying her/his emotional life in the effort (Britzman [1991] 2003, 2006; Taubman 2006). Others draw attention to the fantasy of being abandoned by the student who surpasses the teacher (Freud [1936] 1993) or, alternatively, persecuted by the student who does not learn (Appel 1999; Farley 2012; Matthews 2004). We might all recognise, too, the fear of being 'found out' for all that one does not know and that casts a shadow on yet another pervasive fantasy of the all-knowing teacher (Pitt and Britzman 2003). But there are also consolatory fantasies, such as the fantasy of orderly learning that occurs, as Tamara Bibby (2011, 114) playfully writes, 'preferably before examinations roll around'. Whatever the construction, proponents of psychoanalysis agree with Sigmund Freud's psychoanalytic insistence long ago: that the fantasies generated through the unconscious are not falsities but rather psychical *realities* that animate conscious efforts to teach, to learn and to live.

And yet, where psychoanalysis offers a theory of conflict as the foundation of emotional life, education tends to 'explain competence as the absence of conflict' (Britzman [1991] 2003, 7). Indeed, when it comes to education, Deborah Britzman (2006) notes that the conflicts of human interiority are more often fended off in 'an avalanche of material on helping', in policies designed to exit the 'bad' or 'burnt out' teacher and in the diagnosis of students (130). 'Too rarely', she writes, 'do we speak of the teacher's depression and anxiety, preferring instead to diagnose the learning problems of students and to idealize the statue of the teacher' (131). At the same time, this statue quickly crumbles when teachers, novice and experienced, recall their most memorable experiences of education. Invariably, it would seem, the most impactful memories are shot through with disparaging teachers, sad teachers, angry teachers, hateful teachers and crazy teachers (Britzman 2006; Lawrence-Lightfoot 2003). And then, almost as invariably, these bad memories become the fuel to teach and the reason to get it right. Caught in a loop of disparagement and idealisation, where the ideal teacher 'springs forth' from a terrible past, the profession cannot seem to tolerate the ordinarily devastating effects of trying to teach and learn from each other (Britzman 2006, 118).

In this paper, I theorise the significance and effects of depression, feelings of emptiness and even emotional death as part of the landscape of education. This is a risky direction to be sure, for a great deal of educational research suggests that its practices and policy ought to set into motion processes that are related to the love of learning and of life, or the happily ever after of education. In the subsequent sections, I enter this relatively unchartered terrain from the vantage of André Green's (1980) concept of 'the dead mother', a term he used to describe the qualities and effects of depression as it signifies in the earliest relationship between mother and baby. While the details of this concept become clear in the pages to come, I wish to note up front that the 'death' does not refer to the actual death of either the mother or the baby, but rather an emotional response to loss and its effects in the maternal environment. The loss could be the loss of a maternal ideal, or the anticipation of such a loss under the gaze of others, or a screaming infant. Or, it could refer to the loss of identity in one's new role as mother, or the loss of culture and language as an effect of migration or historical trauma. The loss could also be an actual other in the world outside the maternal relation: a partner, a parent, a friend or another child. More than the literal fact of death, the 'dead mother' refers to an 'emotional death' (Green 1980, 180) and the unconscious fantasies that mother and baby make and use to cope with their shared affective environment *'absorbed by bereavement'* (177, original emphasis).

Of course, Green's construction is not the only way to view depression. Rather, depression is a hotly debated feeling: its meaning shifts depending on the theoretical framework through which it is understood. In what follows, I sketch out some of the terms of debate that have framed – and changed – the meaning of depression over time and across disciplinary lines. While these debates stand as a reminder of the interpretive quality of knowledge, my discussion nonetheless points to the binary terms by which depression is typically cast: on the one hand, as an effect of physiological imbalances in the brain and, on the other hand, as a construction in history. An offshoot of this last claim constructs depression as a site of *critique* insofar as it materialises forgotten histories of loss. Implied but absent from this binary is a discussion of the psychical effects of depression produced in the inter-generational relationship between adults and children. Here is where I turn to Green to offer a language through which to highlight the relational quality of depression: at once an effect of loss that itself *has effects* on those born into its condition. The relational quality of this psychoanalytic construction, I suggest, offers good reason to re-think the tendency to either denigrate depression as an individual malady or privilege suffering as a site of social critique.

My turn to Green's metaphor considers additional terms through which to think about the experience and effect of pedagogical environments affected by loss and grief. This inquiry is particularly pertinent when we take into account theories that account for all that the teacher and student must lose in the name of education: the loss of connection to language and discourse that does not match that of the school (Delpit and Kilgour Dowdy 2002; Silin 1995); the loss of certainty in the face of conflicting knowledge (Waddell 2000); the lost ideal of chronological learning in the belated time of understanding (Bibby 2011; Britzman 2009); the denial of desire in the socially sanctioned image of the altruistic teacher (Freud [1936] 1993); and the loss of an ideal world in which peace reigns over the violence that constitutes human history (Farley 2009; Simon 2005). To this theoretical discourse of loss incurred through education, I add Green's metaphor of the 'dead mother' to open questions about the cascading effects of negative affect in the context of pedagogical relationships marked by loss. How might depression be read as an effect of encountering loss in education? What does it mean to read curriculum and pedagogy as themselves emotional traces of historical loss? Can the negativity of depression be read in a positive light? What if depression is a defence against the very thought of loss that gives rise to its condition?

Depression: a debatable feeling?

The medicalisation of feelings, depression among them, has come under scrutiny by an emergent body of scholarship drawn from feminist and social and political theory. At least one question emerging from this scholarship asks how medical models of assessment (of which the American Psychiatric Association's *Diagnostic and Statistical Manual of Mental Disorders* [DSM] is one key example) are responsible for 'medicalizing social problems' (Horowitz and Wakefield 2007, viii). The main thrust of this critique is that the meaning and diagnosis of varying mental states has never been objective or neutral, but rather a mirror image of the requisite qualities that a given culture deems worthy and good at a particular point in history. The problem is that with such categorisations come justifications for the exclusion and persecution of persons who do not fit within their normative frames – all in the name of seemingly neutral ideals of happiness and health.

One particularly powerful articulation comes from the emergent 'affective turn' in social and political theory: an inter-disciplinary hub of discourse and practices that seeks to 'de-pathologize' historically denigrated affects such as 'shame, failure, melancholy and depression' not merely as personal problems, but as artefacts of having survived long and painful legacies of colonial violence (Cvetkovich 2012, 5). Not only that, the affective turn re-finds the political in the personal, theorising how new political formations might be 'entwined with and *even enhanced* by forms of negative feeling' (Cvetkovich 2012, 5, emphasis added; see also Ahmed 2010; Eng and Kazanjian 2003). Negative affect, of which depression is one example, therefore signifies in the 'affective turn' both a social critique and political possibility. As critique, Sara Ahmed (2010) suggests that melancholia refuses to forget histories of violence otherwise hidden under the cloak of the nation. As possibility, Ahmed argues further that insofar as melancholia registers 'something missing', it also instigates the search for something else, as she puts it: 'a *potential* to find something, even if what you find will not be the same things that have been lost' (153, emphasis added). Such positive re-readings of negative affect, and melancholia in particular, challenge us to abandon the idea that depression is a personal aberration, and instead to read it not only as a construction in history, i.e. 'a culturally bound syndrome', but also a trace of history's many violent exclusions (*The Guardian* 2013).

For my interests in education, it is important that Paula Salvio (2007) adds a discussion of the teacher's melancholia. Just as the aforementioned scholars find potential in melancholia, so too does Salvio, who finds in the 'dispiritedness' and 'estrangement' of the melancholic teacher 'important resources for teaching and learning', which she describes as 'indices of histories – both personal and social – that we have turned away from or conceal' (14). The teacher's melancholia makes readable the losses implied in becoming a teacher: aspects of the self that had to be given up – desire, or need, or even helplessness – in exchange for the professional role. For Salvio, the psychical losses of the profession are melancholically materialised in the teacher's aesthetic, even the highly prized aesthetic of altruism, which, Anna Freud ([1936] 1993, 122) reminds us, is evidence of 'surrender' or, sacrifice of desire in the name of helping students activate their own.

But if melancholia is viewed here as a resource that productively rearticulates the repressions of social and pedagogical domains, yet another position in the literature asks us to think again about melancholia as itself entrenched in the fantasy that idealises its own capacity to work to such transformative ends. The disagreement that these second thoughts pose is not about whether melancholia manifests the knots left behind by devastating histories of social violence and loss. Nor is the disagreement about whether political and educational projects *ought* to address such histories and their emotional effects. The question is whether melancholia can indeed be read as a viable condition from which new possibilities for learning and living together after loss may emerge. The point here is that while melancholia is indeed an effect of the catastrophic losses that mark this historical moment, Sigmund Freud's (1917) 'cautionary insights' remind us of the catastrophic effects of melancholia itself, a condition that both repeats and retreats from the very losses that animate its persistent condition (Kennedy 2010, 112).

Second thoughts on the productive potential of melancholia take many forms. For instance, Wendy Brown (2003, 459) argues that melancholia forecloses creative potential because its process of internalising loss also converts the loss into an ideal, into a 'fetish' or 'thing' that is more about the ego's desire to consume than it is about ethical regard for the object-loss in its own right. Simon, Rosenberg, and Eppert 2000) take Brown's discussion seriously, suggesting that, in consuming the loss, melancholic identification collapses the distinction between the self and other, and so distorts the ethical capacity to witness *who* has been lost, beyond what the ego wants from it, including the desire to not lose at all (see also Boler 1999; Todd 2003). While a deeply painful identification, melancholia forecloses the more difficult encounter with the ego as it is changed by the loss, for in melancholia, 'the ego becomes the object' (Britzman 2000, 34), and so there is no distance from which to pose this question. Britzman articulates the problem: 'Melancholia is a form of narcissistic identification, where the ego confuses itself with the lost object, becomes split, and then attacks itself and the loss' (34). Consumed and consuming, the ego mistakes the loss for itself and so cannot think of how the loss matters, or how the world matters differently because of the loss.

Where there is the internalisation of loss and the confusion between self and other, there is also the conflict of ambivalence: the simultaneous feeling of love and hate in relation to the same object. Under the condition of melancholia, the passionate drive to preserve the lost other is both heightened by and inseparable from the rage at having been left behind. When the tension produced through ambivalence becomes too much to contain, a split emerges: idealisation protects the beloved other from fury, now turned inward and against the ego in the form of bitter self-reproach for failing to recuperate the loss. What may appear an ethical pursuit to recuperate the lost other is also self-protective insofar as it seeks to restore self-mastery in the face of runaway affects that loss unleashes. RM Kennedy (2010) considers further the implications of these cautionary insights. For him, melancholic attachments work on the idealisation not only of the lost object, but also a fantasied version of the self (and community) that is believed to have existed before the loss. Travelling under the rubric of 'tradition' or 'ethnic nationalism', such formations seek to 'reconstitute a lost "imagined community"' that must exclude 'outsideness' and 'social difference' to preserve idealised notions of identity and belonging (112).

Ironically, then, while melancholia indeed holds open 'a continuous engagement with the past', the process of idealisation, also central to the condition, at the same time freezes the on-going work of making emotional significance from the loss: or, understanding how the self and world are modified, and continue to be, because of the loss. In the attempt to 'restore as unchanged both the lost object and the ego', the idealisation at work in melancholia turns away from the difference that loss makes for those left behind (Britzman 2000, 34). In its refusal of outsideness, melancholic identification relies 'on a rhetoric of hiding that works to thwart, obstruct and distort meaning' (Salvio 2007, 14). Where there is the pain of loss and not yet knowing the significance of its effects, there is a fantasy of power – and even pleasure – in the idealisation of the very thing that wounds the ego's fragile boundaries.

For education, the debates over the meaning and significance of melancholia stand as an important reminder not only of the contested quality of knowledge, but also offer 'cautionary insights' about privileging melancholia as a position of both learning and politics. When loss is melancholically rendered in curriculum, there is a risk of idealising both the lost other and a wishful education that could have prevented trauma that has already occurred. The identifications that characterise melancholia, in Britzman's view, have the effect of holding on to historical loss that at the same time turns away from the loss on the wishful discourse of idealisation. In so doing, melancholia repeats the logic of trauma 'by placing helplessness and loss elsewhere' – that is, away from both the self and education (Britzman 2000, 35).

The implication of pointing to these risks is not simply that education ought to make us happier (Noddings 2003), nor even is it that education ought *not* be melancholic. Rather, the aforementioned dialogue suggests that melancholia is a significant feature of the teacher's emotional life that can find its way into both curriculum and pedagogy. At stake here is a view of pedagogy that inverts the usual story of education: no longer an antidote to misunderstanding, education can itself defend against the very knowledge it seeks to represent in curriculum and pedagogy. As Britzman (2000, 37) writes, the very effort of pedagogy to enlighten 'can also become a defense against thought and against its own capacity for ignorance'. In Britzman's view, education is necessarily affected by its own effort to represent 'difficult knowledge' to others, and is *itself* 'difficult knowledge' insofar as it operates on a stubborn conflict: the affected quality of our attachments to knowledge means that both curriculum and pedagogy stand in precarious relationship to processes that also threaten to upend the very effort to represent history. But there is more, for in Britzman's view, representation can itself be a defense when it promises to tie up loose ends or fill the lack that loss ushers in.

Green's concept of the 'dead mother' offers a framework through which to elaborate this double-edged quality of affectively charged pedagogy: at once a painful immersion in the abyss of loss and a defence against the very thought of the loss that binds the attachment. For Green, 'the dead mother' is a particular form of melancholia, and so, as noted above, refers to a charged identification and entrenched trace of historical loss. But because the concept also refers to the quality and effects of the inter-generational relationship, it opens still other questions about the inhibiting effects of melancholia on newcomers to the world. Thus while Green's concept lends support to the idea of depression as an embodiment of unspeakable loss, he also suggests that its inter-generational inheritance has the troubling effect of hindering the capacity to represent loss in the symbolic realm and in the relation between adult and child.

My turn to Green's concept begins, then, with a shared assumption articulated by both sides of the aforementioned debate: depression is not simply an isolated illness or personal failing but rather an important commentary on the deep and lasting pain of personal, social and historical loss. And yet, where there is a tendency to grant political value to negative affect as an index of forgotten history, Green's emphasis on the inter-generational effects of depression gives us pause to think again. This is because, for Green, when the earliest maternal environment is marked by depression, what is passed on is not necessarily the critical agency that fuels its political use. What is passed on is an unconscious fantasy structure that is emptied of the aggressive life drive that is, for proponents of psychoanalysis, *the* psychical condition on which the capacity to renew the world depends. Drawing from Green, I suggest that the negativity of depression negates another psychical achievement – one that Kristava calls 'matricide' – which she argues is needed to transform the anxiety of loss into the symbolic realm where painful legacies can be represented, contemplated and remembered.

The dead mother: or, the failure of matricide

In *Black Sun*, Kristeva (1989) uses the term 'matricide' to refer to the infantile impulse to maternal destruction. Despite the harsh image, maternal destruction does not equate with literal murder, but rather, an impulse to separate that exists before the social categories through which aggression is typically understood: as anger, or war, or violence, or bullying. For Kristeva, matricide refers to an infantile fantasy of psychical murder that emerges around the time when the mother fails, as all mothers do and must, to meet the baby's every need. Matricide is, then, a psychical strategy that the infant uses to cope with the fact of the mother as a separate person. But in this destructive fantasy, and in the mother's inevitable failure, analysts find good news: matricide is a resource for thought because it sets into motion the reparative impulse that transforms the shock of separation into the symbolic capacity, needed to conceptualise the fragility of love, and of life itself. Kristeva (2001) had this in mind in a later book, *Melanie Klein*, where she suggests that the destructive kernel of matricide is 'the organizing principle for the subject's symbolic capacity' (130).

In the context of education, Alice Pitt (2003) draws from both Klein and Kristeva to argue that matricide is the condition of life itself: 'the suffering this [murder] generates ... brings the search for objects that substitute for the mother and so the possibility of *living a life*' (89, emphasis added). But Pitt also uses the concept as a metaphor of learning. On the condition of matricide, education activates the twin dynamics of psychical murder and its reparation. Mirroring S. Freud's ([1911] 2006) theory of education as channelling erotic impulses into satisfying substitutes, matricide frames learning as a 'search for objects that substitute' the loss of the maternal (Pitt 2003, 89). But where Freud's theory focuses on the threat of punishment and the internalisation of paternal law, matricide sets the learner on a path that, as Pitt (2004, 274) describes, 'propels us toward freedom' insofar as 'the search for objects' re-connects the subject to shards of repressed affects otherwise cut off from representation.

Crucially, while matricide refers to psychical murder, it does not produce the 'dead mother' in Green's sense of the term. Quite the contrary, the 'dead mother' is a psychical structure that *hinders* the dynamics at work in matricide. Where the destructive impulses of matricide generate reparative re-searches for satisfying substitutes, the 'dead mother' sets down a fantasy that the world is too impoverished to survive the aggressive quality of these symbolic efforts. In Kristeva's (1989, 28) terms, what arises from the 'black sun' of depression is not the life drive of aggression but 'its inversion on the self' and the 'melancholic putting to death of the self'. Ironically, depression channels the active quality of aggression into the constant and berating inhibition of the ego's capacity for representation. Green's 'dead mother' foregrounds Kristeva's inquiry into the inhibiting effects of being born under a black sun that destroys the aggressive dimensions of becoming a subject. Indeed, for both analysts, the question is: what can matricide mean if the world one meets is already dead?

Green's response to this question gets to the heart of the condition of the dead mother, which he builds from his reading of Winnicott. While Winnicott had a strong idea of 'the value of depression', publishing a paper with this title in 1963 (Winnicott ([1963] 1986), he also expressed concern about depression as the structuring condition of the maternal environment. Over the course of his career, and particularly after the Second World War, Winnicott came to believe that an impoverished holding environment produced in the baby a defensive psychical organisation oriented to comply with the outside world, and against its own internal pressure, including the aggressive impulses needed to separate from the mother. And so where destructive fantasies (or, matricide) would normally 'come first', Winnicott believed that there emerged instead the experience of 'early disillusion' that crushed the force of the baby's aggression with the stark condition of the mother's dark mood (Winnicott [1939] 1989, 21). The result of 'early disillusion', argued Winnicott ([1963] 1986), is an infantile psychical structure in which 'all hate and destruction is controlled' together with a premature drive to reparation that makes 'fixed and unavailable' to the baby the pain of separation that initiates and marks becoming a subject of the world (79). The effect of the mother's depression is, then, an infantile and manic form of reparation that is different from Winnicott's 'stage of concern' (79). Where concern emerges from the young ego's implication in the painful labour of separation, early disillusion, despite its stark intrusion of mental suffering, produces between mother and baby a wishful fantasy that loss can be prevented through its constant anticipation.

Psychoanalytically, the problem is not the fact of loss itself but rather how to create an environment in which to contain and face feelings – of abandonment or anxiety or sadness – that loss dredges up in surviving others. When it comes to the infant, the environment is particularly crucial and complicated. Because the infant does not yet have boundaries that would constitute a self, it is the mother's gaze that acts as a metronome and mediator – what Winnicott calls a 'mirror' – that regulates and reflects back to the baby evidence of life's continuity in the face of breakdown (Winnicott [1967] 1971, 111). When the baby looks and sees the mother's emotional absence, there emerges a crisis of existence that is experienced not only as the 'loss of love', but as Green (1980, 178) writes, 'the loss of *meaning* ... experienced by the infant as a catastrophe'. The catastrophe is made from a central conflict: the mother is physically present to the point of imposing her own needs and defences, even while she is at the same time emotionally absent and deeply fragile. The effect of this conflict is the atrophy of the infant's ordinary aggressive impulses that gradually marshal creative capacities to affect the world through representation and thought. In Green's words, there is 'an impossibility of diverting destructive aggressivity to the outside on account of the vulnerability of the maternal image' (179).

Shadowing S. Freud's (1917) discussion of melancholia, the child of the dead mother 'endeavours to get rid of the object' by consuming it 'in a cannibalistic manner', even as this very attachment is also what keeps it close 'against one's will' (Green 1980, 179). Loss is here expressed in the manic impulse to repair without any relief of closure. As Green puts it, this is identification 'with the hole left by the decathexis (and not identification with the object), and with this, emptiness' (183). The difference here is crucial, for if matricide activates a 'positive identification' with the lost other that instigates the search for symbolic substitutes with which to represent a relationship to the loss, then the dead mother reverses this into a 'negative identification' with the abject traces of loss that resist representation. In other words, the psychical murder that would give way to the 'search for substitutes' is replaced by the ego's surrender of the self in the name of keeping alive an unnameable loss. As Green writes, 'there is simply a feeling of being held captive which dispossesses the ego of itself and alienates it to an unrepresentable figure' (181). Annexed to an 'unrepresentable figure', the emotional labour of separation is forbidden, and the young ego is without the aesthetic distance needed to represent the loss and the affects it sets into motion. Bound to enliven the other, the child of the dead mother can never quite embody a sense of self. The emotional conflict is one of feeling utterly alone and thoroughly dependent: solitary confinement under an invisible lock and key.

Yet another effect of the 'dead mother', intimated already, is the inversion of the structure of care, for it is the child who is charged to secure the adult's survival. In Green's (1980, 191) words, the usual processes of reparation – 'positive acts which are the expression of remorse' – are replaced by 'a sacrifice of vitality on the altar of the mother'. The difference here is subtle but significant, for where the former signals the creative search for 'substitutes' in a world beyond the mother, the latter instantiates the return to the closed orbit of one's own origins constantly on the verge of ruin. Caught in the snare of the dead mother complex, the psychical achievement of separation, or in Pitt's words, 'living a life', gets equated with betrayal. In short, it is not the child who uses – and murders – the mother in the name of 'living a life', but rather, the mother who uses – and feeds on – the child to keep alive her deadened emotional state. This is an attachment that never lets go, and so cannot enter the world beyond the maternal bond.

To the extent that Green's 'dead mother' describes a psychical structure developed in relationship to a fundamental lack, it can be thought of in terms of S. Freud's concept of melancholia. Indeed, the 'dead mother' is a particular form of melancholia as it signifies in the maternal relationship, or, the earliest environmental provision. In the context of the aforementioned debates over the meaning of depression, I suggest that the 'dead mother' provides further evidence and justification for S. Freud's 'cautionary insights' about reading melancholia as an empowering condition. And so where the affective turn in social and political theory takes literally the critical agency of melancholia, Green's dead mother points to the 'un-representable figure' behind negative affective states – of which depression is one – that resist thought itself. In Green's (1980, 193) words, the 'dead mother' signifies as 'compounds' of 'loaded affects' that both precede and overwhelm the capacity for their representation, and by extension, the capacity to think about the effects of living in the shadow of loss.

In what follows, I consider an example that gives expression to some of the more subtle but no less significant effects of Green's concept as it takes shape in curriculum and the pedagogical relation, particularly when the knowledge on offer references social histories of devastating loss. The example is Britzman's (2006) retrospective essay that recounts her very first experience teaching high school English. Britzman's analysis identifies how the emotional situation of teaching and learning shapes the capacity to represent encounters with loss in curriculum and pedagogy. Like Green's clinical analysis, Britzman's memoir illustrates how the teacher can transfer into pedagogy and on to students not only the knowledge of loss but also, the affective traces of grief and helplessness that loss churns in its wake. Even more, Britzman offers a cautionary tale and a warning against the tendency to equate negative affect with political possibility. Her analysis rather shows how depression can drive the very insistence that 'everything is political' and, in so doing, defend against the representation of affective states activated in encounters with loss (118). Finally, Britzman's analysis returns to 'outsideness' (Kennedy 2010, 112) as a key feature of constructing meaning from loss, and not negative affect alone. For Britzman, loss becomes thinkable when there is the 'outsideness' of time and an other.

Monsters in curriculum

Perhaps the only autobiographic piece in Britzman's vast body of work on the emotional labour of teaching, 'Monsters in Literature' (Britzman 2006) is a testament to 'compounds' of 'loaded affects' as they circulate and overwhelm curriculum, students and the teacher herself. It is also suggestive of how the teacher's furor to teach may be a manic response to the grief of representing loss in curriculum and pedagogy. Britzman does not herself use Green's language, and yet I suggest that her memoir reveals both sides of his relational structure: characterized by a curriculum absorbed by grief and the wish to rescue the students (and the self) from this very condition. The irony is that in this passion, the teacher is emptied of the vulnerability that is also her/his emotional life, which, in turn, empties the students of their own emotional lives in the need for them to sustain her/his own. Indeed, Britzman will show how, in the idealization of curriculum and, for her, the insistence on the political value of historical loss, the teacher may repeat the very inhibiting qualities of education that s/he intends to work against.

On the surface, Britzman's essay is a memoir that recalls her very first high school English curriculum. The aim of the course was to examine, through the analysis of 'monsters in literature', the meaning and effects of the avalanche of losses and exclusions that mark traumatic history. Given the contemporary debates on the meaning and value of negative affect, Britzman's curriculum is prescient insofar as her use of monsters was meant to give representation to the violence and exclusions that are otherwise repressed in the national narrative and its pursuit of happiness. Along similar lines, Britzman describes her curriculum as a critical alternative to normalising tendencies in education, then and now, 'to exorcise from itself what it considers as the monstrous: terrorism, poverty, hopelessness, depression' (114). Britzman's use of literary monsters aimed to bring into the borders of the state and the school untold narratives of suffering on which both institutions are built: 'In my head', Britzman recounts, 'these actual monsters would ... set the stage for encountering something terribly real and literally terrible: the inhumanity of the state apparatus, class inequality, racism, and genocide' (114).

Unthinkable to her at the time, Britzman remembers some of the features of the course from the distance of 30 years' hindsight, and which bear uncanny resemblance to some of the features of Green's fantasy formation: there is the pedagogical environment absorbed by grief, the curriculum crowded by the knowledge of loss, the manic drive to repair, the unfailing devotion to a failing teaching situation and the unconscious uses of both students and curriculum to sustain the self in the midst of it all. 'The symptom in all this mess', writes Britzman, 'monsters' (118). Still, then and now, Britzman stands behind her pedagogical obligation to speak of 'terrible events in the world' (115). And yet, her reflections on these early efforts also narrate an 'emptiness' that she could not see for the furor, and that takes us, in belated time, to the painful core of depression (114). In the margins of her crowded curriculum, Britzman admits her classroom became an empty place. Where there would be the risk of relating to the 'excess' of both the literary and the students, Britzman claims she projected a 'wish to raise their consciousness' through her idealised curriculum. The trouble is, Britzman stumbles on a pedagogical dilemma: that, in this fantasy formation, 'students were missing, as was the teacher' (114). Under the weight of her curriculum, Britzman found a wish for no students at all. As she constructs it, 'there were no students to relate to, and no emotional states to explore' (115).

Here we can detect evidence of one of *the* defining conflicts of Green's 'dead mother' complex, now in the pedagogical relation: where the teacher feels single-handedly responsible for recusing students from a ruined world, and in that altruistic effort, ironically, sustains her/his own existence. Another way to think about the paradox is that the urgency of the teacher's pedagogical presence is marked by absence, or in Green's language, a kind of emotional death. And indeed, this might be what Britzman ([1991] 2003, 123, my emphasis) means in her observation that becoming a teacher can feel like '*not* becoming who you are'. Britzman's (2006) memoir bravely narrates this psychical compromise at the heart of her early efforts in teaching. In trading the complexity of emotional life for the fantasied certainty of the teacher's institutional role, Britzman finds she could not imagine what both teaching and learning could mean outside of the orbit of her own ideals. Indeed, Britzman realises her ideal pedagogy carried the wish that there would be no conflict between learning and teaching. 'I was convinced', she recalls, 'that students who signed up for the course would already be interested in my ideal pedagogy' (114). Not only that, she recalls her wish that the course title alone could magically communicate, 'the whole story of what students could expect to learn' (114) without the thought of what students would want from monsters in literature and from their teacher.

Thinking back to the aforementioned dialogue on depression, there are at least two interpretive points of departure to note: first, Britzman's memoir offers support to the idea that the teacher's emotional life is not simply a private matter but rather touched by the history of the profession and the silent demands of those who inherit its traditions. That is, in narrating her early performance of pedagogical certainty, Britzman calls attention to 'the history of the profession's conflicts' and the deadening ideals of perfect knowledge and authority that teachers 'absorb' and act out 'without even knowing' (117). Under the condition of this unconscious inheritance, the teacher 'absorbs' the profession's history that demands, to a degree, the loss of emotional life and defences against that loss: 'feeling as if they created from their isolation, helplessness and dependency a mythic, heroic and so omnipotent self' (117). From this vantage, the figure of the heroic teacher can be read as a melancholic materialisation of the profession's denial of emotional life, and that the teacher repeats in the performance of invulnerability. And yet, through her fall into a 'depressing curriculum', Britzman parts company from theorists who prop up melancholia as a resource for political possibility, noting how, in her own pedagogy, that very condition defended against encountering the sadness of loss through the idealisation in curriculum (115).

This brings me to a second interpretive layer, for Britzman's narrative also illustrates a central paradox that mirrors the logic of the fantasy formation set down by the 'dead mother'. Intent on rescuing students from past and future ruin, Britzman finds that she was actually rescuing herself from the anxiety she felt in the face of her failing omnipotence. The paradox is that in rescuing the other, Britzman recognizes that she had tried to sustain her fragile ego boundaries. On this one-way street, student resistance was read as further evidence of the need for the teacher's rescue fantasy, or, in Britzman's construction: 'what I thought of as replacing their denial of false consciousness with my depressing truth' (115). But her one-way street was perhaps also a dead end, for Britzman claims she could not admit that the 'subversive activity' she wanted for her pedagogy harboured 'something conservative' (118), which demanded allegiance to her existing views. Caught in the glare of idealisation, Britzman admits that her younger self could only defend against the failure of her curriculum to change her students' minds. Every Monday morning, there was Britzman's disappointed pedagogy and her students' eager defiance.

Britzman did not find relief from her teaching until her university supervisor recognised her trouble and offered an interpretation. Through this interpretive support entered the witness, or 'outsideness', needed for the teacher to find distance from herself and make insight where there was the loss of meaning (Kennedy 2010, 112). As Britzman (2006, 119) recalls: 'The supervisor's interpretation of my struggle fell into one sentence: "Deborah, not all monsters are political"'. At first, Britzman admits that she was too angry to make sense of this intervention. But it was perhaps through this aggression, and her supervisor's survival of it, that Britzman could, many years later, bring insight to the absence of her beginnings, which she had at the time 'filled in' with monsters (Green 1980, 183). Through a belated symbolisation of the other's interpretation of her teaching trouble, Britzman (2006) could begin to mourn the loss of idealisation that had protected her from representing a relationship to pedagogy's lack. Here, in the capacity to think about her depression, she writes, she learned that her furor had been a defence against the very thought of loss – and the loss of thought itself – in the effort to represent its significance in curriculum. Her defence, as she puts it, 'was to render everything political' (118) rather than encounter the teacher's 'use of her own unconscious wishes' in the production of curriculum and pedagogy (108).

Cast in relation to the aforementioned discussions of melancholia, Britzman's memoir stands as evidence of negative affect as an effect of the many and devastating losses that make up history. But, taken through the lens of Green's 'dead mother', it also illustrates the negativity of melancholia's effects. That is, while Britzman's curriculum can be read as an emotional response to the historical losses she wanted to represent, she does not privilege melancholia as a site of learning or critique. Rather, Britzman's memoir stands as evidence of the negative effects of negative affect in the pedagogical relation. The point here is that in the materialisation of historical and social loss in curriculum, the students may also encounter the teacher's dis-connection from the emotional states that loss ushers in. And so while Britzman's memoir lends support to the idea that negative affect is an important reminder of forgotten history and a residue of encountering social and political conflict, it also shows how the insistence on its political valence hinders emotional insight: in Britzman's case, the furor to teach hindered her capacity to notice how students *did* make a relationship to historical loss, in spite of her idealisation of curriculum. What emerges from Britzman's memoir is, then, a story of teaching trapped in uncanny time, where 'loaded affects' overwhelm the capacity to make emotional insight from loss, producing instead idealisations that defend against the risk of forging new attachments, to history and to students, in the aftermath of what is no longer here.

Britzman's pedagogy came alive many years later, when she says she finally could let go of some of the glamour of her young curriculum and allow herself to feel the sadness of that effort. Her charged pedagogy came alive after she could mourn the 'loss of omnipotence' in the face of historical loss and in her own effort to teach (115). After such loss, Britzman claims that she could then face the vulnerability and lack she covered over with the defensiveness of her helping hand. But, if Britzman made insight from her 'childhood of teaching' (108), it was not on the electric current of affect alone. Indeed, *precisely because* Britzman was so affected by her curriculum, she argues that she could not yet know its emotional significance for the students or for herself. In this way her memoir cautions against the rush to affect as the foundation of insight. She reminds us that the ground of insight is the capacity to work affect through language, and that requires the distance afforded by time and the other, and in particular, the other's survival of aggression. In the case of Britzman, survival came in the form of non-retaliatory supervision and in her students' non-compliance. Only when she could let inside the outsideness of the other could Britzman narrate a history made from the emotional situation of losing one's footing in trying to get a hold on – in order to teach – a world of lost others.

When Britzman could let go of her idealized curriculum, she began to see that both she and her students had minds of their own. And, because Britzman 'could not take credit for their existence' (117), she recalls learning what the students *did* learn in spite of her fantasied intentions:

> They were mesmerized by split personalities and often felt like Dr. Jekyll and Mr. Hyde. They took great pleasure in narrating this monstrous change in parents and teachers and had a great deal to say about the insecurity of their own emotional states. And no matter how difficult the prose, how archaic the English, they read on, enjoying the suspense, identifying with what was monstrous in themselves and others, but not because they needed to change the world. Just the opposite, they wanted the world to take them in. (117)

In the end, Britzman learns that her students used monsters in literature to identify with what was monstrous within themselves. And in her learning, Britzman comes to understand why it is important for adults, too, to 'care for' what is monstrous in their efforts to care for others (116). Where idealisation was, the vulnerabilities and losses of the pedagogical relation could now be. There, too, traces of historical loss could now be picked up and renewed in the imagination of generations left behind. And, from this emotional insight, Britzman could now write a history not about what students failed to learn, nor even what they learned correctly because of their teacher, but rather, how learning itself emerges belatedly from the failure of the teacher's idealisation of knowledge to stave off the uncertain 'emotional situation' that curricular encounters with loss also generate (Britzman 2009, xi).

An un-dead ending: toward a lively education

Education is a rich site for a whole range of fantasy formations: if we are willing to go deep enough we can uncover the Oedipal desire, matricide, 'dead mother' and other 'monsters' silently waiting to occupy the teaching relation. The 'dead mother' narrates a story of how negative affect sets down a fantasy structure that turns away from the pain of loss even if its plotline repeats some of what has been repressed in the form of splitting and idealisation. The fantasy turns monstrous not only in the idealised effort to rescue history from what has already occurred, but also in the use of students to rescue the teacher from her/his own aggressive tendencies: embodied in the fantasies of rescue. But there is more, for as Pitt intimates, the teacher who denies her own aggression hinders the students' matricidal rite of passage needed to become a self and to forge emotional bonds to the world. The fact that Britzman's students did not comply with her curriculum suggests that she did, in fact, embody enough aggression to allow for their experiments in matricide. Thinking back on this experience, Britzman pinpoints the moment her students came alive to her, and she to herself: when she realised that both her supervisor and students could survive the aggressive reach of her efforts, without the certain ruin that she imagined and then tried to fend off in the tireless effort to teach. That is, Britzman found that in the face of historical loss, learning could survive. There, the frozen truths of her idealised curriculum could be enlivened and renewed by the 'distressing, unbearable, deadly and exhilarating' qualities of trying to live after and learn from historical loss (Kristeva 2010, 5).

In bringing the 'dead mother' to the scene of education, I am not referring to an actual teacher who is 'burned out' or to blame for difficult experiences in learning. Rather, through Green's concept and Britzman's memoir, I am describing some of the features of fantasy and defense produced in the context of pedagogical relationships affected by loss. The lesson of the 'dead mother' is difficult: where the teacher cannot let go of idealised knowledge, including the idealised knowledge of loss, s/he does so at the risk of deadening the complexity of emotional states, including her own, that loss also calls forth. Negative affect cannot be a condition for learning when it is a conduit for idealisation, which, in Britzman's memoir, took shape as politicisation. Her memoir compels because it narrates teaching as a dilemma of making meaning from affects that both animate pedagogy and elude significance at 'the time of their unfolding' (Britzman 2006, 107). In hindsight, Britzman teaches us that such insight is only possible in belated time, once the duration of time and the survival of the other can loosen the spellbinding quality of melancholia. From the aesthetic distance afforded by these conditions, Britzman could encounter the anguish of loss that she argues her insistence on the political fended off. But for all this discussion of failure, there is also a story of hope: when the teacher can bear the loss of her own omnipotence, then there can begin the interminable work of facing in thoughtful ways the fragile, and at times monstrous, foundations of being in the human profession of education and learning from the myriad losses of history encountered there.

References

Ahmed, Sara. 2010. *The Promise of Happiness*. Durham: Duke University Press.
Appel, Michael. 1999. "The Teacher's Headache." In *Psychoanalysis and Pedagogy*, edited by Michael Appel, 133–146. Westport: CT.
Bibby, Tamara. 2011. *Education – An 'Impossible Profession'? Psychoanalytic Explorations of Learning and Classrooms*. New York: Routledge.
Boler, Megan. 1999. *Feeling Power: Emotions and Education*. New York: Routledge.

Britzman, Deborah. 1991/2003. *Practice Makes Practice: A Critical Study of Learning to Teach*. Revised Edition. Albany, New York: State University of New York Press.

Britzman, D. 2000. "If the Story Cannot End: Deferred Action, Ambivalence and Difficult Knowledge." In *Between Hope and Despair: Pedagogy and the Remembrance of Historical Trauma*, edited by Roger I. Simon, Sharon Rosenberg and Claudia Eppert, 27–58. New Jersey: Rowan & Littlefield.

Britzman, Deborah. 2006. "Monsters in Literature." In *Novel Education: Psychoanalytic Studies of Learning and Not Learning*. New York: Peter Lang.

Britzman, Deborah. 2009. *The Very Thought of Education*. Albany: State University of New York Press.

Brown, Wendy. 2003. "Resisting Left Melancholia." In *Loss: The Politics of Mourning*, edited by David Eng and David Kazanjian, 458–466. Berkeley: University of California Press.

Cvetkovich, Ann. 2012. *Depression: A Public Feeling*. Durham: Duke University Press.

Delpit, Lisa, and Joanne Kilgour Dowdy, eds. 2002. *The Skin That We Speak: Thoughts on Language and Culture in the Classroom*. New York: The New Press.

Eng, David, and David Kazanjian. 2003. "Mourning Remains." In *Loss: The Politics of Mourning*, edited by D. Eng and D. Kazanjian, 1–28. Berkeley: University of California Press.

Farley, Lisa. 2009. "Radical Hope: On the Problem of Uncertainty in History Education." *Curriculum Inquiry* 39 (4): 537–554.

Farley, Lisa. 2012. "An Essay is Being Written: Between Aggression and 'Just words'." *Changing English: Studies in Culture and Education* 21 (3): 21–43.

Freud, Anna. 1936/1993. "A Form of Altruism." In *The Ego and Mechanisms of Defense*, trans. Cecil Baines, 122–136. London: Karnac.

Freud, Sigmund. 1911/2006. "Formulations on the Two Principles of Mental Functioning." In *Penguin Freud Reader*, edited by A. Phillips, 414–421. London, UK: Penguin.

Freud, Sigmund. 1917/2005. "Mourning and Melancholia." In *On Murder, Mourning and Melancholia*, edited by A. Phillips and translated by, S. Whiteside (trans), 201–218. London, UK: Penguin.

Green, André. 1980. "The Dead Mother." In *Life Narcissism, Death Narcissism*, trans. edited by Andrew Weller, 170–200. London: Free Association Books.

Horowitz, Allan V., and Jerome C. Wakefield. 2007. *The Loss of Sadness: How Psychiatry Transformed Normal Sorrow into Depressive Disorder*. Oxford: Oxford University Press.

Kennedy, RM. 2010. "National Dreams and Inconsolable Losses: The Burden of Melancholia in Newfoundland Culture." In *Despite This Loss: Essays on Culture, Memory, and Identity in Newfoundland and Labrador*, edited by A.M. Ursula A. Kelly and Elizabeth Yeoman, 103–116. St. John's, NL: Iser Books.

Kristeva, Julia. 1989. *Black Sun: Depression and Melancholia*. New York: Columbia University Press.

Kristeva, Julia. 2001. *Melanie Klein, Trans*. R. Guberman. New York: Columbia University Press.

Kristeva, Julia. 2002. *Intimate Revolt: The Powers and Limits of Psychoanalysis, Trans*. Jeanne Herman. New York: Columbian University Press.

Kristeva, Julia. 2010. *Hatred and Forgiveness*. New York: Columbia University Press.

Lawrence-Lightfoot, Sara. 2003. *The Essential Conversation: What Parents and Teachers Can Learn from Each Other*. New York: Random House.

Matthews, Sara. 2004. "Some Notes on Hate in Teaching." *Psychoanalysis, Culture and Society* 12: 185–192.

Noddings, Nel. 2003. *Happiness and Education*. Cambridge: Cambridge University Press.

Pitt, Alice. 2003. *The Play of the Personal: Psychoanalytic Narratives of Feminist Education*. New York: Peter Lang.

Pitt, Alice. 2004. "Reading women's Autobiography: On Losing and Refinding the Mother." *Changing English: an International Journal of English Teaching* 11 (2): 267–277.

Pitt, Alice, and Deborah Britzman. 2003. "Speculations on the Qualities of Difficult Knowledge in Teaching and Learning: An Experiment in Psychoanalytic Research." *International Journal of Qualitative Studies in Education* 16 (6): 755–776.

Salvio, Paula. 2007. *Anne Sexton: Teacher of Weird Abundance*. Albany: State University of New York Press.

Silin, Jonathan. 1995. *Sex, Death, and the Education of Children: Our Passion for Ignorance in the Age of AIDS*. New York: Teachers College Press.

Simon, Roger I. 2005. *The Touch of the Past: Remembrance, Learning, Ethics*. New York: Palgrave.

Simon, Roger I., Sharon Rosenberg, and Claudia Eppert. 2000. "Introduction." In *Between Hope and Despair: Pedagogy and the Remembrance of Historical Trauma*, edited by Simon, Roger I., Sharon Rosenberg, and Claudia Eppert, eds. 1–15. New Jersey: Rowan & Littlefield.

Taubman, Peter. 2006. "I Love Them to Death." In *Love's Return: Psychoanalytic Essays on Childhood, Teaching and Learning*, edited by Paula M. Salvio and Gail M. Boldt, 19–32. New York: Routldge.

The Guardian. Last successful download 20 May 2013 from: http://www.guardian.co.uk/science/blog/2013/may/20/mental-illnesses-depression-pms-culturally-determined

Todd, Sharon. 2003. *Learning from the Other: Levinas, Psychoanalysis and Ethical Possibilities in Education*. Albany: State University of New York.

Waddell, Margot. 2000. *Inside Lives: Psychoanalysis and the Growth of the Personality*. London: Karnac.

Winnicott, D. W. 1939/1989. "Early Disillusion." In *Psychoanalytic Explorations*, edited by Clare Winnicott, Ray Shepherd and Madeleine Davis, 21–23. Cambridge: Harvard University.

Winnicott, D. W. 1963/1986. "The Value of Depression." In *Home is Where We Start from: Essays by a Psychoanalyst*, edited by Clare Winnicott, Ray Shepherd and Madeleine Davis, 71–79. New York: W. W. Norton & Company.

Winnicott, D. W. 1967/1971. Mirror Role of Mother and Family in Child Development. In Playing and Reality, 111–118. New York: Brunner-Routledge.

Explorations in knowing: thinking psychosocially about legitimacy

Anne Chappell, Paul Ernest, Geeta Ludhra and Heather Mendick

School of Sport and Education, Brunel University, London, UK

> In this paper, we look at what engaging with psychoanalysis, through psychosocial accounts of subjectivity, has contributed to our struggles for legitimacy and security within our ways of knowing. The psychosocial, with its insistence on the unconscious and the irrational, features as both a source of security and of insecurity. We use three examples drawn from our own empirical research to explore the entanglement of the researcher with the researched and how this can offer a re-imagined sense of legitimacy for our work. In elaborating our argument, we discuss our experiences of 'being captured' by data and participants, and of negotiating the ethics of analysing participants' accounts.

Introduction

As the Brunel Education Theory Reading Group, we have been engaging with writings that offer perspectives on the relationship between structure and agency. In particular, we have become interested in psychosocial accounts of 'identity', subjectivity and 'voice'. Poststructuralist accounts of subjectivity have resonated most with us in our discussions, although we have struggled to come to terms with and sometimes overcome the essentialist assumptions about meaning and knowledge in some everyday and academic discourses (Davies and Petersen 2004; Henriques et al. 1998; Rose 1989). We are grappling with theories that offer lenses through which to interpret our research, in relation to the objects and subjects of our studies, and our own identities as researchers. As a group, we have posed questions about: *Ontology* – what is psychosocial being? *Epistemology* – how and what can we know and what are the limits to our knowledge and knowing? *Methodology* – what means of knowledge construction can or should we use? *Ethics* – in 'reading' our participants' narratives, to what degree do we impose our meanings over theirs? Running through our conversations are questions about legitimacy and processes of legitimation – of our-selves, our research and this paper itself. It is these questions on which

---

This is an Open Access article. Non-commercial re-use, distribution, and reproduction in any medium, provided the original work is properly attributed, cited, and is not altered, transformed, or built upon in any way, is permitted. The moral rights of the named author(s) have been asserted.

we focus here, looking specifically at how engaging with the psychoanalytic within psychosocial frameworks can help us to explore them. So, while there are differences in our positions, we came to a collective voice built within the Theory Reading Group activities and extended through this interactive writing process.

Some of these questions are addressed by theoretical perspectives under the umbrella of poststructuralism. We welcomed the poststructuralist acknowledgment of the multiple codings and meanings in texts, thus including both the structural and the personal. It also acknowledges that all human knowledge consists of disciplined narratives with their own legitimation criteria, challenging universal standards (Lyotard 1984). But poststructuralism does not provide us with adequately articulated conceptions of 'identity' or subjectivity. The way subject positions are called up within it has been termed the 'jukebox' theory of identity (Wetherell 2012, 122), failing to address how people come to take up one position rather than another. Theorists using psychoanalysis provide ways of exploring how people become drawn to some discourses rather than others (e.g. Henriques et al. 1998; Walkerdine 1997).

This is why psychosocial approaches appeal to us. As Bibby (2011, 9) says 'we are psychosocial beings ... to study either sociology or psychology ... is a form of splitting and misses the ways in which the internal and the external, the private and public, the individual and the social are deeply mutually implicated'. In addition, psychosocial approaches acknowledge the central role of the unconscious in supplying human desires, motives and actions that follow 'irrational' logics, different from the dominant logic of reason. As Butler (1997, 86) argues, the psyche 'is precisely what exceeds the imprisoning effects of the discursive demands to inhabit a coherent identity, to become a coherent subject'. Our idea of unconscious is a socially embedded one, in which 'psychic processes form a central component of how social and cultural fantasies work' and through which the discursive environment becomes a 'melting pot of psychical conditions of possibility' (Walkerdine 1997, 184–5). However, we still have a shared ambivalence about the unconscious. As something that is fundamentally unknowable, how can we legitimately include it in our research except as something negative – the dark absence that surrounds our lit-up domains of knowledge?

Despite such doubts, we were captured by the theme of the 2012 Psychosocial Studies Network Conference (which was the point of origin of this special issue) – connected to our shared readings – and by each other – exploring the relationship between the social and the individual – and the need to think both together. But we had concerns about our own legitimacy within the space: engaging in psychosocial thinking without a psychoanalytic background. We still have those concerns. Here we are picking up on them in relation to one set of questions posed at the Conference: Do we need the authority of legitimised institutions and regularised methods to build secure knowledge? What might it mean to build insecure edifices of knowledge?

Articulating the psycho and the social together is the basis for our discussions. Our understandings of legitimacy are through discourse, knowledge/power and subjectivity in a psychosocial sense. By discourse we mean not only all the semiotic forms of representation and communication entailed, but also the illocutionary force of language that enacts power, makes positions available/unavailable, and socially and psychologically positions speakers and listeners. We are each aware that the social world is saturated with powerful formations of knowledge that colonise individual and institutional identities. Some knowledge emerges as legitimised and authoritative; other knowledge is resisted or repressed. Thus, we are aware that showing the personal in our research reports is risky and can lead to struggles over what is acceptable as legitimate knowledge for publication. But even this liberalisation of our narratives involves a further, hidden repression of the personal. Several of us are suffering with work-induced stress and overtiredness as we write this paper. We are working in the English university context, under the weight of Ofsted inspections of Initial Teacher Education, the Research Excellence Framework that audits research outputs, and other forms of surveillance, 'accountability' and control. Being rendered silent by the weight of an institution that demands superhuman workloads and outputs is not a legitimate topic for discussion (rare exceptions are the papers by Davies and Peterson [2004] and Sparkes [2007]). Despite well-established psychological research that excess pressure and stress kill creativity, the knowledge monster demands to be fed.

As a group, we draw on our own histories and understandings in discussing and responding to our shared readings; we identify how these feed into the examples in this paper below. Engaging in reflexive research foregrounds issues of our-selves as knowers and experts. How do our subjectivities shape our research, and how aware are we of this? How confident are we entitled to be about our interpretations of both our readings and our data? What insecurities emerge around the limits of our knowledge? We each have different positions, as academics and human beings, and different narratives about our-selves. We each have allegiances to different professional and personal communities, and seeing ourselves as central or, more often peripheral, within them, has a significant impact on our perceptions of the security of our knowing.

To keep silent about our own active engagement in our research is to sacrifice honesty about the limits of our knowing in a quest for spurious authority and objectivity. It is to suppress doubts and anxieties about the legitimacy of the stories we tell and our right to tell them. Protocols of academic publication often demand the depersonalisation and objectification of our stories but here we let the presence of the researcher – with her self-awareness, doubts and assumptions – show through.

About us and our contributions

Paul is the most experienced academic in the group and feels that he is viewed as a reservoir of knowledge by the others. He has self-doubts about the legitimacy of his positioning as a philosophical expert within the group and within mathematics education circles. However, he is excited by new theories and ideas, and enjoys discussing and sharing them with the reading group, describing what he gains as 'intellectual entertainment'. The discussions help him to question his own long-held assumptions and reframe his understandings of issues. The idea of inserting oneself into a research narrative, as here, appeals as a way of making reporting more honest and self-aware. A central theme in Paul's work has been to question the received view of mathematics as infallibly certain. A psychosocial perspective enables him to see that that the assertion of absolutism in mathematics is not merely a rationally held position, but a defence against the threat of the unbearable knowledge that mathematics, like all other knowledge, is irrational, fallible and socially constructed (Walkerdine 1988).

Geeta was drawn to the psychosocial through an interest in the embodied self and her narrative study with 12 'successful' South Asian girls (Ludhra and Chappell 2011). The interactional aspects of her fieldwork acted as a catalyst for revisiting 'girlhood ghosts' and entering the 'darker' areas of the psyche (Walkerdine, Melody, and Lucey 2003). Initially, Geeta felt uncomfortable about writing the self into her research, particularly within the dominant research culture where legitimacy and secure knowledge are read in ways that exclude the personal. In the first section of this paper, we will draw on her experiences to discuss the psychological impact of repression, and learning what not to say (Billig 2006). We will discuss the process of becoming a different type of researcher – one that feels more 'ontologically secure' (Laing 1960) and acknowledges the researcher's own subjectivities – through entering particular research spaces that provide opportunities for 'breathing' and 'thinking' beyond discursive accounts. Finally, we will discuss particular episodes of 'being captured' by research participants whose experiences connect with aspects of the researcher's life. Being captured is an affective response to data described by MacLure (2013), who invokes us to spend more time with those data 'hot spots' which 'glow' as we engage in fieldwork and analysis.

Anne is concerned with developing knowledge about teachers' experiences of professional learning through a sociological approach. From her experiences of working in school, she had felt that teachers were 'missing persons' in both policy and practice (Evans 1999), which she sought to address through her methodology. Her key methodological concern was to understand the teacher's narrated experiences and the meanings they made of these (Craib 2001; MacLure 1993). In the second section of this paper, we will share data from one of the teachers, whom Anne has called Nell, to illustrate the way in which the research process appeared to have 'worked' and the subsequent methodological disruption that resulted following discussions within the Theory Reading Group. The exploration of psychosocial, and specifically psychoanalytic, ideas prompted a way of looking at the analysis differently (MacLure 2006). Taking account of possible psychosocial readings of both process and data troubled Anne by posing a challenge to the legitimacy that could be claimed (Bibby 2009; Henriques et al. 1998).

After some 'identity work', Heather has positioned herself as a sociologist of education. She is drawn to psychoanalytic ideas for what they offer to her thinking about 'agency' and, in particular, for how they offer 'thought experiments' that have the potential to move her to other than 'commonsense' understandings. For example, she has argued that they can challenge us to see ignorance as an active refusal of knowledge rather than as a passive, negative state (Mendick 2006): 'in this question, the desire for ignorance is performative rather than cognitive. It is indicative of the incapacity – or the unwillingness – to acknowledge one's own implication in the material studied' (Luhmann 1998, 149). In the third section, we will discuss Heather's analysis of 'someone else's data'. We will explore how she 'was captured' by one participant, whom she has called Lola, and how this capturing can offer a form of legitimacy. We also use Heather's analysis of Lola to raise some tensions that we experience between psychoanalytic and sociological explanations within the psychosocial.

Although we have written this paper in a single voice, there are tensions between these accounts. In particular, Geeta's sense of 'ontological security' contrasts with Anne and Heather working in parallel with two different interpretations.

Becoming 'legitimate' and feeling 'secure': acknowledging the unconscious

In this section, we will discuss how psychosocial approaches can offer necessary alternatives to objectivity as a means of gaining legitimacy and security in our knowing. We do this through exploring Geeta's changing relationship to her narrative research with 12 academically 'successful' South Asian girls. When Geeta began her study, the routine completion of the university ethics form did not engage her in the 'deeper' psychological difficulties associated with becoming tangled in 'herstory'. But the processes involved made this inevitable (Ludhra 2011; Ludhra and Chappell 2011). At times, resurrecting 'girlhood ghosts' felt painful and emotionally overwhelming, and she felt a desire to 'put a lid' on them. These emotional engagements with her data provoked the following reactions from some senior academic others: 'That's contamination!'; 'Beware of falling into that trap – it's risky!'; 'You could lose respect for writing like that'. These discursive utterances were embodied, and made Geeta feel apprehensive and insecure about asserting the contribution to knowledge that emerged from her subjective, more insecure ways of knowing.

Skeggs (1997) writes powerfully about white working-class women's negotiations of respectability through dress, voice, talk and social life generally. In similar ways, Geeta, in attempting to become academically 'respectable', learned to repress parts of her-self. We can understand this in two ways. First, we draw on our collective reading of Billig's (2006) re-interpretation of Freudian repression. Billig acknowledges the importance of what is unsaid, but rejects Freud's idea of unconscious repression, adapting repression from something that is 'psychic', 'ghostly' and 'hidden', to 'an activity that is constituted within everyday language' (22). Billig's adaptation usefully focuses on the discursive processes through which repression happens, where language is both expressive and repressive. He draws our attention to the discursive process of 'learning to repress' within dominant cultures (22). This social behaviour serves to 'other' individuals, potentially making them feel 'inferior' or 'insecure' about their knowledge contributions. It also serves to 'other' some ways of knowing in preference for those that work alongside dominant discourses.

Our collective discussion of Billig helped us to understand the processes through which 'objectivity', 'elimination of bias' and 'uncontaminated data' have become dominant goals within educational research. However, his ideas did not seem enough to encompass what happens when our own repressed experiences are ignited through research interactions. So, in a move to which we imagine Billig would object, we supplement his discursive conception of repression with a psychic one (Frosh 2001).

The critical utterances mentioned above were tied to Geeta's institutional position and led her to believe that it was wrong to write or publicly discuss the self within particular spaces as it could challenge her position as a secure, legitimate and respectable academic. These complex emotions of 'unleashing' repressed experiences – whilst not knowing what to do with them when they were 'out in the open' – complicated her readings of the data. This made it feel dense, cloudy and difficult to analyse, as she got involved in 'conversations' with her participants, which we discuss later through the stories of Rohini and Maheera. This denseness slowed her progress and was experienced through a constant weighted feeling in the body and mind. Within what felt like a mess, Geeta felt a constant desire to detangle, almost to decontaminate the data, by removing any imprints of the self. These messages, about the need to decontaminate were being conveyed by those who shared dominant research positions; so Geeta learned to hold back and write apprehensively, with caution, 'hiding' those more insecure areas of experience. This proved an impossible task, and so began a quest to understand the unreasonable, the unconscious and unsaid (Frosh 2001). We have all had similar experiences to Geeta, and other work supports the assertion that people's lives are 'fraught with uncertainties, anxieties and puzzles' (Craib 2001, 72). The question lies in how individuals professionally manage those uncertainties of inner lives when academic structures and practices encourage us to *repress*, rather than *express*.

Engaging with the past through writing in her research journal, and through discussions with significant others (her husband and a few close friends), felt therapeutic and emancipatory (hooks 1996; Hollway, Lucey, and Phoenix 2007). This suggests the relationality of legitimacy and how it is negotiated within diverse communities. For Geeta, it was the start of a journey where she actively sought research spaces and academics (through collaborative writing experiences like this paper) that opened up avenues for her own subjectivity and expressive thinking. Geeta (with Anne) joined the British Sociological Association Auto/Biography Study Group. This is a small, yet highly experienced, group of researchers who value narrative research and different ways of thinking and reflecting on their-selves. Their annual conference provided an innovative platform for experimenting in these areas. Geeta presented there (Ludhra and Chappell 2010; Ludhra 2011, 2012) and the group have led her towards literature that opened up her 'sociological imagination' (Wright Mills 1959). Like Bibby (2011), Geeta found herself feeling dissatisfied with theories from educational and sociological literatures alone, as the discursive and structural elements restricted her explanations of experience (Frosh 2001).

Geeta engaged in discussions with Brunel youth work colleagues and they directed her reading towards feminist work, particularly literature that acknowledged psychosocial dimensions (e.g. Walkerdine, Melody, and Lucey 2003). Geeta was particularly drawn to the work of Black feminists and the ways in which they wrote and spoke with honesty, conviction and openness (Bhopal 2010; hooks 1996; Maylor 2009; Mirza 2009, 2013). She met some of them in person, and saw their work as brave, yet secure. They gave her confidence to write with greater authority. These Black feminist writers have discussed theory in ways which moved beyond sociological meanings of structure, gendered oppression and patriarchy, to incorporate 'embodied intersectionality' and deeper psychological experiences (Mirza 2013, 5; see also Ahmed 2009; Maylor and Williams 2011).

As signposted in the introduction, as four authors, we are part of the Brunel Theory Reading Group. Our monthly discussions have provided a critical, yet 'safe' space for being creative and experimenting. Both Geeta and Anne came together before the group formed, through their methodological connectedness in narrative research. They started to write together and provided mutual moral and psychological support (Ludhra and Chappell 2011). These and many others have provided an enhanced sense of legitimacy about writing about those more ethically challenging areas of research (Rogers and Ludhra 2011). These collaborations led Geeta towards acknowledging her own subjective identifications with her participants, and how she felt herself 'being captured' by two of them.

Maheera and Rohini were catalytic in igniting aspects of Geeta's girlhood. They were of Muslim religious background and grounded in Islam in very different ways – Maheera seeing it as a 'supportive and colourful religion', whereas Rohini compared it to a 'culture knife' and 'poison', depicting it as some oppressive being. In very different manners, they (like Geeta) discussed notions of respectability, doing the 'right' thing for others, struggle and sacrifice – aspects that Geeta could relate to, although she had never felt grounded in religion. Both girls aspired to become lawyers, and discussed their desire to 'fight for justice' and equality; interestingly, Geeta perceived them both as suffering from particular injustices. The fundamental difference between the girls was how they perceived and articulated aspects of their gendered and religio-cultural subjectivities.

Geeta identified with Rohini and Maheera in multiple ways: they evoked feelings of pity and worry, and a genuine (maternal) concern for their possible futures, particularly how they would manage their academic and career choices, alongside being successful in the extended family and community. She admired their strong work ethic, stamina and desire to become successful in challenging circumstances; Geeta's 'success journey' mirrored aspects of their desires and experiences. Like Geeta's girlhood, both girls carried heavy household responsibilities – both practical and psychological. They were expected to have 'arranged marriages' within 'traditional' Islamic families. Rohini was a resistor, challenger and questioner – she would get angry, frustrated and annoyed when she saw injustice or inequality, but she said that she only shared these emotions with Geeta. While vocal and authoritative in the school and research contexts, at home she described embodying these feelings in silent psychological ways, banking them for the right moment – when, as she put it, she would possibly 'explode'.

In contrast, Maheera conveyed a spiritual sense of calmness to Geeta, and she seemed to embrace aspects of her religion, culture and family in very positive ways. She described the carer role that she adopted for her sick father and younger siblings (particularly her new baby brother), as something that she enjoyed, and from which she gained satisfaction. Aspects of this evoked pity in Geeta, yet made her feel angry too, as she sensed that Maheera could achieve so much more academically, if she was given the time and space to do so. But who was Geeta to comment on either of them? Yet, the fact that she had once travelled their roads, and been accepting of injustice herself, seemed to offer her a particular type of legitimacy through entanglement, rather than contamination. Maheera reminded Geeta of her pre-marital and early married years of womanhood. In contrast, Geeta connected to the anger of Rohini, who reminded her of her later married years of psychologically challenging and resisting particular cultural structures and norms. She found that her research journal began to include these personal evocations and records of her emotions, through interacting and reflecting on the girls in her study.

Another fundamental shared experience with both girls relates to feelings of having/being a girl, and the inequalities associated with facets of girlhood. Rohini talked openly about the responsibility associated with being the older sister to two 'spoiled' brothers and a traditional father. She talked at length about her lack of status in the family. Maheera spoke adoringly of her baby brother being born after two teenage sisters, and the joy of having a son in the family for her parents. There was an absolute adoration of this son/brother. This desire for a boy was something to which Geeta could relate as she had embodied and repressed particular messages from more authoritative others within her family after the birth of her two daughters. This parallels how she had resisted writing to suit authoritative others in the academic space; she resisted living her life for authoritative others in the family, simply to suit cultural expectations.

Geeta's story suggests the potential of psychosocial approaches for developing a sense of legitimacy within the educational research community. It shows how they opened up a space to explore the irrational that exceeds the discursive. Anne's story, in the next section, describes her contrasting experience, in which thinking psychosocially disrupted her nascent understanding of the legitimacy of her re-presentations of her participants.

Methodological legitimacy: a self-fulfilling prophecy?

In this section, we consider the extent to which participants can be understood to recognise themselves through particular research processes, and the potential for a researcher's desires to become self-fulfilling (Henriques 1998; Walkerdine 1988). If the individual is understood as 'neither totally powerful or powerless but fragmentary and positioned and repositioned from one moment to the next' (Henriques et al. 1998, 225), what can be known and knowable about our participants? How do we address this question when we have a significant sense of personal responsibility to the research process, and accountability to our participants from first contact through every subsequent stage (Andrews 2007)? We explore these questions through Anne's study with teachers. We begin by detailing her methodology to give a sense of how this responsibility was enacted and the depth of the disruption that the psychosocial can bring.

Anne was committed to finding an 'alternative' methodology to generate knowledge about teachers' understandings of their professional learning. In response to the neoliberal policy climate and the 'missing persons' in policy and practice (Evans 1999), the key challenge of the research process was for her to be able to explore 'the relationship between the state, the ideologies of professionalism, and lived interiority' (Hey and Bradford 2004, 693). This was a project arising both from Anne's own experience as a teacher in a secondary school and her theoretical interest in the substantive concern. On the basis of the policy context and the literature, Anne was concerned to avoid a reduction of the teacher-participants' experiences. This deep commitment to reflexivity about the philosophical and ethical stance of the researcher is shared by each of us in slightly different ways. In Anne's case it raised a crucial methodological question about the spaces we can create for our participants' self-analysis and how we can reflect these in our co-constructed re-presentations of them.

Anne's intention in undertaking three research conversations with each of her participants at fortnightly intervals over a six-week period was to facilitate narrative accounts of experience and meaning making (MacLure 1993). In order to focus the participants on the meaning they made of their experiences, they were given an audio-recording and written transcript of the previous conversation and invited to consider it before meeting to talk further. Each conversation was led by their reflections on the previous conversation(s) (Ludhra and Chappell 2011).

This attempt to enact a deep ethical commitment brought with it anxieties and fears about the legitimacy of working with an untried process. However, as Anne spent time engaged in the conversations, she felt that the extent to which the participants were able, or perhaps enabled, to talk and explain themselves was significant and began to feel a new-found confidence in the process and its potential.

One such example comes from Nell, who offered an account that suggested she understood herself in a very specific way as being boring. This was apparent from the outset of the first conversation when she said 'Yeah, I'm just worried about boring you like I said'. When she was thanked at the end of the conversation with a comment from Anne that 'it had been really interesting', she responded with 'Liar'. At this stage in the research, Nell's identification of herself as boring was interpreted as being offered unreflexively. In the second conversation, she began to narrate her thoughts when commenting on listening to the transcript of the first. She said 'obviously last week chatting through, that was alright, obviously I did, I was worried about being boring'. Later in that conversation she returned to her understanding of herself when she asked Anne, 'are you bored yet?' Subsequently, she went on to offer an account of the way in which she understood herself to have chosen a particular presentation of the self. This started to pose questions about the extent to which she sought to offer an explanation for some of the content of the previous conversation:

> I started, at university I started a bit of a nasty habit of being quite self-deprecating and slightly putting yourself down so nobody else had the opportunity to, so I'd rather ... Do it to yourself than you know have people go 'oh God, you know, she's crap at that'. I'd ra- ..., I'd much rather be open and then people have nothing to ... But then the down side of that is it sometimes gets too much and you bash yourself into the ground.

She provided a context for her concerns about being boring by referring to an encounter that she felt was significant to her understanding of herself:

> going back to school really, secondary school, I wouldn't say I was bullied *per se*, but I had a five-week window probably, five or six weeks in my life where I was bullied by one particular girl who is actually a very good friend of mine now, we, but it was because of sport, and I found that really hard, because I went swimming after school every day, I was boring, and that idea of being boring has definitely stayed with me. So I think as a key moment or moments, that one person in terms of personality and how you worry about things, she definitely had an impact ... Yeah, I mean you know as a teenager who liked sport it was hard because she used to tell us off, this girl ... you know for trying in PE [physical education] and stuff, and it was just ridiculous, and so you know it takes a while for you to actually become your own person and go, actually no I do like PE, I actually want to teach it! So sort of stick you really! I like sport, take it or leave it really.

Nell subsequently explained how this particular girl had remained part of her life and offered a brief insight into their conversation about the encounter. She shared her interpretation of the response of the other girl and connected this to her reflections at this stage in her life:

> But all of those things around being a girl and a teenager and the pressures to conform are so, so true I think. I have given her lots of abuse since, over the years! 'You've ruined me! A wonder I'm still living and breathing.' ... She just gets really embarrassed and says 'oh I don't know what I was thinking, you know, mm you know, it was just teenager whatnot, we were only 12 or so, so it wasn't.' ... And she did it to other people as well, it was you know, yeah, alpha female pushing her weight around on everybody else and you know power struggles and whatever, all of that.

Nell reflected on the issue of being perceived as boring and the impact she feels it has had on her view of life and teaching:

> it's probably relevant to my career and such but it's relevant to my life ... I was boring, not because I was a boring person, I was boring because I went swimming straight from school every day, so therefore I didn't hang out with everybody in the park or whatever. So it was boring in a different context. But I think I have taken boring to mean all sorts of things.

The outcome of the methodological process is data that challenge us in a number of ways when we begin to consider psychosocial approaches. On the surface Nell appears to be an effective teacher of physical education, able and willing to 'deliver' the curriculum as required by current education policy. Inside Nell seems to be a mass of self-doubts and inadequacies that erode her self-confidence and ability to make her teaching interesting. How does she reconcile these tensions? Does she manage to repress the negativities? As the interpretation above suggests, the data indicate that Nell offers different types of explanations of herself. The missing person in the policies appears to be a self-denigrating subject in the case of Nell. But what right has a researcher to make such strong claims and to what extent can a researcher accept at 'face value' such accounts of different levels of self-awareness? To what degree does the unconscious render impossible such acceptance? What legitimacy can we attribute to Nell's account and to Anne's re-telling of it?

As the Theory Reading Group considered the role of the subject, subjectivities, repression and the unconscious, Anne developed an interest in the extent to which these could 'get in the way' of knowledge claims in the representations she was committed to offering. The conversations with Nell had a particularly profound impact upon Anne's view of the project and the dilemmas with which she was faced. On one hand, there was evidence of a rational subject who knew and could articulate herself, offering plausible explanations for her experiences and meaning making. On the other, there was concern about the importance of repression and the unconscious, and the wishes and desires of both the participant and researcher. This takes us back to the question of what can be 'known and knowable' (Bibby 2011, 123) and, in this case, Anne's uncertainty about what could be claimed from the teachers' narratives of experiences and the explanations they offered of and for their accounts. Psychosocial readings of the data raised concerns both in relation to the notions of legitimate knowledge and the associated ethics.

Nell appeared to be able to think about and articulate her experiences in a way that offered a new 'legitimate' knowledge and which demonstrated that the interview process had 'worked' to make 'missing persons' visible. However, the disruptive new perspective created for thinking generated concern about the extent to which Anne's wish and desire for a process that satisfied her particular methodological and substantive concerns impacted upon the reading and articulation of data. The key issue was whether it was operating in a self-fulfilling way by constructing a particular reading of Nell. This process of thinking 'differently' as a result of the psychoanalytic disturbance left Anne with doubts about the rational subject who can know herself and raised significant questions: To what extent are we or should we be compelled to critique what we can say about Nell and her account of herself? Wertz et al. (2011), in *Five Ways of Doing Qualitative Analysis*, provide multiple ways of reading one dataset, but Anne feels unsure about how to pursue this within her thesis. Is it academically possible and reasonable to accept and present the original reading as just one version of events? Do we have a responsibility to take up the challenge offered here to better understand the way in which the 'socially produced individual is not merely moulded, labelled, pushed around by external forces; but is formed by a process which treats neither society nor individual as a privileged beginning, but takes interior and exterior as problematic categories' (Henriques et al. 1998, 9).

In the next section, we seek to offer some resolutions to the tensions between how the psychosocial figures in Geeta and Anne's research journeys by taking up Frosh's (2001, 630) recognition that there is 'no knowledge of the other without the engagement of the self'.

'Being captured' as a source of legitimacy and security

In this section, we revisit the tensions between the rationality with which we are (usually) required to present our research and the unreasonable desires which (also) drive it. To do this, we reflect critically on Heather's experience of analysing 'someone else's data', embedding our discussion within the example of Lola's interview data.

Lola was the pseudonym given to a student who was interviewed as part of a study of the Mathematics Enhancement Course (MEC). The study was funded by King's College London and led by Jill Adler. The MEC is an English initiative set up to address the shortage of qualified mathematics teachers. It provides a one-year booster course in mathematics for those people without an undergraduate degree in the subject, but who still wish to train as secondary mathematics teachers. Heather was not involved in the initial research process and therefore she never met Lola in person. She began working collaboratively on the MEC study data when she moved institutions and found herself sharing an office with one of the team members, Sarmin Hossain. Together, Sarmin and Heather explored how participants negotiated their identity in relation to the MEC demand that students acquire an 'in-depth understanding' of mathematics in order to become good-enough mathematics teachers (Hossain, Mendick, and Adler 2013). This demand is foundational for the MEC programme and an article of faith for many mathematics educators (e.g. Ma 1999).

As Heather read through the 18 interview transcripts with MEC students, she felt herself 'being captured' by Lola – as Geeta was by talking with Maheera and Rohini, and Anne was by Nell. Heather, who describes herself as being a *difficult* person, was conscious of being attracted to Lola's story because she was a *difficult* participant – the student who, as we show next, was the most resistant to taking up the dominant MEC discourse that values acquiring an 'in-depth understanding' of mathematics.

While other students were overwhelmingly positive about the MEC, Lola simply described it as 'okay'. She then acknowledged and critiqued its rationale: 'The whole idea is for us to get a deeper understanding and sometimes we are rushed, so it's not very efficient'. In the space of the interview, she ascribed 'in-depth understanding' to her lecturers, and aligned herself with an oppositional 'we' who have 'lived with' a different approach and 'still do well':

I was a bit resistant ... We've lived with this; we still do well ... But, at the end of the day, you have, you have to look at the other side as well, but people find it difficult, because our lecturer said, 'If someone coming from the primary school has already known that ... multiply by 10, you just add zero...' but where I'm coming from, I don't feel like that that person is dumb.

In this extract, we can see how Lola, while making some concessions to 'the other side', constructs herself as part of a collective 'we' who are viewed as 'dumb' within MEC discourses. In their paper, Sarmin and Heather (Hossain, Mendick, and Adler 2013) justified their focus on Lola in relation to how she interrupts and problematises debates within mathematics education. Here, Lola's position as *trouble* within the MEC, corresponds with Heather's desire to *trouble* mathematics education. But, what is lost in this account of how/why Heather became captured by Lola in the way she was?

As Geeta found, psychosocial approaches provide breathing and thinking spaces, in this case to reflect on how we are drawn towards some data/participants rather than others. But having opened up this space, does connecting Heather's identification as difficult with her identification of Lola as also difficult then foreclose it even as it hints at something else? 'What we are taught to see as "natural" in the human condition, the capacity to use reason, is only a small part of the story: behind every action is a wish, behind every thought is an unreasonable desire' (Frosh quoted in Bibby 2011, 7). Heather's point of connection with Lola is likely to have led to a desire to positively inscribe her 'difficultness' and so may have drawn her to foreground the social over the psychic. However, our aim here is not to unpick the wishes and unreasonable desires which may or may not lie 'behind' Heather's fix(at)ing on Lola and her subsequent actions and thoughts. Instead, we wish to draw attention to: the consequences of these for the types of knowledge we produce and what disappears when we feel compelled to offer 'rational' accounts in order to legitimate our academic work. If we are drawn to data that resonate with us and feel comfortable, what constraints does this place upon the arguments that we develop? As in our account of Anne's work above, do 'unreasonable' desires for certainty render some things unknowable? And how does this include some and exclude others? (Walkerdine 1988). The resolution, if it is one, that runs through all our accounts, is 'that realistic understanding of others comes from a process of unconscious reflection in which the subjectivity of the [researcher] is intimately engaged' (Frosh 2001, 630).

As suggested above, through such a process, Heather (and Sarmin) came to understand Lola's resistance to the dominant MEC discourse as being related to aspects of her cultural background, rooted in early educational experiences in Nigeria. Using 'we', Lola inscribes herself within a Nigerian 'imagined community' (Anderson 1983). This is apparent in the following interview extracts:

> I learned outside this country, the way of teaching is totally different ... the concept that we knew and just applied. Coming here, you need to understand why the concepts came about, how they came about, and you get a deeper understanding. Whereas the kind of knowledge and teaching I've been accustomed to is you get a formula, you understand, you just know the formula, you apply the formula, and get results.

> I think the culture plays a lot of role in the way people are taught there, because in Nigeria, for instance, it's rude to ask an elder, 'Why?' ... and what I understand here is that, as a teacher, you need to know all the ways because the, the student might understand one way better.

Sarmin and Heather argued that the MEC positioning of 'in-depth understanding' as the 'right' way to learn and teach mathematics challenges Lola's investment in her Nigerian identity. They read her resistance to the MEC as part of her construction of a diasporic cultural identity and as resistance to a (post)colonial gaze that disfigures and destroys the 'pasts' of oppressed peoples (Hall 1992). They located this within wider processes of Othering in which subjectivities are constructed via 'establishing opposites and "others" whose actuality is always subject to the continuous interpretation and reinterpretation of their differences from "us", and where this designation of Others re/produces hierarchical power relations' (Said 1995, 332).

However, through renewing her engagement with psychosocial approaches within the reading group and with other collaborators, Heather reflected that we might also/alternatively understand Lola as a defended subject: the idea 'that the self is forged out of unconscious defences against anxiety' (Hollway and Jefferson 2000, 19). Within this reading, Lola's resistance to the dominant discourse can be explained as an instance of splitting: the way 'in which both people and events are experienced in very extreme terms, either as unrealistically wonderful (good) or as unrealistically terrible (bad)' (Waddell 2002, 6). In Melanie Klein's work, splitting is linked to the very early processes of feeding, in which the baby:

> takes in the sense of having a bad mother. He [sic] has a bad mother within him. When she comforts and feeds him, and he has a good feeling, his mother again becomes good. He 'projects' his bad feeling and identifies her with it. He 'introjects' his experiences of her as calm, satisfying and good, and he himself acquires a good feeling within. He feels himself to be 'good'. (Waddell 2002, 254)

Juxtaposing these two readings of Lola raises questions for us. While Anne's concern was whether a researcher is 'entitled to do more than seek honestly to represent what participants are trying to say' (Frosh 2001, 638),

Heather – like Geeta – did not worry about inserting her own analysis. But, how do we legitimise knowledge produced through reading data against the conscious understandings of 'our' participants and in ways that could anger or distress them? Heather, not having met 'Lola', found this an easier process than did her co-authors, particularly Jill, who had interviewed Lola. Jill, having also set up the study in collaboration with four MEC tutors, had more investment in a particular way of knowing about the MEC. On one level we are seeking/gaining legitimacy through publication, but is this (ever) enough?

We can also see, in these two readings of Lola, the challenge of doing justice to both the social *and* the psychic in our work. Frost and Lucey (2010, 3) write:

> psychosocial studies have a broad theoretical commitment to the notion that psychological issues cannot be validly abstracted from social, cultural and historical contexts and to the task of accounting for the social shaping of subjective experience without deterministically reducing the psychic to the social. Equally, they have a parallel commitment to the notion that social and cultural worlds have psychological dimensions and to the task of accounting for the ways in which the latter shape these worlds without deterministically reducing the social to the psychic.

How do we, as researchers, balance the social and the psychic, given that we often feel more at home in one than the other? Hollway (2012) has argued that, in the rush towards the psychic, the social got lost in her classic work with Jefferson, *Doing Qualitative Research Differently* (Hollway and Jefferson 2000). How far does an engagement with psychoanalytic ideas reduce the space for, and the force of, our social critiques? Once again we are returned to the question of the ethics of our analysis.

Concluding thoughts

> It hardly needs saying: psychoanalysis radicalizes knowledge by asserting its transformative nature ... from the inauguration of this method, this theory, there is a vivid construction of a way of knowing that leaves everything touched, changes it all. (Frosh 2001, 627)

In this paper, we have explored how our own ways of knowing have been touched by psychoanalysis and by our engagements in different institutional spaces, including those for discussion of our research.

We are aware that our different end points in these sections, with Anne and Geeta seeking more certainty in their interpretations than Heather or Paul, relate to our different levels of experience and institutional positions. We have argued that legitimacy is relational and achieved through struggle, emerging from a range of academic practices which often reproduce dominant ways of knowing that require depersonalisation. The psychosocial provides ways of troubling these, and being troubled, through alternative epistemological positions, roads less travelled. We have found psychosocial research to be risky but rewarding, as we, as researchers, have 'become captured' in the process of engaging with our own emotions and entanglements with our 'objects of study'. It is through these engagements, and through working collaboratively to understand them, that we have experienced some security in both what we know and how we know it. Even as we have generated more questions than we have answered,

> psychoanalysis demonstrates the virtues of a 'good-enough' theory, one which acknowledges the insistence of irrationality and emotion at the heart of knowledge, yet tries to say something helpful all the same. 'Let us not get too tied up in our inadequacies,' it seems to say, 'we can at least act in a principled way.' (Frosh 2001, 633)

This paper is not a report of our findings, but a discussion of research processes. In it, we have balanced our interests in our shared experience within a reading group, with a commitment to our individual research projects. Our meetings have engaged us in creative dialogues between these projects and our collective reading, interleaved with our reflexive accounts of ourselves as researchers. The balance between the social group and the individual researcher both parallels the twin foci of psychosocial research and shows up the false naïve dichotomies between the politcal and personal, public and private, sociological and psychoanalytic. Without resolving these tensions, we are aware of the primarily ethical nature of psychosocial research which engages the researcher. We believe that by adding reports of our self-concerns, doubts and subjective experiences as researchers, we open them up to greater methodological transparency and ethical scrutiny. By positioning ourselves and including dimensions which exceed the discursive in our research, we potentially become more reflexive. Acknowledging one's personal role in the knowledge-generation process, rather than assuming an external Archimedean point, makes the research enterprise ethically more defensible.

Acknowledgements

Geeta and Anne would like to thank their research participants. Heather would like to thank Jill Adler and Sarmin Hossain, her collaborators on the original work about Lola. We would all like to thank our colleagues in the Brunel Education Theory Reading Group who have supported us in thinking differently and Tamara and Claudia for inviting us to contribute to this special issue.

References

Ahmed, Sara. 2009. "Embodying Diversity: Problems and Paradoxes for Black Feminists." *Race, Ethnicity and Education* 12 (1): 41–52.
Anderson, Benedict. 1983. *Imagined Communities: Reflections on the Origin and Spread of Nationalism*. London: Verso.
Andrews, Molly. 2007. *Shaping History: Narratives of Political Change*. Cambridge: Cambridge University Press.
Bhopal, Kalwant. 2010. *Asian Women in Higher Education: Shared Communities*. UK: Trentham.
Bibby, Tamara. 2009. "How Do Pedagogic Practices Impact on Learner Identities in Mathematics? A Psychoanalytically Framed Response." In *Mathematical Relationships in Education: Identities and Participation*, edited by Laura Black, Heather Mendick and Yvette Solomon, 249–276. New YorkNY: Routledge.
Bibby, Tamara. 2011. *Education - An 'Impossible Profession'?: Psychoanalytic Explorations of Learning and Classrooms*. London: Routledge.
Billig, Michael. 2006. "A Psychoanalytic Discursive Psychology: From Consciousness to Unconsciousness." *Discourse Studies* 8 (1): 17–24.
Butler, Judith. 1997. *The Psychic Life of Power*. Stanford: Stanford University Press.
Craib, Ian. 2001. *Psychoanalysis- A Critical Introduction*. Cambridge: Polity Press.
Davies, Bronwyn, and Eva Bendix Petersen. 2004. "Intellectual Workers (Un)Doing Neoliberal Discourse." *International Journal of Critical Psychology* 13 (1): 32–54.
Evans, Mary. 1999. *Missing Persons*. London: Routledge.
Frosh, Stephen. 2001. "On Reason, Discourse and Fantasy." *American Imago* 58: 627–647.
Frost, Liz, and Helen Lucey. 2010. "Editorial." *Journal of Psycho-Social Studies* 4 (1): 1–5.
Hall, Stuart. 1992. "New Ethnicities." In *'Race', Culture and Difference*, edited by J. Donald and A. Rattansi, 252–259. London: Sage.
Henriques Julian. 1998. Social Psychology and the Politics of Racism. In Changing the Subject: Psychology, Social Regulation and Subjectivity (Second Edition), ed. Julian Henriques, Wendy Hollway, Cathy Urwin, Couze Venn and Valerie Walkerdine, 60–89. London: Routledge.
Henriques, Julian, Wendy Hollway, Cathy Urwin, Couze Venn, and Valerie Walkerdine. 1998. *Changing the Subject: Psychology, Social Regulation and Subjectivity*. 2nd ed. London: Methuen.
Hey, Valerie, and Simon Bradford. 2004. "The Return of the Repressed? the Gender Politics of Emergent Forms of Professionalism in Education." *Journal of Education Policy* 19 (6): 691–713.
Hollway Wendy. 2012. Psychoanalysis as Epistemology: Developments in Psycho-Social Methods. Paper Presented at Doing Qualitative Research Differently Seminar at, 22 November, Birkbeck, UK.
Hollway, Wendy, Helen Lucey, and Ann Phoenix. 2007. *Social Psychology Matters*. Maidenhead: Open University Press.
Hollway, Wendy, and T. Jefferson. 2000. *Doing Qualitative Research Differently: Free Association, Narrative and the Interview Method*. London: Sage.
hooks, bell. 1996. *Bone Black*. London: The Women's Press.
Hossain, Sarmin, Heather Mendick and Jill Adler. 2013. Troubling "Understanding Mathematics in-Depth": Its Role in the Identity Work of Student-Teachers in England. *Educational Studies in Mathematics Online First*. http://link.springer.com/article/10.1007%2Fs10649-013-9474-6.
Laing, Ronald David. 1960. *The Divided Self*. Harmondsworth: Pelican.

Ludhra, Geeta. 2011. Exploring the 'hidden' Lives of South-Asian Girls: A Critical and Ethical Reflection on the Representation of 'voices'. Paper Presented at the Annual British Sociological Association's (BSA) Auto/Biography Study Group, 7–10 July, University of Reading, UK.

Ludhra, Geeta. 2012. 'Bet You Think This Thesis is 'Bout YOU': Striving for 'harmony' amongst a Choir of Complex Voices. Paper Presented at the Annual British Sociological Association's (BSA) Auto/Biography Study Group, July 12–14, University of Reading, UK.

Ludhra, Geeta and Anne Chappell. 2010. "'You Were Quiet. I Did All the marching': Research Processes Involved in Hearing the Voices of South Asian Girls." Paper Presented at the Annual British Sociological Association's (BSA) Auto/Biography Study Group, 7–9 July, University of Leicester, UK.

Ludhra, Geeta and Anne Chappell. 2011. "'You Were Quiet. I Did All the marching': Research Processes Involved in Hearing the Voices of South Asian Girls." *International Journal of Adolescence and Youth* 16 (2): 101–118.

Luhmann, Susanne. 1998. "Queering/Querying Pedagogy? or, Pedagogy is a Pretty Queer Thing." In *Queer Theory in Education*, edited by William F. Pinar, 141–155. Mahwah, NJ: Lawrence Erlbaum Associates.

Lyotard, Jean-François. 1984. *The Postmodern Condition: A Report on Knowledge*. Manchester, NH: Manchester University Press.

Ma, Liping. 1999. *Knowing and Teaching Elementary Mathematics*. Mahwah, NJ: Lawrence Erlbaum.

MacLure, Maggie. 1993. "Arguing for Yourself: Identity as an Organising Principle in teachers' Jobs and Lives." *British Educational Research Journal* 19 (4): 311–322.

MacLure, Maggie. 2006. "A Demented Form of the Familiar': Postmodernism and Educational Research." *Journal of Philosophy of Education* 40 (2): 1–17.

MacLure, Maggie. 2013. "Classification or Wonder? Coding as an Analytic Practice in Qualitative Research." In *Deleuze and Research Methodologies*, edited by Rebecca Coleman and Jessica Ringrose, 164–183. Edinburgh: Edinburgh University Press.

Maylor, Uvanney. 2009. What is the Meaning of 'black'?: Researching Black Respondents. *Ethnic and Racial Studies* 32: 369–387.

Maylor, Uvanney, and Katya Williams. 2011. "Challenges in Theorising 'Black Middle-class' Women: Education, Experience and Authenticity." *Gender and Education* 23 (3): 345–356.

Mendick, Heather. 2006. *Masculinities in Mathematics*. Maidenhead: Open University Press.

Mills, Wright, and Charles. 1959. *The Sociological Imagination*. Oxford: Oxford University Press.

Mirza, Heidi. 2009. *Race, Gender and Educational Desire: Why Black Women Succeed and Fail*. London: Routledge.

Mirza, Heidi. 2013. "'A Second skin': Embodied Intersectionality, Transnationalism and Narratives of Identity and Belonging among Muslim British Women in Britain." *Women's Studies International Forum* 36: 5–15.

Rogers, Chrissie, and Geeta Ludhra. 2011. "Research Ethics: Participation, Social Difference and Informed Consent." In *Research Methods for Youth Practitioners*, edited by Simon Bradford and Fiona Cullen, 43–65. London: Routledge.

Rose, Nikolas. 1989. *Governing the Soul*. London: Routledge.

Said, Edward. 1995. *Orientalism: Western Conceptions of the Orient*. London: Penguin.

Skeggs, Beverley. 1997. *Formations of Class & Gender*. London: Sage.
Sparkes, Andrew C. 2007. "Embodiment, Academics, and the Audit Culture: A Story Seeking Consideration." *Qualitative Research* 7 (4): 521–550.
Waddell, Margot. 2002. *Inside Lives: Psychoanalysis and the Growth of the Personality*. London: Karnac.
Walkerdine, Valerie. 1988. *The Mastery of Reason: Cognitive Development and the Production of Rationality*. London: Routledge.
Walkerdine, Valerie. 1997. *Daddy's Girl*. Hampshire: Macmillan.
Walkerdine, Valerie, June Melody, and Helen Lucey. 2003. "Uneasy Hybrids: Psychosocial Aspects of Becoming Educationally Successful for Working-class Young Women." *Gender and Education* 15 (3): 285–299.
Wertz, Frederick J., Kathy Charmaz, Linda M. McMullen, Ph D Ruthellen Josselson, Rosemarie Anderson, and Emalinda McSpadden. 2011. *Five Ways of Doing Qualitative Analysis: Phenomenological Psychology, Grounded Theory, Discourse Analysis, Narrative Research, and Intuitive Inquiry*. Hove: Guilford Press.
Wetherell, Margaret. 2012. *Affect and Emotion: A New Social Science Understanding*. London: Sage.

Going spiral? Phenomena of 'half-knowledge' in the experiential large group as temporary learning community

John Adlam

South London and Maudsley NHS Foundation Trust, London, UK

> In this paper I use group-analytic, philosophical and psycho-social lenses to explore phenomena associated with the convening of an experiential large group within a two-day conference on the theme of 'knowing and not-knowing'. Drawing in particular on the work of Earl Hopper, two different models of large group convening - in which the chairs for the group are arranged either in concentric circles or in spirals - are described 'topographically' and compared in terms of the tasks which each model might address. I argue that the spiral topography may be more suited to the attempt to construct what the conference organisers posited as 'insecure edifices of knowledge' and I borrow from the letters of Keats on 'negative capability' to suggest that phenomena of 'half-knowledge' may be generated and fleetingly perceived within the dynamic processes in the dilemmatic spaces of experiential large groups thus constituted.

In December 2012 a conference was convened at the Institute of Education by the Psychosocial Studies Network to explore the theme of '[K]nowing and Not Knowing: Thinking Psychosocially About Learning and Resistance to Learning'. The conference call for papers opened with the observation that the social world is 'saturated with powerful formations of knowledge that colonise individual and institutional identities. Some knowledge emerges as legitimised and authoritative; other knowledge is resisted or repressed'. The conference organisers asked the question: 'What might it mean to build insecure edifices of knowledge?'

On each afternoon of the two-day event, delegates were invited, as one of two options within the conference structure, to elect to attend an experiential large group, which I was asked to convene. In the conference programme I offered the following description of this group:

The Experiential Large Group is a work group within the temporary learning community of the Conference. Its task is to come together for ninety minutes each afternoon to reflect upon the Conference theme of 'knowing and not knowing' ... An Experiential Group has itself as its own object of study and research ... Its objective is to learn from its own experience something about the nature of opportunities for learning – and resistances to learning – that may emerge within the unstructured spaces of the Group.

By virtue of this invitation to join one or other of two events on a given afternoon, it follows that membership of this Experiential Large Group was self-selecting from within the wider membership of the Conference community. By taking up membership in and of the group, the individual conference delegate was taking up his or her membership of the wider system of the Conference-as-a-whole in a particular way. Hopper and Weyman (1975) observe that a given group is charged with limited aims and that therefore:

> a group must exist within the context of a larger social system on which it depends for the solution of those problems with which it is not concerned directly ... Furthermore, the limitation of its aims makes a group a relatively transitory system, no matter how long it has been established. Permanence requires institutionalisation. (Hopper and Weyman 1975, 177)

These limits in time and scope need not be construed as disadvantageous. In this paper I play with the notion that the work of a large group such as this might be recognised as providing a particular form of temporary accommodation for unhoused minds (Adlam and Scanlon 2005; Scanlon and Adlam 2011a) within the wider system of the conference (and the wider systems within which the conference itself was more or less securely housed).

Whereas other parts of the conference aimed to find new ways to address the needs of the membership for other more familiar forms of experience, such as for example, presentation and discussion of research, administration, networking, the Experiential Large Group offered a form of insecure housing that could then be understood as potentially productive of a particular kind of 'insecure edifice of knowledge', interdependent and impermanent – ephemeral even – that was then made available to the temporary learning community of the conference.

Spiral (adj) winding in a continuous and gradually widening (or tightening) curve ... around a central point on a flat plane. (*Oxford Dictionary of English* 2005)

In experiential large groups the available chairs are generally placed either in concentric circles or in a spiral formation. They are thus distinguished from plenary large group sessions, in which either all the chairs are in one circle or all chairs face towards a podium at the front of the hall, in(viting) dependence upon a Chairperson at a lectern. Stiers describes the structure of a particular series of experiential large groups thus:

> the chairs are arranged in a spiral shape, spanning out from a few chairs in the center into larger and larger spirals until there are enough chairs for the entire membership and the consultants. Given the size and the configuration of this large group, face-to-face interactions with all the group members are difficult to maintain. (Stiers 2012, 10)

Stiers proposes a model of 'dialogical learning' based on the work of Paolo Freire (1996) and he argues that the group is experiential in that it aspires to 'an acquisition of insight from experienced happenings'. We might then say that the *experiential* quality of such groups is brought into being and structured by the topography of the chairs on the plane of the floorspace at the given event and the human geography of what it is like to be invited/challenged to take up one's membership of such a group by seating oneself within its borders.

Different topographies invite or invoke different qualities of experiential learning. Hopper (2002) emphasises the importance of distinguishing between varieties of large group projects: an experience, a demonstration or a consultation to the organisation. In a later paper (Hopper 2006), he echoes this point and makes the intriguing suggestion (one to which I shall return later) that a spiral arrangement

> is more appropriate for large groups who have been organised in the service of learning more about the dynamics of them, and concentric circles are more appropriate for groups who have been organised in the service of discussing matters of concern to the participants in them. (Hopper 2006, 13)

The spiral topography perhaps promotes less secure modes and edifices of learning and Hopper gives a vignette that might be used to illustrate this point. In one particular Large Group event he was convening, he set out a spiral topography, despite going on to announce that the group's task was 'to discuss matters of concern to us': in Hopper's terms, a task more appropriate to the circular layout. On the second day of the group, one participant said that 'she was glad that the group had returned to the co-centric circles that she was used to. In fact, this had not actually occurred, but *she had made herself more at home by ignoring the spiral pattern*' (Hopper 2006, 13, my italics).

The potentially disconcerting nature of the spiral topography (where is the centre of the spiral? where does its outer boundary lie?) is reflected in a certain type of leadership that also generates and/or elucidates unconscious phenomena in the large group setting. The convenor(s) reflects upon demands for leadership from the group in a semi-structured meeting with no agenda, but does not necessarily act upon them. There is something disturbing about the experience of facing some fellow group members while staring at the backs of others, whether in circles or spirals, without receiving 'secure' modes of direction from the figure identified as the convenor of the group. For these reasons, Hopper (2006) argues that when the project of the large group is experiential, interpretation 'should be directed towards helping the participants learn from experience' (13) and that the attentive silence more commonly associated with more psychoanalytic or group analytic projects (and, by extension of his own point, with the circular topography) 'can be oppressive and even persecuting' (13) when misapplied to the experiential large group.

> Each individual is a component part of numerous groups, he is bound by ties of identification in many directions ... Each individual therefore has a share in numerous group minds – those of his race, of his class, of his creed, of his nationality, etc – and he can also raise himself above them to the extent of having a scrap of independence and originality. (Sigmund Freud [1921] 1991, 161)

Large groups have dynamics all their own (Freud [1921] 1991; Kreeger 1975b), so that part of the experience of the membership has to do with numerical considerations: although, as Freud first noted, sheer numbers do not of themselves generate instincts that did not pre-exist the formation of the group in question. Kreeger (1975a) considered that his book treated of groups of more than 40 members; Foulkes (1975), in the same volume, thought that large group phenomena came into view at around 30 members; Hopper and Weyman (1975) suggest a membership of more than 50. Finally, Main (1975) has the threshold figure at 20. These variations are important but there seems to be consensus that beyond a certain number of bodies being in the room – sufficient that small group dynamics are effaced and not all members can see each other's faces – the *idea of the existence of an object known as a large group* enters into the discourse.

This 'idea' is immediately disturbing, as numerous authors have attested (see especially Turquet 1975). Miller, discussing (and defending) the Leicester Conferences (a particular tradition of group relations events featuring large and small group and intergroup events) reports that 'many individuals feel disturbed at times, and some may exhibit seemingly bizarre behaviour – hardly surprising in a setting that is quite unconventional' (Miller 1990, 183). Main writes that 'in *large* unstructured groups ... projective processes may be wide-spread and can lead to baffling, even chaotic situations, which can bring the group's work to a standstill' and that members 'do not have their full thinking-capacities at their own disposal' (Main 1975, 60). Hopper notes that 'when anxious, which in a large group is usually the order of the day, because identities are always under threat, people oscillate between operational, concrete thinking, on the one hand, and "excessive symbolism" and metaphorical thinking, on the other' (Hopper, 2006, 13).

Bion (1961) argued that a group is intrinsically a phantasied object in the mind of the individual (that is to say, the relationship of self to group is the unconsciously represented mental expression both of instinctual impulses and of defences against such impulses; Hinshelwood 1991) and he suggested that a group encourages regression in the mind of the individual because a group (whether small or large 'in reality') presents to the mind as a large object – associated with a bigger body – in relation to which one immediately feels small. This generates the unconscious experience of a feeding relationship to what, following Lévi-Strauss ([1955] 2011), we might term a frightening, anthropophagic/anthropoemic mother figure: a figure threatening either cannibalistic incorporation of the vulnerable needy self, like Kronos/Saturn feeding off his young in the ancient Graeco-Roman myth, or violently casting out the unwanted hungering mouth. This relates to the tendency in large groups to seize upon stereotyped sub-groups experienced as 'other', because the large-group-as-a-whole is such a vast object in the mind (Turquet 1975). The sub-group is then constituted as a problematically different but somehow more 'manageable' other and the feared fate of the individual (to be consumed or to be expelled) is projected into it.

Lévi-Strauss ([1955] 2011, 388) described a process of (anthropoemically) 'ejecting dangerous individuals from the social body and keeping them ... in isolation'. In this scenario there is no difference left to trouble us, for the threatening object of the large group has been broken down into hated part-objects or sub-groups that have then been expelled from consciousness. However, if the large group is appropriately constituted and convened and the membership can retrieve aspects of its capacity for emotional thinking, the perception of difference – of individuals and of sub-groups – can re-emerge. There is then the potential for Freud's 'scrap of independence and originality' or even Foucault's 'insurrection of subjugated knowledges' (Foucault 1980, 81) – the emergence of discourses other than those which overtly or covertly dominate – even if repressive or colonising (anthropoemic or anthropophagic) responses may also follow in their turn.

...I mean *Negative Capability*, that is when man is capable of being in uncertainties, Mysteries, doubts, without any irritable reaching after fact & reason – Coleridge, for instance, would let go by a fine isolated verisimilitude caught from the Penetralium of mystery, from being incapable of remaining content with half-knowledge. (John Keats, from a letter to his brothers, George and Tom Keats, December 1817).

In the Conference programme, the above passage from Keats' letters (Keats 2002, 41–2) was used to introduce the task of the Experiential Large

Group and to hint at possible overlaps between 'method' and 'outcome'. There is a hint at method, because groups of this kind are 'unstructured' and follow no agenda of business but proceed associatively and therefore 'uncertainties, mysteries and doubts' confront the membership from the outset. The possible outcome of 'half-knowledge' is evoked, because perhaps the route towards the verisimilitudes of the 'Penetralium', the 'inner sanctum' of learning from experience is not a secure one and neither knowing nor not-knowing offer the key. I used the Conference programme to suggest to the potential membership that the Experiential Large Group 'provides a setting and a quality of experience in which the "irritable reaching after fact and reason" may be set aside – or the resistances to so doing may emerge to become the object of study'.

Keats' letter of December 1817 is the only point at which he is known to have made explicit written reference to his idea of negative capability. Indeed, there is some question of the accuracy or at any rate completeness of the text of the letter, which comes down to us only via transcription (Ou 2009). However, Ou analyses the corpus of Keats' letters to show how he evoked and developed what for him was specifically an *aesthetic* of negative capability: 'I can never feel certain of any truth but from a clear perception of its Beauty', he writes in 1818 (Keats 2002, 175). In the same passage he avers that 'I have made up my Mind never to take anything for granted'. The following winter he writes again to his brother and sister-in-law:

> ... Dilke was a Man who cannot feel he has a personal identity unless he has made up his Mind about every thing. The only means of strengthening one's intellect is to make up one's mind about nothing ... Dilke will never come at a truth as long as he lives; because he is always trying at it. (Keats 2002, 303)

This condensation of the idea of negative capability (don't 'try at a truth' if you want to 'come at one') is directly referenced and echoed in Philip Pullman's *His Dark Materials* stories, particularly in the passages in which Lyra discovers how to use the 'alethiometer' and Will is taught to wield the 'subtle knife' (Pullman 2000). Ou (2009) writes that 'to be negatively capable is to be open to the actual vastness and complexity of experience' and therefore 'to abandon the comfortable enclosure of doctrinaire knowledge' (2). Negative capability is '*fundamentally experiential*, aiming to encompass and convey the ... complexity of experience, as opposed to an idealist stance, which seeks to abstract ideas or doctrines from experience' (4–5, my italics).

Bion (1970) used the idea of negative capability to illustrate his notion that the psychoanalyst needs to approach the encounter with the patient in a frame of mind in which there is a 'positive discipline of eschewing memory and desire' (31) in pursuit of a shared 'Language of Achievement' (125) – this latter term being an echo of Keats' depiction of Shakespeare as a 'Man of Achievement' 'so enormously' possessing the quality of negative capability (Keats 2002, 41). Scanlon (2012) suggests that negative capability may be a necessary response to what Honig (1994) calls 'dilemmatic spaces'. For Honig, all moral subjects are situated in dilemmatic spaces that constitute them: the subject is 'positioned on conflictual axes of identity/difference such that her agency itself is constituted by and daily mired in dilemmatic choices and negotiations' (568). Dilemmas are spaces rather than events. They do not come from nowhere; rather, they are 'the eventual eruptions of a turbulence that is always already there ... the periodic crystallisations of incoherences and conflicts in social orders and their subjects' (569). In this argument, she anticipates Žižek's distinction between subjective violence (the perceived violent event) and objective violence (the violence, symbolic and systemic, that is the background context for all our lives) (Žižek 2008). There is also an echo here of Bion's comment that resistance to growth is 'endo-psychic and endo-gregious; it is associated with turbulence in the individual and in the group to which the growing individual belongs' (Bion 1970, 34). I suggest that Honig is giving an account, albeit in very different language, of the large group dynamics mapped out by the group analysts and other social theorists referred to in the previous section of this paper.

An experiential large group, if we link and follow through these ideas, not only is then experienced as a particular dilemmatic space, in which ideas of difference and identity are unstable and troubled and contested: it is also a space in which the dilemmatic nature of the larger social system of the temporary learning community around it may be glimpsed and become apparent. Seen in this light, moreover, the idea of a 'secure edifice of knowledge' becomes highly problematic – for how could such a building be constructed in such a conflictual space, inhabited by such unhoused and bewildered subjects, without saturating it with rigid and enclosing formations of knowledge that are fenced off from too much interrogation and exclusive of those not held to be initiates? For the membership of such a group (and here I mean on principle to include the convenor as a member, albeit one with an apparently distinct allocated role), an insecure half-knowledge may be the safest experiential learning outcome.

...each of us is, as it were, circumscribed by many circles; some of which are less, but others larger ... the first, indeed, and most proximate circle is that which everyone describes about his own mind as a centre, in which circle the body, and whatever is assumed for the sake of the body, are comprehended. For this is the smallest circle, and almost touches the centre itself. The second from this ... is that in which parents, brothers, wife, and children are arranged. The third circle from the centre is that which contains uncles and aunts, grandfathers and grandmothers ... Next ... is that which contains the common people, then that which comprehends those of the same tribe. Afterwards that which contains the citizens; and then two other circles follow, one being the circle of those that dwell in the vicinity of the city, and the other, of those of the same province. But the outermost and greatest circle, and which comprehends all the other circles, is that of the whole human race ... it is the province of him who strives to conduct himself properly in each of these connections to collect, in a certain respect, the circles, as it were, to one centre, and always to endeavour earnestly to transfer himself from the comprehending circles to the several particulars which they comprehend. (Hierocles 1822).

How then can the experiential large group afford to its membership the best opportunity for the emergence of Freud's 'scraps of independence and originality'? I return now to the question of the topographical difference between concentric circle and spiral arrangements of the chairs in the room. My colleagues and I have explored the dynamics of 'metropolitan' systems of care and of government, concentrating upon the ways in which such systems and discourses exclude the out-group by the terms on which inclusion is offered by the in-group (Pelletier 2011; Scanlon and Adlam 2011b; Scanlon and Adlam 2013). We have made particular use of the figure of Diogenes the Cynic, who, when asked where he came from, replied 'I am a citizen of the world' ('*kosmopolites*') (Diogenes Laertius 2005, 6.63).

Diogenes may have coined the term 'cosmopolitan' but he was no proponent of ideological systems of any description and it was the Stoics, in particular Zeno of Citium, who started to teach in Athens around 300 BC, who developed a coherent philosophy of cosmopolitanism. Martin (forthcoming; see also Scanlon and Adlam 2013) quotes Plutarch's description of Zeno's position:

The much admired *Republic* of Zeno ... is aimed at this main point, that our household arrangements should not be based on cities or parishes, each one marked out by its own legal system, but we should regard all men as our fellow citizens and local residents, and there should be one way of life and order, like that of a herd grazing together and nurtured by a common law. (Martin forthcoming, quoting from Plutarch, *On the Fortune of Alexander* 329A–B)

Martin goes on to re-examine the Stoic doctrine of *oikeiosis*, which asserts a fundamental primitive attachment to one's self and one's own constitution as a living being. The Stoic philosopher Hierocles, writing possibly in the first half of the second century AD, offers the image, quoted above, of concentric circles, the smallest being the mind of the individual, expanding outwards through familial and tribal and citizenship ties to the largest circle: the human race itself. Although Hierocles wrote that the dilution of blood ties would naturally correspond to a diminution in warmth of attachment ('for something of benevolence must be taken away from those who are more distant from us by blood; though at the same time we should endeavour that an assimilation may take place between us and them' (Hierocles 1822)), the ethical challenge, if we accept this metaphor of concentric circles, concerns whether or not it is possible to aspire to a communalism within which all are equally connected or interdependent and no-one needs to measure their distance from the centre in order to 'know their place'.

God loves from whole to parts: but human soul
Must rise from individual to the whole.
Self-love but serves the virtuous mind to wake
As the small pebble stirs the peaceful lake;
The centre mov'd, a circle strait succeeds,
Another still, and still another spreads;
Friend, parent, neighbour, first it will embrace;
His country next; and next all human race …
(Alexander Pope 1734, from *Essay on Man, Epistle IV*)

These precedents would therefore appear to offer a previously unformulated rationale for the concentric circles of a certain type of large group, tasked, as Hopper (2006) suggests, with deliberating matters of shared concern. In this way of understanding the dynamics of learning from experience within the large group, the figure of the convenor represents or signifies a practice, not only of negative capability but also of inclusion. This figure then *potentially* allows each member of the large group, whether in the 'inner' or 'outer' rings, to feel themselves in an equal position from which to take up their membership (or what Hopper conceptualises in a particular sense as their 'citizenship', evoking the concept of *koinonia* or 'impersonal fellowship'; Hopper 2000, 2002; see also de Maré 1975) in original and independent ways. But what then are we to make of the idea that experiential learning is best pursued in the spiral topography and that concentric circles are in comparison a familiar formation, upon which one might fall back in relief? Perhaps the Stoics and their Cosmopolitan successors have still not entirely escaped from the seemingly benign but covertly oppressive 'Metropolitan' practice of 'inclusion'.

The fragmented and agonised and excluded subjects depicted by Honig (1994) or Judith Butler (1997) are perhaps more unsettled by the spiral topography because their subjection is potentially more apparent to them and, at the same time, the possibilities for at least a momentary reconstitution of self are more tangible and even tantalising. For a spiral has a notional centre and a notional rim – a chair that is apparently closest to the middle and another chair that appears to sit at the outer limit – but at the same time, the topography evokes infinite continuations in both 'directions'.

It winds inward towards the centre of the flat plane that one can never be certain of reaching and it winds outwards towards what is in essence an arbitrarily marked perimeter (one runs out of chairs, or runs up against the walls of the room, but the shape of the arrangement of chairs evokes its own indefinite continuation).

It is not quite obvious, in short, that there is an inside or an outside to the spiral – even though these ideas are frequently referred back to by the membership in their initial disorientation. The spiral of the experiential large group therefore could be said to exist outside of both 'metropolitan' and 'cosmopolitan' practices and models of inclusion or inclusivity, in a particular kind of dilemmatic space in which secure forms of knowledge can be interrogated and insecure edifices of learning can be developed. In the spiral topography, the convenor is much more of a member than in the concentric circle model. Undoubtedly, she has power *a priori*, for it is she who sets out the chairs in the first place and names the time when the work of the group begins and ends. The conference space is also saturated with formations of knowledge that would covertly insist that she is the leader (and therefore a 'front person' for the oppressor(s)) of the group – and one must cautiously note that both permanence and impermanence, rigidity and chaos, have equal status as fantasies to be explored, rather than as facts to be assumed *a priori*.

But there is room here for optimism – not perhaps to the extent that Pope was proposing in his *Essay on Man*, but nonetheless something like a glimpse of what Rancière ([1987] 1991) terms a 'practice of equality'. Rancière tells the story of Jacotot, the nineteenth-century schoolteacher exiled from post-Napoleonic France who discovered that if he discarded the 'saturated' idea of the knowledge/power differential between himself and his Flemish pupils, he could enable them to learn French, even though he spoke no Flemish. The experiential large group is more dialogical than didactic. Its concentric circles in exploration of 'matters of concern' to its membership are Cosmopolitan but its spirals in pursuit of learning from experience are more egalitarian; the challenge (the impossible task?) for the convenor is to try to hold the realisation that all the agonised subjects temporarily housed in the space of the group are equal in their common humanity and intellect and that all half-knowledges, all experiments in learning from experience in the group, including her own, are of equal validity and authority.

Acknowledgements

I am very grateful to Dr Claudia Lapping and Dr Tamara Bibby for inviting me to convene a large group at the Psychosocial Studies Network conference and for their editorial encouragement and guidance. I am also very much indebted to Dr Earl Hopper, who generously shared with me some of his writings and ideas around this theme and who helpfully commented on the first draft of this paper. Any lingering conceptual confusions are very much my own.

References

Adlam, J., and C. Scanlon. 2005. "Personality Disorder and Homelessness: Membership and 'Unhoused minds' in Forensic Settings." *Group Analysis* 38 (3): 452–466.

Bion, W. R. 1961. *Experiences in Groups*. London: Routledge.

Bion, W. R. 1970. *Attention and Interpretation*. London: Karnac.

Butler, J. 1997. *The Psychic Life of Power: Theories in Subjection*. Stanford, CA: Stanford University Press.

Foucault, M. 1980. "Two Lectures." In *Power/Knowledge: Selected Interviews and other Writings 1972-1977*, edited by C. Gordon, 78–108. New York: Pantheon.

Foulkes, S. 1975. "Problems of the Large Group from a Group-Analytic Point of View." In *The Large Group: Dynamics and Therapy*, edited by L. Kreeger, 33–56. London: Karnac.

Freire, P. 1996. *Pedagogy of the Oppressed*. London: Penguin.

Freud, S. [1921] 1991. *SE Group Psychology and the Analysis of the Ego*. 18: 65–143. Reprinted in S. Freud (1991) *Civilization, society and religion*, pp. 91–178. London: Penguin Freud Library (Vol. 12).

Hierocles 1822. *Ethical Fragments of Hierocles, Preserved by Stobaeus*. Trans. Thomas Taylor. Kindle Edition. http://www.amazon.co.uk/Ethical-Fragments-Hierocles-Preserved-Stobaeus-ebook/dp/B0062COJUM/ref=sr_1_2?ie=UTF8&qid=1383481234&sr=8-2&keywords=Hierocles.

Hinshelwood, R. 1991. *A Dictionary of Kleinian Thought*. 2nd ed. London: Free Association Books.

Honig, B. 1994. "Difference, Dilemmas and the Politics of Home." *Social Research* 61 (3): 563–597.

Hopper, E. 2000. "From Objects and Subjects to Citizens: Group Analysis and the Study of Maturity." *Group Analysis* 33 (1): 29–34.

Hopper, E. 2002. "Response to Walker Shield's 'the Subjective Experience of the Self in the Large Group: Two Models of study'." *International Journal of Group Psychotherapy* 52 (3): 433–436.

Hopper, E. 2006. "Some Thoughts about the Large Group for the *Imagine* Conference in Israel and about My Convening of It." *Group-Analytic Contexts* 32: 11–15.

Hopper, E., and A. Weyman. 1975. "A Sociological View of Large Groups." In *The Large Group: Dynamics and Therapy*, edited by L. Kreeger, 159–189. London: Karnac.

Keats, J. 2002. *Selected Letters*. Oxford: Oxford University Press.

Kreeger, L. 1975a. IntroductionIn the *Large Group: Dynamics and Therapy*, edited by. L. Kreeger, 13–29. London: Karnac.

Kreeger, L. ed. 1975b. *The Large Group: Dynamics and Therapy*. London: Karnac.

Laertius, Diogenes. 2005. (3rd century BCE). The life of Diogenes of Sinope. Reprinted in L. Navia, *Diogenes the Cynic*. New York: Humanity Books.

Lévi-Strauss, C. [1955] 2011. *Tristes Tropiques*. London: Penguin Classics.

Main, T. 1975. "Some Psychodynamics of Large Groups." In *The Large Group: Dynamics and Therapy*, edited by L. Kreeger, 57–86. London: Karnac.

De Maré, P. 1975. "The Politics of Large Groups." In *The Large Group: Dynamics and Therapy*, edited by L. Kreeger, 145–158. London: Karnac.

Martin, W. Forthcoming. Stoic Transcendentalism and the Doctrine of *Oikeiosis*. In. *The History of the Transcendental Turn*. edited by S. Gardner and M. Grist. Oxford: Oxford University Press

Miller, E. 1990. Experiential Learning in Groups I: The Development of the Leicester Model. In *The Social Engagement of Social Science: A Tavistock Anthology, Vol. I: the Socio-Psychological Perspective*, edited by E. Trist, H. Murray and B. Trist. 165–85. Baltimore MA: University of Pennsylvania Press.

Ou, L. 2009. *Keats and Negative Capability*. London: Continuum.

Pelletier, C. 2011. "Beating the Barrel of Inclusion: Cosmopolitanism through Rabelais and Ranciere – a Response to John Adlam and Christopher Scanlon." *Psychodynamic Practice* 17 (3): 255–272.

Pope, A. 1734. *Essay on Man*. Accessed November 13. www2.hn.psu.edu/faculty/jmanis/a~pope/onman.pdf.

Pullman, P. 2000. *His Dark Materials (Trilogy)*. London: Scholastic.

Rancière, J. 1987/1991. *The Ignorant Schoolmaster: Five Lessons in Intellectual Emancipation*. Stanford, CA: Stanford University Press.

Scanlon, C. 2012. "The Traumatised-Organisation-in-the-Mind: Opening up Space for Difficult Conversations in Difficult Places." In *The Therapeutic Milieu under Fire: Security and Insecurity in Forensic Mental Health*, edited by J. Adlam, A. Aiyegbusi, P. Kleinot, A. Motz and C. Scanlon, 212–228. London: Jessica Kingsley Publishers.

Scanlon, C., and J. Adlam. 2011a. "Defacing the Currency? a Group-Analytic Appreciation of Homelessness, Dangerousness, Disorder and Other Inarticulate Speech of the Heart." *Group Analysis* 44 (2): 131–148.

Scanlon, C., and J. Adlam. 2011b. "Cosmopolitan Minds and Metropolitan Societies: Social Exclusion and Social Refusal Revisited." *Psychodynamic Practice* 17 (3): 241–254.

Scanlon, C., and J. Adlam. 2013. "Knowing Your Place and Minding Your Own Business: on Perverse Psychological Solutions to the Imagined Problem of Social Exclusion." *Ethics and Social Welfare* 7 (2): 170–183.

Stiers, M. 2012. Toward a Dialogical Learning Community: The National Group Psychotherapy Institute. Accessed Nov 13. http://www.magps.org/conferences/archive/2012%20spring/conferences_spring_2012.html

Turquet, P. 1975. "Threats to Identity in the Large Group: A Study in the Phenomenology of the individual's Experiences of Changing Membership Status in a Large Group." In *The Large Group: Dynamics and Therapy*, edited by L. Kreeger, 87–144. London: Karnac.

Žižek, S. 2008. *Violence*. London: Profile Books.

Index

Note: Page numbers in *italics* represent figures

2012 Psychosocial Studies Network Conference 138–9

abjection as a concept 3, 23–4, 26–8, 30–2, 34–6
absolutism in mathematics 140
academic abjection 34–5
affective turn, the 120–1
Agamben, Giorgio 104
alcohol as an abjecting effect 27
aloofness as a mode of critical distance 9–14, 18
archival spaces 6–7
archive, the 1–2, 97, 99, 100–1
Archive Fever (book) 1, 99
archons as guardinas of official documents 1–2
Azoulay, Ariella 105, 108, 113

Bataille, Georges 49, 50, 51
Battaglia, Letizia 97, 101–8, 110–13; and the photograph of Rosario Schifani 108–10, *111*, *112*
Battaglia, Vincenzo 105
'being captured' by other data participants in research processes as a source of legitmacy 149–51
Bernstein, Basil 44, 52, 85
Beyond the Pleasure Principle (essay) 13
Black Sun (book) 124
Bodenheimer, A.R. 16, 18
Borsellino, Paulo 103
'bringing up gender' as an action 21–2, 24–6, 30–6
British Sociological Association Auto/Biography Study Group 143
Britzman, Deborah 35; and the emotional labour of teaching and the knowledge of loss 118, 127–33; on melancholia 122, 123, 130

Brunel Education Theory Reading Group 137
  see also research process into sense of legitimacy through psychosocial accounts of subjectivity
Butler, Judith 27, 32

calligrams 57
Capaci assassinations, the 108–9
case study of student narratives and photography in their engagement with university space 61–2, 67, 69–77
cataloguing system of the methodological archive 2
Cavarero, Adrianna 101, 112
Central State Archive, Rome 98, 100
choice in education 83, 91–2
complementarity 51–2
concentric circles as an image and *oikeiosis* 164–5, *166*
concept of natality 111–12
concept of the 'dead mother' 119, 120, 123–7, 132–3
conflict of ambivalence, the 122
Cosa Nostra: A History of the Sicilian Mafia 98
cosmopolitanism 164, 166
Course in General Linguistics (book) 41, 42–3
credit system in the function of schools 94
crime in Palermo 102–3, 105
crisis heterotopias 73

DeCarlo, Marina 104
deconstruction and writing 52, 58
depression, significance and effects of 120–7; through the emotional labour of teaching and the knowldge of loss 118, 127–33
Derrida, Jacques: and the archive 1–2, 99; on the definition of metaphor 28–9, 30; sense of writing or grammatology 39, 41–2, 48–50, 51, 52, 53, 57

INDEX

destruction of memory and the archive, the 99
destruction of presence through writing, the 49
Diagnostic and Statistical Manual of Mental Disorders 120
dialectical tradition in foreign language pedagogies 45–50, 52
'dialogical learning' and topography of chairs in experiental groups 159
Dickie, John 98, 100
digitisation of the archive, the 100
dilemmas as spaces for moral subjects 163, 166
Diogenes the Cynic 164
disavowal by the Italian state of Mafia infiltration into civil society 98–9
disconnect between the written and spoken word 11–12
distance between authorial intent and reader's reception 11–12, 13–14
distributive rules and pedagogic devices 44
Docklands Campus topography 63, 69
Doing Qualitative Research Differently (book) 152
Douglas, Mary 30
drive, the *see* Lacanian notion of the drive, the
drug addiction in Palermo 102–3

educational settings and the anxiety of speaking 12–13
education theory and psychoanalysis 117–18, 123, 124–5, 127–33
ego's desire to consume loss through melancholia 121–2
Essay on Man (poem) 166
everyday practices and 'inner' subjectivity 65–6
evolutionism 80
exclusion in education as a contingent occurrence 82–3
extimacy *see* Lacanian notion of extimacy, the

failure in the official discourse of education 5, 81–2 *see also* research into failure in mathematics education
Falcone, Giovanni 103, 108, 110
fantasy and reality 117–18
foreign language pedagogies 3
formations of knowledge 1, 157–8
Foucault, Michel 161
Four Fundamental Concepts of Psychoanalysis (book) 63, 67, 68
Freire, Paolo 159
Freud, Sigmund 18, 118, 124–5; conceptualisation of melancholia 5, 121, 127; and repression and denial 98, 142; 'scraps of independence and originality' theory 161, 164 *see also* aloofness as a mode of critical distance
Freudian ego, the 64

gender as a factor in professional discourse 21–2, 24–5 *see also* 'bringing up gender' as an action
Gender Trouble (book) 27, 32
German school system, the 83–4, 94, 94n1, 95n3
Giaconia, Giovanna 109
grammatology *see* science of writing, notion of a
Green, André 119, 120
Growtowski, Jerry 102, 104

Hashimoto, Kayoko 53–4
Hegel, Georg 49, 52; Hegelian dialectics 43, 50
heliotropic metaphor, the 3, 30, 32
Hierocles 164–5
Hopper, Earl 159, 160–1, 165
human rights violations and organised crime 99, 113 *see also* Mafia, the
hypothesis of belonging 61, 62 *see also* case study of student narratives and photography in their engagement and sense of belonging with university space

ideology in educational practice 80, 81–2, 88–91
ignorance as a refusal of knowledge 141
Imaginary order of existence, the 64, 70–1, 74
inclusion and equity as educational ideology 4–5
in-group/out-group binary logic 54–5
'inner' subjectivity and everyday practices 65–6
insecure half-knowledge as experiential learning outcome 161, 162, 163–4
internalisation of speech, the 47

Japanese politics of internationalisation 53–4

Keats, John 161–3
knowledge and psychoanalysis 152–3
Kristeva, Julia 4, 117, 124, 125; and the notion of the abject 23, 24, 26–8, 35–6; phobia as 'métaphore manquée du manque' 29, 32, 33

Lacan, Jacques 64–5, 67, 68, 72, 75, 80
Lacanian notion of extimacy, the 4, 65–6, 70, 72, 85
Lacanian notion of the drive, the 62–3, 65, 67–8, 71, 75, 76
Lacanian psychoanalysis 62
language and metaphor 28–9
language as a system of signs 41, 42–3, 48
learning obstacles in education 79–80

INDEX

legitimacy and the psycho and the social 139
  see also research process into sense of legitimacy through psychosocial accounts of subjectivity
Leicester Conferences, the 160
Le Lionnais, François 56
Linthout, Lorenzo 108, 109
logocentrism 41
L'Ora (newspaper) 102, 111
loss and depression 119, 120, 131–2, 133

Mafia, the 98, 102–6, 108–9, 110, 113
mathematics education 4–5, 79, 81–2
'matricide' and the dead mother 124–6
MEC (Mathematics Enhancement Course) *see* 'being captured' by other data participants in research processes as a source of legitimacy
mediating capacity of educational texts 12–13
medicalisation of feelings, the 120
melancholia as a reparative politics 5–6
mental *semantic normativity* 43–4
metaphor, the 28–30; and the heliotropic metaphor 3, 30, 32; and 'métaphore manquée du manque' 29–31, 32–3
'métaphore manquée du manque' 29–31, 32–3
methodological implications for research questions and the spatial organisation of subjectivity 66
microtexts as pedagogies 56–7
modes of not-knowing in the classroom 10
Monsters in Literature (essay) 128

narrative of female rebellion against the Mafia 101
negative affect and depression 120–1
negative capability as an experiential idea 162–3
normalisation of pedagogic practices in language 42–3
numerical considerations for the dynamics of large learning groups 160

obscenity of asking questions, the 15–16, 18
Oedipus complex, the 63–4
oikeiosis and the image of concentric circles 164–5
omerta (code of silence) 106, 109
orders of existence, the 62, 63–5, 70–1, 74, 76
Oulipo (Ouvroir de Littérature Potentielle) 56

Palermo and the Mafia 102–3, 105–6
Paratheatre 102
Parra, Nicanor 56
pedagogic device and language 44
Phenomenology of Spirit (book) 48, 50

phobia as 'métaphore manquée du manque' 29–30
photography and the spatial organisation of enjoyment 68–9, 74, 76
photojournalism as form of public pedagogy 101–8, 110–13; photograph of Rosario Schifani 108–10, 111, 112
Pipitone, Marina 110
Plutarch 164
poiesis 56–7
Pope, Alexander 166
poststructuralist accounts of subjectivity 137–8
Powers of Horror (book) 23, 24, 26, 28, 29
presence and the meaning of absence 75–6
processes of idealisation in melancholia 122–3
productiveness in restricted and general economies 49
psychoanalysis and education theory 117–18, 119–20, 123
psychoanalytic technique 13
psychological functions and language 46–7
psychosexual desire 11, 14
psychosocial approaches to the social and the individual 138–9 *see also* research process into sense of legitimacy through psychosocial accounts of subjectivity
Psychosocial Studies Network Conference, London 1, 2
psychosocial thinking about learning *see* research through an Experiential Large Group to determine opportunities and resistances to learning
Pullman, Philip 162
Purity and Danger (book) 30

Queneau, Raymond 56

Real order of existence, the 64, 65, 66, 72, 74, 76
relations in restricted economies 49
repercussions of 'bringing up gender' 31–2
repression and denial 98, 142
research into failure in mathematics education 80–2, 84–91, *87,* 93–4
research process into sense of legitimacy through psychosocial accounts of subjectivity 140–5, 149–53; and self-recognition through research 145–9 *see also* subjectivity and legitimacy and post-structural psychosocial approaches
research through an Experiential Large Group to determine opportunities and resistances to learning 158–63
re-storying of photojournalist shots 111–12
Ricoeur, Paul 28–9
Rieff, Philip 15–16

INDEX

Rule of Metaphor, The (book) 28–9
Ruta, Carlo 102

Sangiorgi, Ermanno 98
Saussure, Ferdinand de 41, 42–3
Saviano, Roberto 113
Schifani, Rosaria 108–10, 111, 112, 114n5
science of writing, notion of a 40, 51–2, 57
'scraps of independence and originality' theory 161, 164
self-recognition through research methods 145–9
shame and the failure of distance 11, 14–18
significance of space for students *see* case study of student narratives and photography in their engagement and sense of belonging with university space
SLA (Second Language Acquisition) 42–3
social justice and mathematics education 79–80
social milieu that shape and are shaped by language 43
social other and shame, the 17
social protective shield, the 99–100, 101, 112
sovereignty in the act of writing 58
space, notions of 4, 6–7; space of the self and shame scenarios 17, 18 *see also* case study of student narratives and photography in their engagement with university space
spatial organisation of enjoyment, the 62, 66, 67–8, 70, 71–6, 90–1
spiral arrangement of chairs in experiential large groups 158–60, 165–6
splitting and resistance to a dominant discourse 151
spontaneous concepts in linguistic instruction 47–8
Stille, Alexander 103
Stoics, the 164

streaming in the German school system 83–4, 94, 94n1, 95n3
structuralist and cognitive notions of language 44–5, 49
sub-groups as 'other' within a large group 161
subjectivity and legitimacy and post-structural psychosocial approaches 137–40
Sublime Object of Ideology, The (book) 14–15
superego and the failure of the Law, the 91
Symbolic order of existence, the 63–4, 65, 74, 75
systematic repression of writing, the 41–2

theatre of participation 102
topography of chairs in experiential groups 159, 164–6
totalitarian power and the obscenity of asking questions 15
'transference neurosis' 13, 18
Tre Donne (photograph) 111

vomit as a metaphor for gender 31–3
Vygotsky, Lev 3–4, 45–6, 47, 48, 50–1, 52

Walsh, Julie 2–3
Wertsch, James V. 47, 48
writing 49; as an encounter with being 2–3, 51; as a pedagogic process in a foreign language 40–2, 45–7, 51, 53–8

Young-Bruehl, Elisabeth 99–100, 107

Zecchin, Franco 102, 103
Zeno of Citium 164
Žižek, Slavoj 90, 92, 163; on contingencies within universal principles 82, 83; shame as a consequence of asking questions 11, 14–15, 18
ZPD (zone of proximal development) 46, 58
Zupancic, Alenka 16, 18